THE PHILOSOPHY OF DEATH

The Philosophy of Death is a discussion of the basic philosophical issues concerning death, and a critical introduction to the relevant contemporary philosophical literature. Steven Luper begins by addressing questions about those who die: What is it to be alive? What does it mean for you and me to exist? Under what conditions do we persist over time, and when do we perish? Next, he considers several questions concerning death, including: What does dying consist in? In particular, how does it differ from aging? Must death be permanent? By what signs may it be identified? Is death bad for the one who dies? If so, why? Finally he discusses whether, and why, killing is morally objectionable, and suggests that it is often permissible; in particular, (assisted) suicide, euthanasia, and abortion may all be morally permissible. His book is a lively and engaging philosophical treatment of a perennially fascinating and relevant subject.

STEVEN LUPER is Professor and Chair of the Philosophy Department, Trinity University. He is the author of *Invulnerability: On Securing Happiness* (1996), and his most recent edited volumes include *Essential Knowledge* (2004), *The Skeptics: Contemporary Essays* (2003), and *Existing: An Introduction to Existentialist Thought* (2000).

THE PHILOSOPHY OF DEATH

STEVEN LUPER

CAMBRIDGE
UNIVERSITY PRESS

CAMBRIDGE UNIVERSITY PRESS
Cambridge, New York, Melbourne, Madrid, Cape Town, Singapore, São Paulo, Delhi

Cambridge University Press
The Edinburgh Building, Cambridge CB2 8RU, UK

Published in the United States of America by Cambridge University Press, New York

www.cambridge.org
Information on this title: www.cambridge.org/9780521709125

First published 2009

Printed in the United Kingdom at the University Press, Cambridge

A catalogue record for this publication is available from the British Library

Library of Congress Cataloging-in-Publication Data
Luper, Steven.
The philosophy of death / Steven Luper.
p. cm.
Includes bibliographical references and index.
ISBN 978-0-521-88249-1 (hardback)
ISBN 978-0-521-70912-5 (pbk.)
1. Death.   2. Death–Moral and ethical aspects.   I. Title.

BD444.L87 2009
128′.5–dc22

2009010743

ISBN 978-0-521-88249-1 hardback
ISBN 978-0-521-70912-5 paperback

For Mara

Contents

Acknowledgments

In writing this book, I have incurred a number of debts. Christine Gerakaris helped greatly by tracking down relevant materials. I thank her. Curtis Brown read the entire manuscript and gave me a great deal of extremely helpful feedback and suggestions. He saved me from making many errors, including errors in the formulation of comparativism. The book is much better as a result of his comments, and I am grateful. Eric Olson read chapter 2; his feedback helped me to make many improvements, for which I owe him thanks. Lawrence Espey also read chapter 2 and made helpful suggestions. I am grateful to him as well.

Chris Belshaw invited me to speak at a conference at York University, called "Death: What it is and Why it Matters," held in July of 2008. There I received useful feedback concerning my views on suicide. I thank Chris and the participants in the conference.

I have drawn on various publications. The overall structure of the (first part of the) book is based loosely on "Death," in the online *Stanford University Encyclopedia of Philosophy*, ed. Edward N. Zalta, 2002 (revised 2006). Much of the material in chapter 5 is based on my "Posthumous Harm," *American Philosophical Quarterly* 41.1 (2004), 63–72, and "Past Desires and the Dead," *Philosophical Studies* 126.3 (2005), 331–345. Chapter 6 is a revision of my "Mortal Harm," *Philosophical Quarterly* 57 (2007), 239–251.

PART I

Dying

CHAPTER I

Introduction

Suppose that in one hour you will utterly cease to exist. It would make no sense for you – the present you, the person reading these words – to make plans for the future you. Normally, when you look forward to your life to come, you imagine yourself carrying on with the plans you presently have for your future self, and you imagine your future self creating and launching new plans which you cannot yet know of, or acting spontaneously, perhaps simply enjoying the sun setting over the ocean. The prospect of these things to come prompts you to act now, to take some time out of your busy day to do things that will make things possible for your future self. Your future self is, after all, you. At the same time your future self is like a child whose life you are shaping now; you want your child to be happy, and to be someone of whom you can be proud, and who will think back to you fondly. Much of what you do is meaningful only if this child will thrive. Annihilation, ceasing to exist, would bring all of this planning and nurturing to an end. There would be nothing in life to look forward to – no pressing on with the things you presently take to be significant, no fresh undertakings, no future self to look after, no *you* at all.

It seems that if death means annihilation, then for most of us, most of the time, dying would be a very bad thing.

The first part of this book is a philosophical meditation about death. Perhaps death is actually a transformation by which the life with which we are familiar is followed by some sort of afterlife in which our existence is continued. In this book I do not discuss this possibility. Instead, I simply assume that death is the end of us. I try to clarify what sort of ending it is, and what significance should be attached to it. Even those who think that death is a continuation, and not an ending, can benefit from contemplating the implications of annihilation. That annihilation would be bad for them explains why it is important to live for ever: it is the only way to avoid the evil of annihilation. If, on the other hand, annihilation would not be bad for them, the question arises as to why they value the prospect of immortality.

In dying, we are deprived of the good things we would have enjoyed had we lived on. It even precludes our regretting our loss, and our loss can be great. However, not everything death takes from us is good. It takes the bad with the good, and life can get very, very bad indeed, as anyone who suffers from the devastating loss of a loved one, or painful degenerative diseases, or the prospect of oncoming progressive dementia, is aware. In allowing us to escape these, death, it seems, can be a very good thing for us.

So perhaps death is bad for us when living on would have been good for us, and good for us when living on would have been bad for us. Most contemporary theorists who write about death defend some version of this view. It has many plausible consequences. For instance, it would be good to extend our lives significantly, if doing so permitted us to have more good life. This may well be possible, as the mechanisms behind aging are coming more clearly into view. The prospect of indefinitely extended life, under favorable conditions, is welcome indeed, in that it would make our lives as wholes – our lives from beginning to end – better.

There is another consequence of the view that the evilness of death derives from the goodness of the life death takes from us: disquiet concerning death is the other face of love for life. It would be absurd to avoid a tragic death by making our lives bad, or so mediocre we would not mind losing them, and doing this would only make our predicament far worse. We would be left with lives that are not worth living. Better to live well, and risk a tragic death.

Nevertheless there are some surprisingly persistent objections to the proposition that living well entails risking a bad death. Some of these objections were developed by philosophers in the ancient world who believed that we can live better, more tranquil lives if we rid ourselves of certain disturbing but erroneous beliefs, such as that dying might be bad for us, and certain misguided desires, such as the yearning for immortality. My own view is that these efforts, or at least the ones of which I am aware, backfire: they leave us with greatly impoverished lives. The ancient Greek philosopher Epicurus was one of the people who tried to help us by convincing us to give up the desire for immortality and the belief that death can harm us. Of course, many people (such as Socrates) have said that death is harmless because it is a portal to an afterlife in which we will continue to live well, and in that sense unreal. But that is not Epicurus' approach. For Epicurus, the difficulty is to identify a subject who is harmed by death, a clear harm that is received, and a time the harm is incurred. Assuming, as Epicurus does, that the dead no longer exist, these tasks are daunting. According to him, death can harm the one who dies only while she is alive or later. Opting for the second answer is problematic, given the lack of a subject at that time. On the first answer, it is easy to find a subject, but far harder to see how death is bad for her.

The first part of this book, called "Dying," is largely devoted to the discussion of these Epicurean objections, but it is also an attempt to work out a general account of what is in, and what is against, a person's interests. Before these discussions can get under way, however, it is necessary to say some things about what you and I are, and what it means for us to exist. Since existing is bound up with living, this will require saying something about what life itself is. It will also require working out views of humanity and personhood. I try to provide this preparatory material in chapter 2.

There (in chapter 2) I maintain that living things include organisms and their organs and tissues. All known organisms are creatures that can maintain themselves through certain distinctive processes. These are their vital processes, and they are controlled by DNA. Conceivably, life forms might be discovered or engineered that are based on some mechanism other than DNA. Whether these will count as living beings will depend on whether the alternative mechanism is sufficiently like DNA; it would need to be a replicator with the properties necessary for it to evolve over time in the way DNA has.

Living things cease to exist when they die, as they are no longer able to maintain themselves through their vital processes. However, whether you and I exist or not depends on what we are, and on the conditions under which we persist over time. There are many ways of understanding what we are. I will discuss three; the first, which I call *animal essentialism,* is the view that we are essentially animals; the second, which I will refer to as *person essentialism,* says we are essentially self-aware beings; and the third, *mind essentialism,* is the view that we are essentially minds. Likewise, there are various accounts of our persistence conditions, including the *animalist account,* which says that we persist, over time, just when we remain the same animals; the *psychological account,* according to which our persistence hinges on our psychological attributes and the relations among them; and the *mindist account,* on which we persist just when our minds remain intact.

All of these views appear to have flaws. It is difficult indeed to give a precise and accurate account of what you and I are, and of what is required for us to persist. The animalist views explain many familiar facts about us; for instance, we can survive the loss of a limb, and we certainly appear to be human beings, which are animals. However, there are certain thought experiments that seem to constitute decisive objections to animal essentialism and the animalist account of persistence. Transplantation is one: suppose your cerebrum was removed from your body, and surgically transferred, successfully, to another body, whose own cerebrum has been removed and destroyed. Upon completion of the operation, the surgeons wake their patient, and she (or he) says that she is you, and indeed she has your memories and personality traits. Isn't it obvious that she *is* you? Not on the animalist views. A cerebrum is not even an organ; it is part of an organ, and it seems clear that neither an organ nor its parts is an animal. Whether you survive the operation depends on what has happened to the body from which your cerebrum was taken: it might have been kept alive; a body with an intact brain stem can live for years despite the loss or death of its cerebrum, as cases of persistent vegetation, made famous by people like Nancy Cruzan and Terry Schiavo, illustrate. Animalism seems to imply that if it is still alive, it is you. Yet the patient with your cerebrum violently disagrees!

Person and mind essentialism, and the psychological and mindist accounts of persistence, are better positioned to handle the Transplantation case, but they face worries of their own. What should we say about fetuses that have yet to develop minds? Were you ever such a creature? Not if person or mind essentialism is right. Nothing that is essentially a mind or person can ever have been anything else. But the fetus is something. Let us say it is a human being. What happens to that human being when your existence as a mind or person begins? Presumably it does not cease to exist. Surely a human being will not cease to exist just because it develops a mind or a personality. So apparently person and mind essentialism suggest that there are two creatures sharing your body right now – the human being who was once a fetus, and *you*, the mind (or you, the person). Can this really be true? Worries like this make animal essentialism look much more inviting.

In chapter 3 I discuss what death is. I examine how it differs from aging, whether it must be permanent, by what signs it may be identified, and whether lives can be suspended and then revived. I also distinguish some ways in which the term 'death' is ambiguous. Chief among these is death considered as the process of dying, and death considered as the state into which the dying process puts its victim.

Some theorists say that people remain in existence after they die. This is nothing to get excited about, since the posthumous existence of which they speak is one we spend as corpses. I say they are wrong. Being a corpse is not a way to continue our existence. But must death be permanent? We can shed light on the matter by distinguishing between reviving life and restoring it. The former happens in nature countless times a year; seeds are essentially plants whose vital processes are in suspension until April showers revive them. Also, frogs, and even human embryos, can be frozen, suspending their vital processes, and then thawed, at which time those processes begin again. So lives may be suspended then revived. Similarly, the process by which a creature dies may be suspended or reversed, as we shall see. But once the dying process has run its course, and a creature has ceased to exist, it is not possible to reverse the dying process, or to revive that creature. The restoration of life is another matter. Restoration is bringing a creature, which is dead and which no longer exists, back to life. I will suggest that restoration is conceivable, so that death need not be permanent. For you and me, death will be the irreversible cessation of the vital processes that sustain us.

Chapter 4 lays out Epicurus' reasons for claiming that neither death, nor events following death, can harm the one who dies. It also considers an argument by his follower Lucretius to the same end, namely his asymmetry argument: prenatal nonexistence is not bad for us, and is saliently identical to posthumous nonexistence, so the latter is not bad for us either. I will suggest that we have good reason to have different attitudes about prenatal nonexistence and posthumous nonexistence. Epicurus' own concerns are harder to deal with. He notes that because death marks our transition from existence to nonexistence, it is difficult to see that it, or posthumous events, can affect us at all, much less in a way that really matters. The only thing that is really harmful, Epicurus thought, is pain, whether mental or physical, but we cannot experience pain once we have ceased to exist. Of course, this argument leaves open the possibility that death could harm us at the time it occurs, but it would be remarkable if its harm were limited to any pain we receive then. Could it really be that a painless death cannot harm us?

In chapters 5 and 6 I consider replies to the challenges proffered in chapter 4. The main task in chapter 5 is to develop a theory of prudential value. We shall need to know something about what welfare consists in and how this relates to our interests. I defend the standard view, which I call comparativism. Comparativism holds that something is in our interests just when it benefits us or when it would benefit us if it occurred, and that something benefits us just when it makes our lives better than they would have been. Similarly, a thing is against our interests just when it does or would harm us, and it harms us just when it makes our lives worse than they would have been. This analysis of our interests is compatible with a range of views about the nature of well-being.

I will sketch three analyses of welfare. Positive hedonism, the first, says that only one thing is good in itself, or intrinsically good, for us, namely our pleasure, and our pain is the sole intrinsic evil for us. According to preferentialism, what is intrinsically good for us is the pairing of two things: desiring that some state of affairs, P, hold, and P's holding; and what is intrinsically bad for us is desiring that P hold when the denial of P holds. Pluralism is the position that the things that are intrinsically good for us or bad for us are not limited to those countenanced by hedonists and preferentialists.

In the latter part of chapter 5, I look at how the competing accounts bear on the possibility of being harmed by death or posthumous events. Those who defend the harmlessness of death tend to say that harm reduces to pain; they say, roughly, that dying deprives us of the capacity for pain, and hence cannot harm us. But this is an overly narrow conception of harm. Theorists who say that death may harm us defend the idea that we are harmed when deprived of goods, not just when we are made to suffer.

Chapter 6 is devoted to leading solutions to Epicurus' timing puzzle. I also examine the presumption that things harm us *only* if there is a time at which, because of them, we are worse off than we otherwise would have been. I will argue that this presumption is false; death or a posthumous event can be bad for us even if there is no time at which we are worse off as a result of it. Because we die, our *lives* are worse than they otherwise would have been. Nevertheless, I will suggest, usually there are times when we are worse off as a result of death or a posthumous event, namely while we have the interests which dying is against, and that is while we are still alive.

In the second part of the book, called "Killing," I discuss the significance of killing. More specifically, I ask why and when killing is *prima facie* wrong due to its effects on the one killed, rather than because of any side effects it might have. Chapter 7 takes on this theoretical issue directly, whereas 8 and 9 consider whether suicide, euthanasia, or abortion is wrong.

The wrongness of killing surely has something to do with its harmfulness, so conclusions reached in the first part of the book will bear on the second. But if your death would not be bad for you, does it follow that killing you is not morally objectionable? The matter will take some careful thought. There are three widely discussed views concerning why and when killing is objectionable. The Harm Account claims that the wrongness of killing is a matter of the harm done to the one who dies. The Consent Account says it comes down to the individual's not having competently consented to being killed. And the Subject Value Account explains killing's direct wrongness in terms of the intrinsic value of the subject who is killed. Each of these views is worth considering, and I treat them sympathetically. Of them, the Subject Value Account is probably the most popular, but it is also the most difficult to develop with any precision. Too, if we say that individuals have specific values as subjects, we are immediately confronted with puzzles such as: How many sheep together have subject value equivalent to that of one human being? If two people together have twice the subject value as one, is it permissible to kill one (who has done nothing untoward) in order to save two?

In my view the most defensible analysis is a fourth view which I call the Combined Account. Unlike the Subject Value Account, it does not say that individuals have specific values as subjects. Like the Consent Account, it says that killing competent persons is wrong just when they have not made an informed choice not to be killed. And like the Harm Account, it says that killing incompetent subjects is wrong just in case (and to the extent that) it harms them. (Throughout the book, I will use the term 'just in case' as a stylistic variant of 'if and only if.' For example, 'killing incompetent subjects is wrong just in case it harms them' is equivalent to 'killing incompetent subjects is wrong *if* it harms them and killing incompetent subjects is wrong *only if* it harms them.')

In chapter 8 I consider arguments for the view that suicide and euthanasia may not be chosen rationally and morally. It seems clear that choosing either one can be rational, if a means is available that is painless, fast, and reliable, and if living on is against our interests. But there are various complications to consider.

The best argument against the moral permissibility of suicide and euthanasia appeals to the absolutist version of the Subject Value Account, which says that human beings have a kind of value that overrides all other sorts. However, the Subject Value Account is implausible unless qualified to allow for the possibility that some killings are beneficial enough to outweigh lost subject value. For example, it needs to be adjusted in the face of the evident fact that euthanizing animals is permissible. I argue that, suitably adjusted, it must also allow for the possibility that killing people can be beneficial enough to outweigh their lost subject value. If that is correct, then suicide and euthanasia will not always be wrong. I go on to suggest that the best account of killing, the Combined Account, supports the conclusion that suicide, assisting in suicide, and euthanasia all can be morally permissible.

Chapter 9 discusses the issue of whether, and if so why, abortion might be morally objectionable. The strongest case against abortion is that killing fetuses harms them by depriving them of lives like ours, and such harm is wrong. However, it is not so clear that the argument succeeds. Person and mind essentialists tend to reject it. They want to say that fetuses are not deprived of lives like ours. *We* were never fetuses; fetuses are some other sort of creature, with a different sort of life.

The issues in chapter 9 bring us full circle, and back to the difficult questions tackled in chapter 2, which is coming up next, concerning what life is in general, and what sort of creatures you and I are, in particular.

CHAPTER 2

Life

In the introduction to *Leviathan* (1651), Thomas Hobbes offers a view of life which is remarkably forward-looking considering that he wrote in the midst of the seventeenth century:

Seeing life is but a motion of limbs, the beginning whereof is in some principal part within; why may we not say, that all 'automata' (engines that move themselves by springs and wheels as doth a watch) have an artificial life? For what is the 'heart,' but a 'spring'; and the 'nerves,' but so many 'strings'; and the 'joints,' but so many 'wheels,' giving motion to the whole body, such as was intended by the artificer?

Hobbes says that what lives is alive because its motion springs from within. This makes you and me, and other living things, automata. We are like pocketwatches, ticking away, passing time, rewinding at mealtimes. It also makes creating life a very simple matter; any watchmaker can do it.

Hobbes means to demystify living things by reducing them to self-movers. His idea of life is oversimplified. Nevertheless, his idea helps to illustrate an important point: to understand death we need to understanding life in some detail, since a death occurs when a life ends. If Hobbes's simple conception of life were correct, death would be an equally simple matter: we would die when our 'movements' fail, and motion ceases to come from within.

In this chapter I would like to clarify the property, *alive*. However, the task is a large one, and the issues involved are complex. I must settle for a very sketchy account of life indeed. Having provided it, I will consider a particular sort of living thing in more detail, namely the sort of creature you and I are. The question I will ask about us is: What are we? It seems obvious that we are human beings, that we are persons, and that we are conscious beings. But these different characterizations of ourselves differ in important ways, and can affect our understanding of what it is to die. Death itself I will begin to discuss in chapter 3.

The chapter has two sections. In the first, I ask what it is for something to be alive. In the second, I sketch views of humanity and personhood, since, for you and me, being alive, or *being*, is tightly bound up with our status as human beings and as persons.

LIFE AND LIVING THINGS

All of us can name things that clearly are alive and other things that clearly are not. We can also find or imagine things that are difficult to classify, as are viruses. To be useful, an account of living things must tell us what is distinctive about things that clearly are alive. It should also help us to deal with other, less obvious cases, such as viruses, either by suggesting how they should be classified, or at least why it is unclear whether they are living things. In this section, I sketch such an account, drawing on some of the basic discoveries of evolutionary and molecular biology.

Life

The key mechanism behind the evolution of living things is the DNA molecule. DNA governs processes by which it, and the things of which it is part, develop, maintain themselves, reproduce, and evolve through natural selection (where natural selection is understood to include endo-symbiosis, about which more presently). DNA has made the evolution of living things possible by performing four key activities:

1. It *replicates*: it makes copies of itself.
2. It *mutates*: over time, its copies differ significantly from the originals.
3. It *augments* itself; that is, it constructs and integrates itself with structures that promote its longevity and copying process. Call these *replicator bodies*.
4. To its copies it *bequeaths* mutations, including mutations of features by which it shapes its replicator bodies: these are *inherited*, or copied by the copies it makes of itself.

It is not clear how DNA first came to be, but it is likely that it evolved from simpler replicating molecules. Eons ago, when the planet was devoid of life and oxygen, the atmosphere would have had water and gases such as hydrogen, methane, ammonia, and carbon dioxide. Mixtures of these would have been exposed to lightning and ultraviolet light from the sun. By simulating these conditions within flasks, it is possible to produce amino acids, the chief components of proteins, and purines and pyrimidines, the fundamental components of nucleic acids such as DNA and RNA (Miller 1953, Kobayashi 1986). The earliest replicating molecules might have emerged in such a soup of organic molecules (Haldane 1929, Oparin 1952), perhaps with the assistance of minerals serving as scaffolding and catalysts (Cairns-Smith 1982). DNA itself might well have evolved from RNA; in the 1980s Thomas Cech and Sidney Altman showed that RNA can splice together copies of itself, making it a replicator in its own right (Gilbert 1986).

However it originated, the first DNA-like molecule replicated, mutated, and bequeathed mutations to its copies, and eventually began to augment itself, constructing replicator bodies. These primordial combinations of DNA with replicator bodies were complex compounds which we might characterize as *protoorganisms*. At some point in evolution, by degrees, protoorganisms made the transition to (micro)organisms. Living things emerged once DNA's replicator bodies came to be individual organisms in their own right (Dawkins 1976; 1987, ch. 6).

The distinction between organisms and protoorganisms is not a sharp one. Unlike protoorganisms, organisms have some degree of autonomy, some measure of independence from the DNA molecules of which they are partly constituted. While DNA shapes the morphology and physiology of a particular simple organism such as a paramecium, it is the individual paramecium that consumes and digests microorganisms, the paramecium that moves about with undulating cilia, and the paramecium that reproduces itself, asexually or sexually. The distinction is clearer in higher organisms. Any dog's brain, vocal chords, respiratory apparatus, and so forth are shaped by the DNA within her, yet it is my dog Mara, not her DNA, who whines for attention, barks at armadillos, and chases beams of light.

Organisms develop or grow, then maintain themselves, keeping themselves intact, by capturing energy and converting it into usable forms (through chemosynthesis, photosynthesis, cellular respiration, and so forth), making repairs (for example, through cell generation and regeneration), transferring nutrients to their various parts, removing waste, sustaining the internal conditions necessary for their physiology (Bernard 1878–9), and so forth. These are vital processes. Some organism *components* contain vital processes that assist in their own maintenance, even though, unlike whole organisms, they cannot do the entire job themselves. For example, the maintenance of our skin depends on vital processes occurring within skin cells, but skin is heavily dependent upon the vital processes occurring in other parts of our bodies. Skin is only partially self-maintaining. By contrast, the water molecules that are also integral parts of an organism lack vital processes altogether, and hence are not alive. Sometimes vital processes are suspended temporarily, as, for example, in endospores, seeds, the eggs of brine shrimp, and frozen embryos. When all goes well, and with some exceptions, organisms also reproduce. The processes by which organisms accomplish these things depend, directly or indirectly, on information contained in DNA.

These observations suggest a tri-part account of life:

An *organism* is an individual that has a substantial capacity to maintain itself using processes governed by durable replicators that are integral to it. A replicator is *durable* just when, like DNA, it can mutate, augment itself, and bequeath mutations.

Vital processes are those by which an organism (or organism component) is developed or maintained and that are governed by its durable replicators.

Something is *alive* just when it has a substantial capacity to maintain itself using processes governed by durable replicators that are integral to it. The vital processes of living things might be active or temporarily in suspension.

For succinctness, we can say that life is constituted by replicator-based self-perpetuation.

The replicator-based account of life helps clarify some controversial issues in biology.

For example, while viruses generally are not classified as living, the matter remains controversial. However, it is easy to locate the source of the controversy. Viruses are not organisms. They lack autonomy. Viruses can exist only by taking control of the vital processes of some organism. But the fact that viruses are not organisms does not show they are not living things, since many living things are not organisms. For example, your blood and muscle, and various organelles within cells of your body, are alive. Nonetheless, we can rule out viruses as living things since they are neither organisms nor *components* of organisms (despite the surprising fact that about 8 percent of the human genome consists of sequences of virus DNA [Lander 2001]). What *are* viruses, then? Instead of classifying them as living, it seems reasonable to view them as surviving examples of proto-organisms.

Nevertheless, the replicator-based account leaves open issues that depend on a more precise account of the notion of an organism. Three such issues are: Must a type of organism be capable of reproduction?

Are colonies of bees or ants organisms? Are multicellular creatures really organisms, or are they perhaps colonies of organisms?

The first question arises for two reasons. First, some organisms are hybrids; they result from crossing organisms from different species. Typical members of a species can reproduce, but usually hybrids, such as mules and hinnies, cannot. Second, permanently sterile castes of workers have evolved among social insects, such as ants, bees, and termites (Andersson 1984). Its sterility does not stop an individual from developing and maintaining a distinctive and stable set of features through the action of its vital processes. Nor does its sterility preclude the evolution of a life form, as the existence of sterile workers in colonies shows. Hence sterile creatures can be organisms.

To see why the second question arises, consider the following excerpt from Lewis Thomas's book *The Lives of a Cell* (1974, 14–15):

Bees live lives of organisms, tissues, cells, organelles, all at the same time. The single bee, out of the hive retrieving sugar … is still as much a part of the hive as if attached by a filament. Building the hive, the workers have the look of embryonic cells organizing a developing tissue … When the time for swarming comes, and the old queen prepares to leave with her part of the population, it is as though the hive were involved in mitosis … Like an egg, the great, hairy, black and golden creature splits in two, each with an equal share of the family genome.

The phenomenon of separate animals joining up to form an organism is not unique in insects. Slime-mold cells do it all the time, of course, in each life cycle. At first they are single amebocytes swimming around, eating bacteria, aloof from each other, untouching, voting straight Republican. Then, a bell sounds, and acrasin is released by special cells toward which the others converge in stellate ranks, touch, fuse together, and construct the slug, solid as a trout. A splendid stalk is raised, with a fruiting body on top, and out of this comes the next generation of amebocytes, ready to swim across the same moist ground, solitary and ambitious.

The creatures Thomas describes are *eusocial.* Eusocial animals, such as various wasps, ants, termites, and bees, are defined as ones that form colonies that feature nonreproducing worker castes, overlapping generations, and the cooperative rearing of offspring. These and other features lead some biologists to say that colonies of eusocial animals are "super-organisms." For a measure of the evolutionary success of eusocial creatures, consider that ants (the insects of the family *Formicidae*) constitute about 15 percent of the entire animal biomass, and while together termites (insects of the order *Isoptera*) and ants are only 2 percent of the known species of insects, they are more than half of the insect biomass (Wilson and Hölldobler 2005).

The replicator-based account does not provide a clear answer to whether a eusocial colony is an organism, since it is vague about when something is an *individual* organism. It is obvious that each of two paramecia has distinctive, stable features which it is capable of sustaining through replicator-based self-maintenance, and that the combination of the two paramecia does not constitute a unit. It is clear that each paramecium is an organism, and that the pair is not. A eusocial colony, by contrast, is a self-sustaining unit. It is not obvious that it does not qualify as an organism. But mightn't we at least say that something is an organism only if it is not composed of units that are organisms in their own right? Even slime-mold slugs are ruled out on this, the *no-component organisms* criterion.

Before we take this position, however, we would do well to consider the third question: Are multicellular creatures really organisms? This issue arises since the cells of such creatures themselves strongly resemble colonies of organisms.

The cells of multicellular creatures, eukaryotic cells, probably evolved when separately evolving organisms *combined* perhaps a billion years ago. Eukaryotes are one of the two main forms of life on the planet; prokaryotes are the other. Prokaryotes (such as the bacteria that cause strep throat) are more primitive than eukaryotes (such as human beings) both in lineage, as prokaryotes evolved about 2 billion years earlier than eukaryotes, and in the structure of their cells: the nuclei and organelles of eukaryotic cells are surrounded by membranes, whereas prokaryotic cells lack nuclei and organelles. Another difference is that only eukaryotes are capable of sexual reproduction, or reproduction by cell fusion. According to the endosymbiosis theory (Margulis 1967, 1991), some of the organelles of eukaryotic cells evolved from prokaryotic bacteria. The bacteria were ingested by cells of prokaryotic organisms and remained, benefiting both. Over time, such cells, packing their bacterial symbionts, evolved into eukaryotes. Mitochondria and plastids such as chloroplasts both probably evolved through this process of endosymbiosis. Chloroplasts are organelles in which sunlight is converted into organic molecules, such as sugar, via photosynthesis, and mitochondria are organelles in which that sugar is converted into adenosine triphosphate, a chemical that powers cellular functions via respiration. The case for their endosymbiotic origins is strong; for example, mitochondria and chloroplasts both carry their own DNA and RNA, which closely resembles bacterial DNA and not nuclear DNA; they reproduce themselves by fission and cannot be produced by cells in which they are absent; and they produce their own protein through a process that appears to be bacterial. To this evidence we might add the fact that secondary endosymbiosis – the ingestion of eukaryotic symbionts by other eukarotic cells – is observable today (Okamoto 2005). Perhaps chloroplasts, mitochondria, and some other cellular organelles evolved from organisms engulfed by larger cells a billion years ago, melding into cells as we know them today. Lewis Thomas (1974, 82–83) is eloquent on the point:

The membranes lining the inner compartment of mitochondria are unlike other animal cell membranes, and resemble most closely the membranes of bacteria. The DNA of mitochondria is qualitatively different from the DNA of animal cell nuclei and strikingly similar to bacterial DNA ... The RNA of mitochondria matches the organelles' DNA, but not that of the nucleus. The ribosomes inside the mitochondria are similar to bacterial ribosomes, and different from animal ribosomes. The mitochondria do not arise *de novo* in cells; they are always there, replicating on their own, independently of the replication of the cell. They travel down from egg to newborn ...

The chloroplasts in all plants are, similarly, independent and self-replicating lodgers, with their own DNA and RNA and ribosomes. In structure and pigment content they are the images of prokaryotic blue-green algae ...

There may be more. It has been suggested that flagellae and cilia were once spirochetes that joined up with the other prokaryotes when nucleated cells were being pieced together. The centrioles and basal bodies are believed in some quarters to be semiautonomous organisms with their own separate genomes. Perhaps there are others, still unrecognized.

So *are* cells colonies? On the no-component organisms criterion the issue hinges on whether or not cellular organelles have ceased to be organisms. Have they? There are some grounds for this position: both mitochondria and chloroplasts require proteins manufactured in their host cells using host cell DNA. Perhaps these grounds suffice, but it is far from clear that they do. It is entirely reasonable to say that the cells of eukaryotes have organisms as components. By the no-component organisms rule, then, no eukaryotes are organisms. That makes eukaryotic cells what? Colonies? And if so, what are eukaryotes like you and me? Colonies of colonies?

There is another option: we could accept that some organelles in our cells are organisms but deny that they are components of our cells. They are intimate symbionts, like the bacteria living in our intestines that supply us with vitamins, or the bacteria inside siboglinid tube worms living in deep-sea volcanic vents. After losing their digestive tracts in the latter part of their lives, siboglinid worms are fed entirely by bacteria. But this option seems desperate, since mitochondria and chloroplasts are as intimate a part of eukaryotic cells as other organelles with foreign origins.

Even more options are possible. For example, we could say that something is an organism only if it is surrounded by a membrane. That would rule out collections of eusocial insects, but it does not help us to decide whether our cells are colonies: while cells have an outer membrane, so do the mitochondria within them. We could insist that everything whose entire existence is spent within the outermost membrane of an organism is part of that organism, and not an organism in its own right, but mitochondria predate the organisms they come to be part of.

It seems best to abandon these attempts to draw clear lines, and accept two surprising propositions which we have been resisting. First, organisms may have component organisms. Second, there is no sharp distinction between an organism and some colonies whose members live in highly intimate association.

There is another surprising proposition to consider, this one unrelated to the way the concepts *organism* and *colony* blur together: given the replicator-based account of life, things that are not alive might be able to reproduce. An entity's status as alive turns on how it perpetuates itself, namely by replicator-based processes. Things that are not replicator-based but which make copies of themselves are therefore not alive.

This possibility is apt to seem worrisome: isn't a thing alive *by virtue* of its capacity to reproduce? Certainly this view has had its defenders. Before DNA was understood, people tried to define life in terms of a wide range of capacities exhibited by living things. For Aristotle this was especially natural, since he defined every sort of thing in terms of its distinctive function or capacity. A clock, for example, is distinctive in that it registers the passage of time; therefore any device that registers time counts as a clock. Similarly, he thought, a thing is living if it performs the characteristic function or functions of living things. On this approach what matters is what a thing can do, not *how* it does it – not the mechanism by which it does what it does.

Unfortunately, there was a problem: living things have many capacities, and some life forms have capacities that are very different from those of other life forms. Among the characteristic capacities of living things Aristotle included nutrition, appetite or desire, growth, reproduction, perception, motion, and thought. If we want to define life in terms of one of these capacities, which one should we select? Aristotle himself opted for a simple solution to the *multiplicity problem* (as we might call it): he claimed that *any* capacity characteristic of living things is definitive. In other words, anything with any one of the listed capacities is *ipso facto* alive (*De anima* 2, 413a22–25).

In recent years many theorists continue to attempt to understand living things in terms of their characteristic capacities. With better information about the inner workings of living things, the cast of capacities has changed somewhat, but the multiplicity problem persists; several capacities vie for the leading role, such as reproduction, growth, movement, response to the environment, homeostasis, and metabolism (Lange 1996). As a consequence, many biologists are skeptical about defining life. Some (notably Pirie 1938) argue that 'life' is indefinable on the grounds that each listed capacity is either unnecessary or insufficient for life. As an illustration, consider motion, which is on the ancient and modern list of the characteristic capacities of living beings. Many things that clearly are not alive move themselves around. At regular times, usually when no one is home, my iRobot Roomba vacuum cleaner starts itself up, vacuums my floor, and returns to its charging dock. It moves autonomously. But it is not alive.

The traditional way of defining life in terms of the capacities life forms display is indeed problematic, not just because of the multiplicity problem, but also because nonliving things have many of the same capacities. The latter has become especially clear with the advancement of technology. That devices can do many of the things listed as definitive of life would not be a problem if those devices were alive, but clearly they are not. As we shall see, the traditional approach counts too many clearly nonliving mechanisms as alive.

Artificial life

Consider a series of thought experiments, beginning with devices that can move autonomously, like my Roomba and most living things, but that, unlike my Roomba, are self-perpetuating to a significant degree.

First up is a robotic truck designed to drive on a circular road. The sides of the road are marked at regular intervals with distinct barcodes. The truck orients itself by remotely scanning this information using barcode readers built into two robotic arms attached to it. The truck is able to replace its own components, so that it gradually rebuilds itself. It is able to do this partly because of features of its environment and partly because of its design: its components are highly modularized, somewhat like Lego pieces, so that they can easily be combined. Next to the road over which the truck moves is a warehouse where truck parts are stored. These parts are marked with barcodes, and the numbers correspond to barcodes on similar parts of the truck. On a regular basis the truck stops on a docking station at this warehouse to replenish its power. Then one of its robot arms removes a component of the truck, replaces it with a corresponding part from the warehouse, and discards the old. The computer controlling the arm identifies parts using the barcode-reader built into the arm. The computer's program enables the arm to apply a given procedure for conjoining parts. For simplicity, let's say the inventory of parts is just this: wheels, electric motor, robot arms, computer (with cables that plug into the two robot arms, as well as a cable that can be plugged into similar computers), two batteries (each with cables that can be plugged into the motor, computer, and robot arms), a heater (turned on by a temperature sensor) to prevent the batteries from freezing, back truck body component (including two built-in axles onto which four wheels can be fitted, a built-in driveshaft assembly, a slot onto which one robot arm fits, and another slot into which the motor fits), front truck body component (including two more axles, a slot onto which a robot arm fits, and a slot onto which the computer fits), and nuts and bolts. Over time, the robot arms remove the parts in sequence, then starts over. Even the robot arms are replaced; one by the other. Perhaps the trickiest job is replacing the front truck body component, since the computer resting on it controls the rear arm that must do the job. But the job can be done if the rear arm remains cabled to the computer.

After its own fashion, this truck is self-perpetuating. It responds to its environment, both while directing its movements and in rebuilding itself, and exhibits crude homeostasis (its heater protects its batteries from freezing during sharp drops in temperature) and metabolism. It is somewhat plant-like, since it perpetuates itself without consuming other self-perpetuating things.

We can call the plantlike truck we just described an R1. Now let us imagine a 'predatory' truck called an R2. Its circular road is populated by R1s, and the basic components of the R1 match those of the R2. Suppose that, using its robotic arms, the R2 can switch off any R1 (but no R2) it encounters and remove a component for use in place of its own. To use an R1 computer, the R2 computer must plug itself, via its cable, into the replacement computer, and reprogram it. R2s perpetuate their existence using components of their prey.

Nonetheless, clearly neither R1s nor R2s are alive. Is this because they are not really capable of nutrition? Carrots, like other plants, are autotrophs, or self-feeders – organisms that make their own food from inorganic raw materials. Autotrophs use sunlight or a chemical energy source to synthesize organic molecules, such as sugars, in which they store usable energy. They use this stored energy to synthesize their tissues. Should we conclude that nutrition necessarily involves the synthesis of food? Surely not; rabbits and wolves are capable of nutrition, but they are heterotrophs; unable to make their own food, they must obtain it from autotrophs. So even in nature nutrition takes very different forms. Admittedly, nutrition in R1s and R2s is far cruder than nutrition in nature. Living things do not swap bits of themselves with ready-made parts found by the wayside. A wolf dines on rabbits but is not a tapestry of bunnies or bunny flesh stitched together like Frankenstein's monster. However, if nutrition is any process by which an entity processes materials for self-construction, self-maintenance, and reproduction, then there are no good grounds for denying that R1s and R2s are capable of nutrition.

Is it the inability to reproduce that deprives R1s and R2s of life? Consider an even fancier robot truck called the R3. One difference between R3s and the other two models is that the truck body components are reversed on R3s: its computer is on the rear body component and it is propelled by the front body component. Another difference is that it dismantles R1s and R2s and uses their components in place of its own. But the third difference is the most important: it assembles arrays of parts into fresh R3s. Its program allows R3s to put parts together, rather than merely adding parts to itself. Once again its own computer reprograms those of its 'prey' so as to enable them to make and control R3s.

R3s replicate. This definitely makes them more lifelike. However, the case for saying that they are alive is still very weak, which suggests that the ability to reproduce does not suffice for life.

What is missing? R3s are devoid of life because none of their components are replicators, i.e., self-copying structures. So the processes by which R3s maintain themselves are not replicator-based. Instead, the R3 is itself a replicator, hence no more alive than DNA.

Might R3s be protolife? That would require the ability to augment themselves with replicator bodies, or structures that promote their longevity and copying process. This R3s cannot do. In fact, only by a real stretch of imagination could we say that R3s could mutate or bequeath mutations to their copies. Their ability to evolve by natural selection is seriously questionable. Many things could change them. A falling branch could break off a wheel; their parts might rust. But it is hard to see in them any mechanism for heritable mutations. The only candidate involves their computer: conceivably, some phenomenon such as a hardware glitch or cosmic radiation might alter its programming, so that, instead of R3s, it builds a slightly distinct type of self-building truck.

But ultimately all its parts come from the warehouse, and even if we imagine that its supply is replenished indefinitely, there are not very many ways to combine these parts, and most of the combinations are not functioning machines at all. Hence it is not plausible to say that random glitches in an R3's programming could lead to alterations that make for improved longevity or copying.

Even though R3s reproduce, there is therefore good reason to deny that they are alive. The ability to reproduce does not suffice for life.

The replicators that shape known forms of life are DNA molecules. But nothing in the replicator-based account requires that living things be based solely on DNA. Somewhere in the universe life might be based on some other sort of replicator. Indeed, it might have been based on RNA here on Earth.

The replicator-based account is also compatible with the possibility of artificial life. Of course, artificialness is a matter of degree, and some existing living things are rather artificial. Through selective and cross-breeding, many artificial creatures have been introduced; for example, poodles, killer bees, and mules. Far more artificial organisms have been introduced by experimenters by altering the genomes of existing organisms. And recently experimenters have managed to transplant the genome of one species of bacteria into another. Eventually they hope to synthesize new genomes and put them in control of organisms (Wade 2007).

Genetically altered organisms illustrate an important fact: some life forms did not actually evolve through natural selection. This fact is compatible with the replicator-based account, which considers a thing alive only if it is based on structures that, under suitable conditions, are capable of replication, mutation, augmentation, and bequest. This is to say that life is based on structures that, like DNA, *could* generate organisms through natural selection. It is not to say that a type of creature is a life form only if it *did* evolve due to a replicating, mutating, augmenting, and bequeathing structure. Living things are based on structures with features that *suffice*, under favorable conditions, for the evolution of organisms by natural selection.

We can conceive, although vaguely and impressionistically, of far more artificial life. Quite reasonably, many people support using technology to extend the human lifespan (Veatch 1979), and using genetic engineering and other technology to extensively enhance the abilities of human beings, even if doing so means altering human nature somewhat (Glover 1984). Self-styled 'transhumanists' (Bostrom 2005) propose transforming human beings into (or should we say: replacing human beings with?) something else, something quite different, which they call "transhuman" or "post-human" beings. In one of their scenarios the improvements would be made by genetic engineering, so that transhumans are living beings, even if highly artificial. On another scenario, human abilities are augmented with gadgets implanted within the body. (Having equipped himself with electrodes by which he can access the internet, Kevin Warwick [2002] declared himself the world's first cyborg; according to Gillian Anderson, he is "Britain's leading prophet of the robot age," but I will reserve judgment until I hear what David Duchovny thinks.) On a related scenario, human limitations are overcome by replacing parts of human beings with machines. Some people dream of taking this project very far: they want to relocate their brains into, and put them in control of, robotic devices that are far more versatile and durable than human bodies. An entity consisting of a human brain inside and in control of a robotic device is sometimes called a cybernetic organism or 'cyborg.' But it would not be an organism at all. When part of the body is replaced with a prosthetic device such as an artificial heart or knee, the result is a living being with an attachment that is not alive. If such replacements are extensive, very little of the resulting being is alive. The brain-in-robot combination (like Darth Vader from *Star Wars*) is really a detached part of an organism – a brain – kept alive within a robot. Thus the project of swapping human parts with gadgets would, if taken far enough, involve replacing human beings with entities that are not organisms at all. If taken farther still – if parts of the brain itself were swapped with improved mechanical versions, or if we abandoned our bodies and "uploaded" our personalities into supercomputers, as Ray Kurzweil (2005) envisions – the point might be reached where none of the resulting being is alive. Human beings would have ceased to exist in the course of replacing themselves with nonliving mechanical beings.

Perhaps one day scientists will invent robots sophisticated enough to serve as the replicators by which things may undergo self-perpetuation as we have characterized it. Perhaps these will be Eric Drexler's (1986) nanobots, or hypothetical microscopic robots that can assemble things out of atoms. Imagine robots with the capacity to construct copies of themselves. Suppose they also construct and integrate themselves with mechanisms that promote their longevity and copying process. Suppose they bequeath mutations to their copies, including mutations of the features by which they construct the mechanisms with which they integrate themselves. And suppose the mechanisms the robots construct are capable of sustaining themselves through processes governed ultimately by the replicating robots which are part of them. Mechanisms that sustain themselves through processes governed by robots with this kind of versatility would seem to be living things – no matter how they came to exist.

Presently, it is difficult to decide how reasonable such speculations are. Help may come from a new field devoted to the study of 'artificial life' or 'alife' for short (Langton 1992). Theorists in this field attempt to use computer simulations to understand the principles by which forms of life might evolve. The principles by which life forms *might* evolve would show how life is possible, and should help clarify how life forms *did* evolve. They would also help clarify what possible life forms there could be.

HUMANITY, PERSONHOOD, IDENTITY

To be human is to be a human being – or a piece of one, like a bone or foot, possibly detached but kept alive, and possibly abnormal, like a teratoma. Human beings, in turn, belong to that species of organisms which biologists have designated *Homo sapiens* ('wise ones'). As members of the species *Homo sapiens* they display a distinctive (though slightly variable) genome. (I put aside issues concerning the notion of a species; for discussion, see Ereshefsky 2001.) A living thing with a substantially different genome, or no DNA at all, cannot possibly be a human being, no matter how humanoid it appears. Can we also say that any being with the genome of *Homo sapiens* is a human being? That is much more controversial. Arguably (as Eric Olson suggested to me), a creature that shares that genome through sheer chance, and whose origin is wholly unrelated to that of organisms on Earth, is not a human being. (A version of Davidson's [1987] Swampman case is a good example: suppose that a lightning strike on some planet far from Earth causes molecules spontaneously to combine to form a creature that, by sheer coincidence, happens to have the genome of *Homo sapiens*.) As we shall see later, it is also reasonable to deny that certain organisms with the genome of *Homo sapiens* are (fully formed) human beings, since they are still developing. However, this much seems clear: necessarily, a creature is a human being only if it is an organism with the distinctive genome of *Homo sapiens*.

What is the relationship between personhood and humanity? One view is that, necessarily, something is a person if and only if it is a human being. Let us call this the *biological conception* of personhood. Another position, which we can call the *psychological conception* of personhood, says that, necessarily, persons are all and only those things that have certain sorts of psychological attributes, among which the most important is the capacity for self-awareness (Locke 1975).

The case against the biological conception of personhood is simple and straightforward. Suppose there are self-aware animals other than human beings (such as chimpanzees and orangutans [Gallup 1970] and possibly bottlenose dolphins [Marten and Psarakos, 1994]), or suppose there are self-aware beings elsewhere in the universe who are not members of *Homo sapiens*, or that, one day, we will construct self-aware machines of some sort. Lacking humanness does not preclude such beings from having self-awareness, and surely self-awareness suffices for personhood. Yet humanness is necessary for personhood according to the biological conception. Clearly, then, the psychological conception is more plausible than the biological conception of personhood.

However, even if we accept the psychological conception of personhood, we can fail to have an answer to further important questions, including this one: If you and I are to exist at some time other than the present, must we be persons at that time? It would be particularly helpful to know what determines whether I, who exist now, am one and the same as (numerically identical with) something that exists at some other time. The answer to the latter question would set out my *persistence conditions*.

In what follows I will consider three views of my persistence conditions: I persist by virtue of psychological continuity; I persist just when I remain the same human being; or I persist just when I remain the same mind. Another possibility is that I simply do not have any persistence conditions. I will not discuss this position, but it is worth mentioning. As we will see, each of the other three positions faces powerful criticisms, given which the fourth alternative might be worth serious consideration.

The psychological account of persistence

One view, which I will call the *psychological account of persistence*, is that my persistence over time is determined by my psychological features and the relations among them (Locke 1975, Parfit 1984). These features include experiences, acts of forming intentions, character traits, and decisions, for example. Two key relations may hold among these features: psychological connectedness and psychological continuity.

Psychological connectedness refers to certain direct relations between features. For example, *having an experience* and later *remembering having that experience* are connected; *forming an intention to plant quince* and later *acting on that intention* are connected; also, having a character trait, and retaining it until later, constitute connectedness. *Psychological continuity*, by contrast, is overlapping chains of strong connectedness. Suppose that, as a child, I got my first puppy; as a youth, I first met my fiancée; and as older adult I got my first gray hair. Suppose, too, that the youth can recall getting the puppy, the older adult can recall meeting his fiancée, but the adult cannot recall getting the puppy. Then the youth is psychologically connected to the child, and the adult to the youth, but the adult is *not* connected to the child (for simplicity, we can pretend that my psychology reduces to memory). However, the adult is *continuous* with the child, since the adult is connected to the youth and the youth to the child.

On one theory, the connectedness view, one's persistence over time is determined entirely by psychological connectedness. This account implies that persistence is a matter of degree. The child probably will have more psychological connections to the youth than to the adult; if persistence is wholly determined by connectedness, and connectedness is a matter of degree, then we may gradually lose our identities. This will seem unacceptable to anyone who believes that identity is all or nothing – that one either is, or is not, the same person over time.

The connectedness view also implies that persistence is not transitive. The youth and the child are the same person, being connected, as are the adult and the youth. But the adult and the youth are not the same person. This result is unacceptable; personal identity must be understood in terms of a *transitive* relation (a relation R such that, if A bears R to B, and B to C, then A bears R to C), since identity itself is transitive.

Transitivity can be preserved if we account for personal identity in terms of continuity instead of connectedness. On the continuity view, one's persistence over time is determined wholly by chains of strong connectedness. This account restores transitivity: if X is strongly connected to Y, and Y to Z, then X and Z are continuous; hence X, Y, and Z are all the same individual.

Both forms of the psychological account of persistence – that my persistence depends on connectedness and the view that my persistence depends on continuity – position us to handle certain puzzling cases, such as the following:

Transplantation: My brain (or cerebrum) is removed from my cranium, destroyed, and replaced with your brain (or cerebrum), which is the only part of your body that remains after a tragic accident. The survivor wakes, and believes that he or she *is* you.

Cerebral death: After a car crash, your brain is deprived of oxygen so long that all of your brain dies except its stem, leaving a body in a persistent vegetative state.

On either form of the psychological account, in the former I travel with my brain and in the latter I share my brain's demise.

However, the psychological account faces problems of its own. One difficulty involves the following example (Wiggins 1967, 50; Parfit 1984, 254):

Division: Half of your cerebrum is transplanted to a body that lacks its own cerebrum and the other half is transplanted to a second body that lacks its own cerebrum. Upon waking after surgery, both survivors believe they are you.

Each survivor is connected to and continuous with you, so both are you, according to psychologism. This is a problem, since two persons cannot be one.

David Lewis (1976) offered a solution to this difficulty. According to Lewis, each survivor is identical to someone who donated his cerebrum, yet the survivors are not one and the same person. Instead, contrary to appearances, *two* persons donated the cerebra in Division. Before surgery, the donors were indistinguishable, and they thought they were just one person: you. They were mistaken. One of them persists in the body that receives their left hemisphere, and the other persists in the body that receives their right hemisphere. While Lewis's solution is coherent, even ingenious, it is also difficult to accept, since it implies that two persons can be completely indistinguishable for most of their lives. As Lewis put the point, it seems to lead to "overpopulation." To see why, let us apply his solution to amoebas. Suppose you put what appears to be a single amoeba into a jug of nutrients, and watch as it divides. Its descendants also divide, upon which there appear to be four amoebas in the jug. You then squish them, and declare the experiment to be over. Question: Did your experiment really begin with one amoeba? Not on Lewis's account. On Lewis's view, your experiment began and ended with the same number of amoebas: four. If you had squished the amoeba in your jug before it could divide, it would have been a single amoeba. Call it A. If you had let one division occur and then squished the two amoebas that result, your experiment would have begun with two amoebas, each indistinguishable from A prior to the division. If you let millions of divisions occur, your experiment would have began with trillions of amoebas, each indistinguishable from A prior to the first division. The pattern is clear: your experiments always begin and end with the same number of amoebas. And what goes for the amoebas in your experiments goes for real amoebas: there are no more amoebas today than there ever were!

There are other options. Proponents of the psychological account of persistence might settle on a two-part response defended by Derek Parfit. First, they can recommend the admittedly strange view that neither survivor of Division is you. This recommendation they can base on the view that a person who exists now is identical to a being existing at some other time T if and only if the latter is the only being at T with whom he is psychologically continuous. On this view, identity consists in *non-branching* psychological continuity. Second, they can explain why their stance seems strange: it is because we do not realize that identity is not what really matters in surviving over time. What is important in survival? When we feel prudential, egoistic concern for someone existing at another time, what is it that we care about? Division suggests that we care about psychological continuity and connectedness. We want there to be some-one in the future who, among other things, inherits our character traits, acts on our plans, and attempts to unify her life with ours. All of this is preserved in Division twice over: it is present in your relationship with *each* of the two survivors. But neither survivor *is* you, so identity is not what matters. According to Parfit's *detachment thesis*, what matters can be separated from identity: Division ends our existence yet preserves the continuity and connectedness that is of egoistic concern to us. Division is baffling since we normally think that the preservation of psychological continuity is the very same thing as the preservation of identity.

I will discuss Parfit's detachment thesis further in chapter 7. It is ingenious, but questionable; while most of us want to share psychological ties with someone in the future, we also want to *be* at least one of these individuals, so that we can continue to have good lives. We cannot have a life at all if we cease to be!

Psychologism faces other objections. According to Jeff McMahan, we get the wrong results if we define our persistence conditions in terms of psychological continuity or connectedness, even if we insist that con-tinuity and connectedness have their usual cause. Consider the following:

> *Isolation*: You develop Alzheimer's disease. Eventually the dementia is so severe that day to day psychologically connections, and continuity, are lost. Nevertheless, an "isolated subject" remains, whose awareness is limited to the moment (McMahan 2002, 65).

Psychologism implies that you will have ceased to exist before the isolated subject appears; the isolated subject is a new being, whose existence begins after Alzheimer's ends the existence of its victim. McMahan says that this result is counterintuitive. Suppose you were in the early stages of Alzheimer's, and were told that, after your disease leaves behind an isolated subject, this subject would be tortured. McMahan (following B. Williams 1970) thinks you would fear the torture, and that this suggests that you think you and the isolated subject are the same individual. (But do we fear for ourselves or is our fear based on empathy for someone we know to be intimately related to us?) If you and the subject are the same, we will need a different account of our persistence conditions.

The animalist account of persistence

The view that you and I are animals (or, more specifically, human beings) is called *animalism* (Snowdon 1990, Olson 1997, 2007). If all animals are essentially animals, in the sense that nothing that is an animal could exist without being an animal, then you and I are essentially animals. Let us call the latter position – that we are essentially animals – *animal essentialism.*

Animalism and animal essentialism are consistent with the possibility, mentioned earlier, that some persons are not human beings. Suppose that there are some self-aware androids, one of whom I will call *Data.* Data cannot be essentially a human being; he is not any sort of animal. But that does not preclude *my* being essentially human. Rejecting the biological conception of personhood is necessary if we are to recognize the possibility of persons who are not human beings. But the possibility of such persons is consistent with saying, of some persons, even all persons who have lived (who may well be confined to Earth), that they are essentially human beings.

If animalism is correct, it seems reasonable to say that my persistence conditions are as follows: I, a human being who exists now, am identical to something that exists at another time if and only if it and I are the same human being. Let us consider whether this account is plausible.

The strongest case against the animalist account of persistence involves examples like Transplantation. In Transplantation, you appear to survive while I do not. However, if biological persistence conditions were applicable, apparently it would be the other way around. The organism you once were is destroyed; only one organ remains, namely a brain. A brain, it seems, is not a human being, not an organism. While it can assist in its maintenance, and is therefore alive, it is not capable of the many vital processes that enable organisms to be as highly self-sufficient as they are.

Or *is* a brain an organism? Peter van Inwagen (1990) argues that, much as an organism can survive the loss of a limb, it can be pared down to a brain. However, as animalists realize, anyone tempted to agree that a brain is an organism can alter the Transplantation case, so that not your brain, but only your cerebrum, or only half of it, is transplanted into my cranium, in which only my brain stem remains of my brain. Or is half of a cerebrum also an organism? If so, which hemisphere is the surviving organism if the two are separated and kept alive?

In the Transplantation case, the animalist account of persistence seems to suggest that I survive and you do not. I am the organism whose brain is removed; I receive a transplant – a brain – which enables me to persist. You, on the other hand, are destroyed; all that remains of you is a single organ. After thinking about this example, most people conclude that *you* survive; you have been reduced to your brain, but then you are given a brainless body, which was once mine. If they are correct, it seems that we must reject the animalist account of persistence.

Another example poses a challenge for the animalist account:

Cerebral Death: After a car crash, your brain is deprived of oxygen so long that all of your brain dies except its stem, leaving a body in a persistent vegetative state.

Apparently, you do not survive the crash. But if you are an organism, you do. You survive as an organism that is no longer self-aware. Hence the animalist view of persistence seems implausible.

The mindist account of persistence

McMahan suggests that you and I are *minds*, defined as entities capable of consciousness. Let us call this view *mindism*. If all minds are essentially minds, it follows that you and I are essentially minds. We can call this latter view, that we are essentially minds, *mind essentialism* (cf. DeGrazia 2005, 129). Given mindism, it seems reasonable to adopt the *mindist account of persistence*, according to which we persist just when our minds remain intact. McMahan's version of the mindist account is that we persist just in case the regions of our brains that are responsible for our capacity for consciousness remain undivided as well as functional enough to make consciousness possible (2002, 66–68; compare Hasker 1999, ch. 7).

He calls his view of our persistence the Embodied Mind Account of Identity.

According to McMahan's mindist account of persistence, you and I survive Isolation: we persist as isolated subjects since the relevant regions of our brains continue to operate well enough to make consciousness possible, even though other aspects of our psychology are lost. We will survive the ravages of extreme dementia, and Transplantation, as long as our brains are capable of consciousness. We could even persist as a Darth Vader-type cyborg. But we could not persist via Uploading or Duplication.

Revisions

Animalists might borrow from Parfit to make their view more plausible. They can acknowledge that mere identity is not valuable. After Cerebral Death, we remain in existence, but our continued existence adds nothing of value to our lives. Our continued existence matters most while we are psychologically continuous beings, which is possible only while we are persons, understood as beings that are capable of self-awareness. Personhood is an episode during the life of a human being, much like infancy. 'Person' is to 'human being' as 'tadpole' is to 'frog': 'person' applies merely during the self-aware stages of a human being's life. In Wiggins's (1980) terminology, 'person' is a phase sortal, not a substance sortal. Substance sortals classify things in terms of their essential properties. A property P is essential to something just in case that thing cannot exist without having P. For example, the property of being a frog is an essential property of frogs: nothing that is a frog could exist without being a frog. Hence 'frog' is a substance sortal. By contrast, phase sortals sort things in terms of properties which they can exist without. A particular frog can be tadpole for a while, and then cease to be a tadpole, without ceasing to be altogether. After being a tadpole, it can remain a frog. Animalists can say that our existence matters most while we are persons, and that the reason we tend to believe that you survive Transplantation, while I do not, is that we find it difficult to detach the continuity we prize from identity even when the two separate; after Transplantation, I retain mere identity, but you enjoy continuity.

These considerations help, but the animalist account of persistence is still open to doubts. Consider an example which epistemologists discuss endlessly:

Brain in Vat: Your body is destroyed except for your brain, which is kept alive in a vat, and attached to elaborate machinery that allows you to communicate with others. Upon waking, the survivor thinks she or he is you, and has reflections just like yours, although these thoughts quickly change when the situation sinks in ("D'oh! I'm a brain in a vat!").

The logic of identity forces us to relinquish the position that the survivors of Division are you. In the Transplantation case, bodily continuity offers some grounds for saying that I survive, and not you. But in the Brain in Vat case, the organism that was your body is destroyed. Someone survives, and that person is the only one who is psychologically continuous with you. This continuity even has the usual cause. If this person is not you, who is it? It does little good to claim that the Vatted survivor merely appears to be you because what matters is preserved. Animalists must accept one of two very implausible conclusions: either that no one survives in the vat, or that the individual in the vat has sprung suddenly into existence. We might call this the *naked brain problem.*

Some of the worries about the psychological account of persistence can be met by moving the view a bit closer to the animalist account. Consider two examples:

Uploading: Your body is killed but not until your personality is 'uploaded' into a machine in such a fashion that psychological connectedness is preserved in the resulting being.

Duplication: Using you as the model, scientists build an organic person who resembles you down to the last detail. This duplicate's life begins at the very instant you fall into a volcano and are incinerated. The duplicate's thoughts pick up where yours left off.

According to the psychological account of persistence as it stands, the psychological continuity that determines whether you survive can have *any* cause. It can be caused by 'Uploading' or by Duplicating your body, for example. I am inclined to deny that you survive in the Uploading and Duplication cases. I know that some will disagree. (Presumably Ray Kurzweil and others who want to be cyborgs adopt the form of person essentialism that endorses survival via Uploading.) However, I think that is because they believe that what happens is nearly as good as survival. (My own response to Uploading is sympathy for the victim; if his [its?] personality is anything like mine, he would respond with horror when his condition became clear.)

The psychological approach may be modified so as accommodate these concerns. Instead of saying that identity-preserving continuity can have any cause, we can demand that it have its usual cause. Parfit (1984, 207–209) argues in favor of accepting any cause, but his official view appears to be that we should not try to reach a decision about which sort of cause is appropriate (see "Note added in 1985" on p. x). For us, the usual cause is a set of processes in the brain; conceivably it will be different for persons who are very different from us, like androids. Uploading and Duplication do not preserve psychological continuity through these cerebral processes. Hence on the refined version of psychologism you do not survive Uploading or Duplication (but you do survive Transplantation).

However, even as refined, the psychological account of persistence implies that we cannot survive Isolation. It faces other problems as well.

One worry about the psychological account is that it says little about *what* you and I are. Suppose that proponents of the psychological account say that we are *persons*, where 'person' is defined as any creature which has the capacity for self-awareness and thought. Call this view *personism*. If all persons are essentially persons, a view we can call *person essentialism* will follow: namely that we are essentially persons. So understood, person essentialism differs from the view we labeled 'mind essentialism,' assuming that some minds, such as those of early fetuses, lack the capacity for self-awareness, and hence are not persons. Person essentialism, like mind essentialism, leaves us with difficult questions.

One such difficulty has been called the *thinking animal problem* (Carter 1982, Olson 2007). If either person or mind essentialism is true, then I am not the human being whose body I travel about with, since it lacked a mind, and was incapable of self-awareness, during its early stages of development, and will possibly lack them again towards the end of its life. The same goes for you, too: neither one of us can be one and the same thing as the human beings whose bodies we share, since these organisms can exist when we do not. However, even if *we* are not human beings, it is obvious that there *are* human beings. They are creatures in their own right. During one very long phase of their lives human beings are an awfully lot *like* us. They certainly appear to develop psychological capacities, such as self-awareness and thought, which are characteristic of persons or minds. One human being seems to be holding the book which you are now reading, and thinking the very thoughts you are thinking at this moment! If all this is true, it is puzzling indeed to say that we are not these beings. How would we know? Do you know you are not one of the human beings now reading this sentence? When you utter the words "I am not a human being," a human being who shares your consciousness would be uttering the same words. *He* would have said something false. But on what basis could you assume that you were not a human being who has just said something false?

Now, we *can* say that human beings really do not develop the ability to think, and that they do not really become self-aware. They are mindless zombies; calling them "*Homo sapiens*" is a gross misnomer. We can base this claim on the assumption that the capacity for self-awareness or thought is essential to whatever bears it. If these capacities are essential to their bearers, then human beings cannot have them – since human beings can exist without them. If we are not them, then each of us shares his or her body with one of these dull-witted, oblivious beings. But this conclusion is hard to believe, and the assumption on which it is based (the assumption that certain psychological attributes, such as the capacity for self-awareness or thought, are essential to whatever bears them) is far from obvious. Why shouldn't we think that psychological attributes are contingent to human beings – properties which human beings develop in the course of their lives? On that view, even if the capacities for thought and self-awareness are essential to 'persons,' animals might also come to develop these capacities, as contingent (nonessential) features.

Some theorists say that while I am not identical to my body, I am *constituted* by (made of the same stuff as) my body, in much the same way that a statue is constituted by a particular bit of bronze. The statue and the bronze are two different things: the former and not the latter is destroyed if melted. But they coincide spatially (and conceivably temporally too, if their existence begins and ends at the same time). Perhaps I am related to my body in the same way: I and my body are spatially coincidental yet numerically distinct. On this view person essentialists could say that persons (like me) and not the bodies that constitute them think (Doepke 1996) or that bodies think in a derivative way – they think by virtue of constituting thinking persons (Baker 2000). However, it is difficult to see why the thinking animal problem does not arise once more (Olson 2007, 60–75). The body that constitutes me is, after all, just like me when I think. On what grounds can we deny that it is thinking? There is another puzzle as well: What determines that I am a person and not a body which constitutes a person?

Might I be a *piece* of an organism, such as a brain? That could provide an answer to the thinking animal problem: my body does not really think;

only a *piece* of my body thinks, namely its brain; my body itself thinks only in the derivative sense that it has a piece – me, the brain – that does its thinking. However, neither person essentialists nor mind essentialists can say that I am my brain, or part of my brain. My brain, and parts of it such as the cerebrum, can exist without being capable of consciousness or self-awareness, as the brains of early fetuses show.

Might I be a temporal *stage* of the organism whose body I share, in much the same way that a tadpole is a stage of a frog? If so, we might say that I am a human-being-while-capable-of-awareness, as compared to a human being *simpliciter*. The former are temporal stages of the latter. Unlike human-beings-while-capable-of-awareness, human beings can lack the capacity for awareness; the latter come into existence precisely when human beings acquire the capacity of awareness and cease to exist when that capacity is lost. But when a frog moves out of its tadpole stage, no one thinks that some creature ceases to exist (unlike 'frog,' 'tadpole' is a phase sortal, not a substance sortal). We think that one and the same creature, a frog, exists during and after its tadpole stage. Yet person and mind essentialists think that I am a creature in my own right, with my own essence; if I am literally a stage of a human being, which is itself a creature, then a creature – I – does indeed cease to exist when another creature – the creature I call my body – loses the capacity for awareness. Why not adopt the simpler view that one and the same creature, namely a human being, exists before and after it is capable of awareness, and that you and I are human beings? Note, too, that the stage approach we are considering leaves us with the thinking animal problem. It is implausible to deny that human beings think on the grounds that only certain of their stages think. To say that a certain stage of a human being thinks is simply to say that a human being thinks at certain times.

Consider, finally, the version of mind essentialism offered by Jeff McMahan. In order to answer the question of what we are, McMahan appears to combine the stage approach with the piece approach, and it is far from clear that the resulting view is a satisfactory answer to the thinking animal problem or to the question of what we are. McMahan says (2002, 92) that you and I are "regions of the brain in certain functional states." (Compare the position of Michael Tye [2003, 143]: we are "brains insofar as those brains are in the appropriate physical states.") This appears to mean that I am *my brain-while-it-is-capable-of-awareness*, or I am *part-of-my-brain-while-this-part-is-capable-of-awareness*. On the combined approach, there is a fundamental difference between a brain that is now capable of awareness and a brain-capable-of-awareness: the former might lack the capacity for awareness at various times, but the latter cannot. The combined view says that I am a temporal stage of my brain (or a temporal stage of a piece of my brain). It gives you and me the odd distinction of being creatures that are temporal stages of parts of other creatures! We are hauled around within human beings of which we are partially constitutive, rather like their mitochondria.

Each of the three essentialist accounts of what we are, and each of the three accounts of persistence, leaves us with daunting problems, bullets to be bitten. I do not know of views of what we are and when we persist that are free of substantial objections. If we deny that we are human beings, we will be stuck with the bizarre view that we share our bodies with human beings with lives of their own. However, examples such as the Transplantation and Brain in Vat cases strongly suggest that we are persons or minds. Personally, I cannot bring myself to deny that I would go with my brain when Transplanted or put into the Vat. I doubt I am alone in this. Hence I will have to remain agnostic on the topic of exactly what we are, and exactly what our persistence conditions are.

A final point: all of the accounts we have considered are consistent with the possibility, mentioned earlier, that an order of wholly nonliving devices could be persons. At the moment, self-aware machines, such as Data from *Star Trek*, are the stuff of science fiction. But it is possible that one day we will construct machines that are self-aware. These will be functioning persons, being self-aware, who are nevertheless nonliving, since either they are not self-perpetuating (they may be wholly unable to maintain themselves), or else their mode of self-perpetuation is not replicator-based.

However, that they are not alive does not imply that they are insignificant. There are two powerful reasons to assign mechanical persons high value.

First, they are important from the moral point of view. The only known self-aware beings are alive; hence it is natural to assume that the only persons with moral significance are those that are (or will be) alive. But assuming that (1) moral standing is that property by which an individual is owed moral consideration, (2) self-awareness is one mark of moral standing, and (3) self-awareness need not depend on vital processes, we must conclude that life is not a prerequisite for moral standing.

Second, even if mechanical persons literally do not have life, they might well be capable of something about as good. We can exploit the important fact that persons are aware of many of the things they do and much of what happens to them. Let us stipulate, of beings who are aware of their existence over time, that they have a *conscious existence*. A being might have the capacity for self-awareness without having the ability to care about its own existence or the ability to plan and shape its activities. But if a mechanical person were equipped with the ability to care about and to shape its conscious existence, it would be the moral equal of similarly equipped live persons.

SUMMARY

On my view, something is alive only if it has a substantial capacity to maintain itself, but not just any form of self-maintenance will serve. The self-maintenance of living things is controlled by durable replicators. These are replicators that are able to mutate, augment themselves, and bequeath mutations. A thing is alive just when it has a reasonably substantial capacity to maintain itself using processes that are controlled by durable replicators within it. An organism, in turn, I have defined as a living individual. This view takes no stand on what constitutes an individual organism. Hence it cannot say whether the mitochondria within us or the colonies of ants in the yard are organisms in their own right. It also leaves open the possibility that living things very unlike the ones with which we are familiar could be developed. Perhaps an order of things could be based on mechanisms that have features much like those of DNA. Then those things, too, might be capable of replicator based self-perpetuation.

We are living things. But on some ways of understanding what we are, we may continue to exist after we are dead. As for what we are, and when we persist, I described three views about what we are, and three views about our persistence conditions. Animal essentialism says we are essentially animals, specifically human beings; person essentialism says the capacity for self-awareness is essential to us; and mind essentialism says we are essentially minds. The animalist account of persistence says we persist just as long as we remain the same human beings; the psychological account says we persist just in case we retain sufficient psychological continuity; and the mindist account says we persist just as long as our minds remain intact.

All of these views seem to face powerful counterexamples. We can pare animals down quite a bit, but it seems counterintuitive to say that they can be pared down to a cerebrum. Yet if our brains are Vatted, or if one of our cerebra is Transplanted, we seem to survive. This problem does not arise if we accept person or mind essentialism, but others do, the worst of which is that we share our bodies with human beings with lives of their own; either these human beings are inexplicably unable to think for themselves, or else their mental lives are indistinguishable from ours, and if the latter is true, it is hard to resist concluding that we just *are* these human beings.

There are ways to bolster each of the views about what we are and what it takes for us to persist, but each requires that we accept counterintuitive conclusions. As things stand, it seems best to withhold judgment.

CHAPTER 3

Death

I have portrayed life as replicator-based self-perpetuation, and human beings as (possibly developing) members of the species *Homo sapiens*. I considered several ways of understanding what we are and the conditions under which we persist before retreating to agnosticism on the matter. In this chapter I discuss death. It seems apparent that a death is the ending of a life, but in several respects the term 'death' is unclear and ambiguous. My first task, taken up in the first section, is to clarify it. In the next section I consider criteria by which we can recognize that an individual's death has occurred. It turns out that the criteria that have been adopted in the United States and in the United Kingdom are not accurate, and it is difficult indeed to see what to put in their place.

DEATH CLARIFIED

In order to clarify what death is, I will begin by distinguishing it from aging. Aging is not the same thing as death, but the two phenomena overlap in fascinating ways. Then I will discuss what it is for a life to end: is it, for example, a process a thing can undergo or is it the completion of that process? I will also contrast life's ending with its suspension; if, like a clock's movement, our vital processes are interrupted but may be restarted, have we died? Next I will consider how ceasing to exist is related to dying: may we cease to exist deathlessly, or die without ceasing to exist? The answer is not as obvious as it might seem.

Aging

When we are shot, stabbed, splashed with acid, or poisoned, the cells in our bodies are killed in a straightforward if messy way. They undergo a form of death called *necrosis*: their membranes stop operating properly, causing them and some of their organelles to swell and burst. One or more systems that are essential to cellular maintenance are destroyed, bringing down secondary systems as well, in a chain reaction. The cells' contents leak into surrounding tissue, causing inflammation and further damage.

In necrosis, the cells do not initiate their own demise; they are killed despite themselves. But cellular death is not always like this. Some of the cells of multicellular organisms self-destruct in an orchestrated process called programmed cell death, or *apoptosis* (Potten and Wilson 2004). Enzymes begin to digest the cells; they shrink, and their organelles, including the contents of their nuclei, break down into fragments that attract phagocytic cells that engulf and consume them, and send out chemical signals that inhibit inflammation in surrounding tissue. Apoptosis has a variety of triggers. Sometimes it is initiated by the cell itself, when it is infected or damaged. It can also have triggers that are external to the cell. For example, the immune system might initiate self-destruction in a cell found to be infected with a virus. Apoptosis is also one of the mechanisms by which developing organisms are shaped; the hands of embryos form fingers when the cells between the digits undergo apoptosis. It is one of the ways in which death plays an integral role in the formation of an organism. In some organisms its role is more striking. For example, the wood that trees grow (their inner xylem) dies soon after it is formed, leaving a strong but wholly dead inner scaffold surrounded by a living skin.

Both of these types of death should be distinguished from biological aging, the process by which organisms are gradually less able to maintain and renew themselves. The aging of organisms involves replicative (or cellular) *senescence*, which occurs in somatic cells, which are the cells of which most of the body (or 'soma') is composed, when these are no longer able to proliferate themselves. They can divide only a limited number of times. It turns out that this limit – Hayflick's limit, it is sometimes called, after its discoverer Leonard Hayflick (1965) – has a genetic basis. Cell division results in the shortening of telomeres, which are repeated DNA sequences at the ends of chromosomes. Unlike the rest of the chromosome, telomeres are not fully replicated; they shrink with each generation of cell division, until eventually cells cannot divide, since their chromosomes have become unstable (Harley 1992). This shrinking can be reversed by an enzyme called telomerase; strikingly, telomerase can rejuvenate a cell line that has reached the Hayflick limit (Bodnar 1998). But telomerase is active only in so-called 'immortal' cells, such as reproductive cells, stem cells, cancer cells, and some unicellular eukaryotes like paramecia. Telomerase is not active in somatic cells. Therefore they are 'mortal' (Harley 2001). Telomere shrinking is not the only trigger for senescence; it can also be initiated, prematurely, by the activation of cancer genes, DNA damage, oxidative stress, and other things, all of which can trigger apoptosis as well (Chen and Goligorski 2006).

Undoubtedly, telomere erosion plays a substantial role in the aging of people, but the specifics are not clear. It is not a simple matter of our chromosomes losing their telomeres, causing our cells to cease proliferating, for our chromosomes never completely lose their telomeres: the telomeres of people who are 100 years old appear long enough to permit perhaps twenty more doublings (Allsopp 1992, Nakamura 2002). Aging also involves the accumulation of damage to macromolecules such as DNA, and to cells and tissues. As a result, the body becomes less and less able to repair and maintain itself, and more susceptible to disease.

Aging sets the stage for death, but is not itself a form of death. Cells that have reached replicative senescence can still repair and maintain themselves for a time. By contrast, apoptosis and necrosis are both forms of death; apoptosis is a process of cellular death, while necrosis is a process by which either an organism or its tissues may die.

Life's end

It seems reasonable to say that death is life's ending, and that a particular death is the ending of the life of a particular thing – the ending of its vital processes. But complications arise concerning the notion of an ending. (As we will see later, other complications arise concerning the relationship between ceasing to live and ceasing to exist.)

A life's ending is one thing, and its having been ended is another. Socrates' life ended – his death occurred – sometime in 399 BCE. Thereafter, his life has remained ended, leaving him dead. Like 'construction,' 'death' is ambiguous; it may be a process or the product (or result) of a process. 'Death' can refer either to the events whereby a life ends, or to the condition or state of affairs of its being over. The latter is relatively straightforward. But let us see if we can get clearer about 'the events whereby a life ends.'

Many theorists construe the ending of a life, the ending of something's (capacity for) vital processes, as a (more or less) momentary event. An alternative view is that it is a process or sequence of events.

Thought of as a process, a death might be compared to a race or a fall. A race begins when something begins racing, and ends when it finishes; a fall is initiated when something begins to move downwards under the influence of gravity, and ends abruptly upon contact with the surface below; likewise, a death begins when something starts dying and ends when the dying process is over; for example, a cell's death might begin when it initiates apoptosis and end when apoptosis is complete. The process view supports two claims about death.

First, it is not instantaneous. In dying, our vital processes are progressively extinguished, until finally they are gone, in a process that stretches out over a period of time, however brief. The poison Socrates drank caused him a relatively quick death. It probably induced respiratory paralysis, which initiated death; after his circulation ceased, the cells in his body would have continued to metabolize for about 4 to 10 minutes, then the membranes within them would have ruptured, releasing enzymes that then digested the cells from within, completing the dying process. Autolysis or self-digestion would have occurred quicker in some organs, such as his cerebrum, than others, and spread through his body. Socrates did not die instantly; it took time for his vital processes to cease.

The second claim is that death lacks clear boundaries. In this respect death is like birth: does a birth begin when the hormone oxytocin initiates contractions? When contractions begin pushing the fetus? (What if the contractions stop, then resume several hours later?) When the child begins moving through the birth canal? (What if its progress ceases for a lengthy interval of time?) Apparently there is no precise time when a birth begins. The boundaries of death are blurry as well. When Socrates stopped breathing, it took some time for his blood to cease to carry oxygen to and remove carbon dioxide from his body's tissues. It also took some time for his tissues to begin dying, and still more time for them to be completely dead. It is an indeterminate matter when, in this sequence of events, Socrates' death started and ended.

However, when some philosophers speak of 'the ending of a life' they mean to refer to a (more or less) momentary event. What sort of event would this be? There are two or three possibilities.

First, 'death' might refer to the completion of the dying process – the loss of the very last of life. I will call this *denouement death*. Here death is comparable to the end of a fire: until the last flame is out, the fire is not extinguished; until life is gone, death has not taken place. In this sense 'death' is not at all like 'race' or 'fall'. It would be absurd to speak a race or fall as occurring only at the very end of the racing or falling process.

Second, 'death' might refer to an earlier point in the dying process. Firefighters might pronounce a fire 'out' if they have battled it until it is beyond revival, even if they know that a few live embers remain beneath well-doused ashes. This way of speaking suggests that a fire ends when reduced beyond a point of no return, not when completely extinguished. Perhaps we should also say that an organism dies, not when its vital processes come completely to an end, but when they reach the point of no return, and death's completion is assured, no matter what is done to forestall it. I will call this *threshold death*. However, reaching this point in the dying process must be distinguished from an event that renders death causally necessary, for a condition can guarantee that a creature will die considerably before it begins to die. One does not die at the moment one's body is perfused with a fatal poison that has not yet begun to undermine one's health, but at that moment one's death may well be guaranteed. Of course, even when threshold death occurs it is likely that much of the dying process has yet to occur.

There may be a third possibility. Many theorists (e.g., Grisez and Boyle 1979, Bernat, Culver, and Gert 1981, Belshaw forthcoming) say that death occurs when the various physiological systems of the body irreversibly cease to function as an integrated whole. I will call this *integration death*. However, it is hard to see why the loss of integrated functioning is a significant point in the dying process, unless the idea is that it entails threshold death. It does seem reasonable to think that integration death entails threshold death, but threshold death can occur before integration death does. For example, irreparable damage to the immune system might bring about threshold death even before the body's integrated functioning has ceased. (A puzzle: Is it possible to kill an individual, say by quickly incinerating or crushing her, after she has reached the point of integration death or threshold death?)

In its earlier stages – before the point of no return – the dying process can be reversed. In a cell, apoptosis may be initiated, then reversed; similarly, an individual organism's respiration and heartbeat may stop for a time, then be resuscitated. In such cases a cell or an individual was *dying*, even though the process was interrupted, and even reversed.

The fact that vital processes can decline before completely ending suggests that the process of dying occurs in degrees, and if the state of death is not just the final product of the process of dying, but also the intermediate products, then dying can put us into a state in which we are only partially alive. That is, at one time the dying process may have just begun, leaving us mostly alive, and at a later time it might be well under way, leaving us only somewhat alive, and so forth.

Thus death can be a *state* (being dead) or the *process* of extinction (dying); it might also be equated with one of two *events* during the dying process: *threshold* death occurs when the dying process reaches the point of irreversibility, while *denouement* death occurs when the dying process completes itself.

Suspension

There are other respects in which 'death' is unclear. It seems somewhat indeterminate whether the temporary ending of life suffices for death, or whether death entails a permanent loss of life. Usually if a life stops, the condition is permanent, but in unusual circumstances it will not be, or it might not be. On the one hand, it seems, a life might be suspended for a while then *revived*. On the other hand it might be *restored*.

When a clock is stopped and restarted later, its action clearly is suspended for a while. Something similar happens to seeds, spores, and frozen embryos, making it tempting to say that their lives are suspended, until reinitiated by a catalyst. However, this is a loose way of speaking. Instead of saying that, in the case of seeds, spores, or frozen embryos, an organism's *life* has been suspended or temporarily ended, let us instead say that its *vital processes* have been temporarily suspended, and that it remains alive while these stop. This is appropriate, because an organism whose vital processes are suspended for a time still has, during that time, the *capacity* to maintain itself, just as a sleeping person retains the capacity for consciousness.

Now imagine a futuristic device:

The Disassembler-Reassembler: This machine gathers information about my structure, then reduces me to small cubes, or individual cells, or even to disconnected atoms, which it stores. Later, using the information it has gathered, it reassembles the components it has stored just as they were before.

Many of us will say that I would survive – my life would continue – after the reassembly. My life would have been restored. But it is quite clear that I would not live during intervals when pieces of me, or my atoms, are kept in storage. *I* do not exist during those intervals, so I am certainly not alive then. (Nor would destroying the machine after my reduction to small pieces kill me, as I am already dead.)

There is an important difference between revival and restoration. An organism (or one of its parts) may be revived if it is in suspended animation. While it is a seed, a plant's vital processes are suspended; the plant is not dead. If we find a way to freeze adult human beings so that they can be revived, as we can embryos and frogs, we should say that their lives, too, are suspended, not ended, while frozen. Their existence would continue while they are held in cold storage. Restoration differs from revival in this respect. Consider another machine:

> *The Corpse Reassembler*: I have a heart attack, and die. My corpse begins to decompose, but my nephew stows it away in a freezer. Centuries later, scientists thaw it and, using a device they call a Corpse Reassembler, return all of its atoms to where they were before I had my heart attack, thus restoring my life.

All this seems conceivable (although just barely!), but the process they use to restore my life is not a way of reviving it. The dying process ran its course. I died, and ceased to exist. So my corpse was not in suspended animation. All freezing it did was slow its decomposition. Let us say that after a creature has ceased to exist, it cannot be "revived," and its death cannot be "reversed"; however, its life may well be *restored*. Restoration is a way of bringing a creature back from the dead. (Would it be theoretically possible to restore the lives of everyone who has died by reassembling the matter of which they were composed when they died? Perhaps. One obstacle is that some of the matter of which one person was composed will be part of a later person; this precludes their simultaneous restoration, but not their resurrections at different times.)

These reflections suggest that something dies not when its vital processes are suspended, but rather when its capacity to maintain itself through its vital processes (which it retains even while in suspended animation) is destroyed. If that is correct, then the Disassembler-Reassembler kills me when it takes me apart, atom by atom, even though it restores my life when it puts the atoms back together. It is tempting to resist this conclusion. The term 'death' seems applicable only when a creature's life is *permanently* ended. If that is true, however, then Disassembly did not kill me: when I am Reassembled, my life goes on, so Disassembly did not end it permanently. Because we are inclined to view death as permanent, it is tempting to say that Disassembly puts me into a state that is not quite death, although it resembles death, much like suspended animation does. However, this option is ruled out by the fact that, while Disassembled, I do not exist. While Disassembled, the being that was alive is there no longer; there is nothing whose life might be suspended. Surely we do not want to say that no matter what brings our existence to an end, it does not kill us, if our atoms can be put back together somehow. It is best to deny that death entails the permanent ending of our lives.

Ceasing to exist

Something's death is the destruction of the vital processes by which it is sustained. May we also equate death with annihilation? Is something's death and the end of its existence the same thing?

Let us begin with one side of the equation, and ask 'Can something die yet continue to exist?' The view that dying entails ceasing to exist has been called the *termination thesis* (Feldman 1992, 2000). Some animalists deny it; they say that organisms may die without ceasing to exist. These writers point to expressions such as 'dead cat' and 'dead cow' to suggest that animals continue to exist, while no longer alive: they continue to exist as animal corpses or carcasses. If we accept this suggestion, presumably we think that an animal continues to count as the same animal if enough of its original components remain in much the same order, and that animals continue to meet this condition for an indefinite time following death (Mackie 1999), until their decomposition is advanced.

Something similar can be said about you and me, assuming, as animal essentialists do, that we are essentially animals: since animals can exist even after dying, so can we. Just as other animals persist as corpses after they die, we, too, will persist, for a time, as corpses. In fact we could prolong our existence indefinitely, simply by arranging to have our corpses frozen or pickled. I will call this the *dead survivors view*. In support of it some animalists cite the expression 'dead person,' which, they say, refers to people while and only while they are dead.

The dead survivors view is vulnerable to criticism. The linguistic support for the suggestion that people and other organisms survive death as corpses is inconclusive at best. The animalists' examples do show that in the proper context 'dead organism,' 'dead animal,' and 'dead person' can refer to corpses. If I am in a morgue and someone asks, 'How many dead people are here?,' it is true that I will start counting corpses. However, normally these terms do not refer to corpses. If I am asked, 'How many dead people can you name?,' I will not count corpses. One dead person I can name is Socrates, and it is clear, in his case, that I am not naming his remains, which ceased to exist long ago. I do not call him a 'dead person' while he is a corpse and not after the corpse disintegrates. It is entirely proper to refer to Socrates as a dead person right now, even though

I know his corpse has utterly disintegrated centuries ago. The dead person I am referring to is someone who lived very long ago. Now suppose Socrates' corpse still exists – squirreled away by Plato, in an urn hidden within a cave. A Plato scholar finds some obscure reference to the event in a manuscript, and digs up the corpse, on which, in clear Greek, appears a metal plaque with the single word 'Socrates.' None of us is going to say, "All these years I thought Socrates had ceased to exist; now I see I was wrong." A grief-stricken woman who says, of her child who died long ago, that 'she wishes she could still hold Timmy in her arms,' certainly does not mean to refer to his corpse moldering in its grave. Similarly, when I refer to my first dog, Jojo, who died decades ago, as a 'dead dog,' I certainly do not mean to refer to a corpse. I mean to refer to the dog I loved when I was a child.

Normally the terms 'organism,' 'animal,' and 'person' refer to beings while they are alive, or while they were alive. We can forestall confusion by making a stipulation. Let us stipulate that 'dead organism,' 'dead animal,' and 'dead person' all refer to beings who lived in the past, rather than to the remnants they left behind. For the latter, 'corpses' is an eminently suitable term.

Since the dead survivors view is false, animal essentialists should accept the termination thesis. Those who embrace McMahan's version of mind essentialism will also accept the termination thesis, since an embodied mind is annihilated when its embodiment dies. Personists, too, may endorse the termination thesis, if they think that the continuity of our identities must have its usual cause. But they will deny it if they think that the continuity of our identities can have any cause, or any reliable cause. In that case we could survive the deaths of our bodies by being Uploaded.

What, now, about the second side of the equation: Can something cease to exist without dying? Certainly. Any contingently existing thing that is not alive can cease to exist without dying, such as soap bubbles that burst, or Christmas tree ornaments that are crushed. Can organisms cease to exist without dying? They can if the ending of their existence is not accompanied by the ending of their vital processes, and precisely this seems possible (Rosenberg 1983, 21). It seems to happen every time an amoeba splits: no vital processes cease, but one amoeba is replaced with two, neither of which is the original (unless Lewis is right that it was at least two amoebas from the start; see the discussion in chapter 2). If a slime mold slug is an organism, it too ceases to exist deathlessly if the amoebocytes of which it consists go their separate ways. Division, too, would appear to end an individual's existence, even though the cerebrum's vital processes continue (chapter 2). And if persons cease to exist when they lose their identities (a view that was criticized in chapter 2), then they, too, can depart deathlessly.

Nevertheless, I see no harm in stretching the concept of death a bit so as to treat splitting and Division and loss of identity as death. We can do this by stipulating that death occurs anytime a living being ceases to exist. While we are at it, we might want to stretch the notion of life and death even further. We could treat a conscious existence (discussed earlier) as, in effect, an honorary type of life. Any person, including any androids there might be some day, can have a conscious existence. If we expand the notion of life to include conscious existence, the demise of any person entails death. If we do not, we will simply have to acknowledge the possibility that one day some persons, such as androids, may come into existence without ever living at all, and go out of existence without dying. Thought of as occurring just when a person ceases to exist, death is unique, and needs a special name, since it may or may not be accompanied by the cessation of that individual's body's vital processes. I will call it *personal death*.

Death for us

What will death be for you and me? The answer I have suggested is that your death, like the death of anything else that is alive, can be understood as a process or as the outcome of that process (the state of death). The process of death ends when your capacity to maintain yourself using vital processes is completely lost (denouement death), after passing through a point at which its completion is inevitable (threshold death).

This characterization of your death could be sharpened if we knew exactly what we are. Unfortunately, the answer to what we are has proven to be elusive. However, we can say something about what death will be on each of the three main accounts of what we are. Given animalism, we are human beings, and death will be the irreversible cessation of the vital processes by which our existence as human beings is sustained. On the mind essentialist view, it is our existence as minds that death will end. For the person essentialist, death ends our existence as beings capable of self-awareness.

As we will emphasize in the next section, each of these views differs from the others considerably. Severe dementia can end our existence as persons without ending our existence as minds. Moreover, we can cease to be minds without ceasing to be human beings, assuming that it is possible to remain a human being after becoming irretrievably unconscious. It may even be possible to cease to be human beings without ceasing to be minds or persons, assuming that minds or persons can survive as bare brains but human beings cannot. These things are possible because the vital processes that sustain minds, persons, and human beings may all differ.

CRITERIA FOR DEATH

It is one thing to specify what death is, and quite another to specify criteria by which death can be verified. The previous section clarified what it is for something to die. In this section I will see if I can supply criteria by which the death of a human being is readily marked. Of course, you and I might not be human beings; we might be persons or minds. So I will also want to see if there are criteria by which the death of a person or mind can be readily verified. Where necessary, I will indicate the sort of being whose death I mean to discuss by speaking of the death of a human being or the death of a mind or the death of a person.

The criteria I seek need not constitute a definition of death for a human being. A good definition must pick out all possible deaths of human beings. I am now looking for conditions that specify something readily identifiable that invariably accompanies the deaths of human beings. These criteria should pick out all and only *actual* human deaths, and need not pick out all and only *possible* human deaths. The criteria would guide physicians in making pronouncements of death. When the criteria are met, it is usually considered appropriate to take various actions, such as ending all medical treatment, transferring the property of the deceased, retrieving some of her organs for donation, if that was her will, and disposal of the body.

Clinical death

Until well into the last century, people and their bodies were considered dead just when their hearts and lungs stopped functioning, at which point they were in a condition called 'clinical death.' (The term 'clinical' means observable by a healthcare worker, as in a clinical setting.) This traditional criterion for death seemed acceptable until roughly the middle of the last century. Until then, it appeared that hearts that stopped beating, and lungs that stopped breathing, would never resume. Individuals pronounced clinically dead stayed clinically dead. But it is now commonplace for physicians to stop and later restart the heart in the course of surgery. New technology makes it possible to sustain a body's respiration and circulation artificially, and in some cases to restore natural heart and lung functioning after considerable periods of time.

Consequently, clinical death is no longer a serious contender as a view of death. At best one might equate death with *irreversible* clinical death. But even this view seems weak, for at least two reasons.

First, even if the heart and lungs irreversibly cease to function, death need not ensue, since their tasks might be performed artificially. This is done routinely by cardiopulmonary machines in hospitals. Blood might also be circulated with the assistance of artificial hearts. Artificial lungs may be possible too. And of course similar things are true of a great many other parts of the body as well.

Second, the heart and lungs are not the only parts of the body that are essential to life. They are not even the only essential organs. If, just to name a few examples, the body's liver, brain, or skin ceases to function, or its kidneys do, death will ensue (albeit less quickly than after heart or lung failure), unless their functions are carried out in some other way. Defining death as the irreversible stoppage of the heart or lungs is little better than defining it as the irreversible failure of the kidneys, liver, brain, or skin.

So how, precisely, is clinical death related to death? Distinctions made in the previous section suggest the following picture: when the heart (or lungs, or liver, and so forth) stops working, the dying process begins. If the heart is kept intact while it is stopped, as during cardiac surgery, the death process is suspended. Restarting the heart reverses the dying process. If the dying process continues, the body's other organs and systems begin to fail, some sooner, some later. One of the earliest to go is the brain.

Brain death

Historically the move away from the clinical view began in the late 1950s when French neurologists noted that some patients on respirators had dead brains; they called the state "coma dépassé," meaning beyond coma (Mollaret and Goulon 1959). A decade later a committee of Harvard Medical School developed influential standards for determining brain death (Ad Hoc Committee 1968), and recommended that patients who meet the standards be considered dead. A few years later two neurosurgeons in Minnesota suggested that irreversible damage to the brain stem was the "point of no return" in death, and developed standards for detecting brain stem death. Soon thereafter, in 1981, the President's Commission for the Study of Ethical Problems in Medicine and Biomedical and Behavioral Research issued a report concerning the legal definition of death. The Commission had been asked to consider "whether the law ought to recognize new means for establishing that the death of a human being has occurred (President's Commission 1981, Introduction)." The Commission concluded that new means should indeed be recognized. They recommended the Uniform Determination of Death Act, which states that

An individual who has sustained either (1) irreversible cessation of circulatory and respiratory functions, or (2) irreversible cessation of all functions of the entire brain, including the brain stem, is dead. A determination of death must be made in accordance with accepted medical standards.

All fifty states now say that people are dead when their brains have ceased to function (Fine 2005).

In the United Kingdom, the official understanding of death has undergone a similar evolution. There, death has come to be identified with brain death, and brain death has been equated with the "permanent functional death of the brain stem" (Pallis 1982, 1488). Hence on this view individuals are dead just in case their brain stems are dead. Several European countries have followed the precedent established in the UK.

In devising its criteria, the President's Commission was guided by a particular concept of death, namely integration death. Drawing on work by Germain Grisez and Joseph Boyle, Jr. (1979), the Commission defined death as "that moment at which the body's physiological system [irreversibly] ceases to constitute an integrated whole." They noted that among the body's physiological systems, three are especially crucial, namely the circulatory, respiratory, and nervous systems. These systems are integrally related; the irreversible cessation of the functioning of any one of the three quickly stops the other two, and thus life, thought of as coordinated functioning of the body's systems, ends. Having focused on integration death, the Commission then defended its two criteria by linking each to a breakdown of the interrelated functioning it considered constitutive of life. Irreversible clinical death suffices to end life since integration requires the capacity for spontaneous breathing and circulation. Brain death suffices because a living brain is also essential for integration. So an individual who has sustained either irreversible clinical death or the irreversible cessation of all functions of the entire brain is dead.

Although the criteria for death currently accepted in the UK differ from those in place in the US, the justification for them is similar. The UK position is that one dies if and only if one's brain stem irretrievably ceases to function. The equation is justified on the grounds that (1) the death of the brain stem suffices for the "death of the patient as a whole" (but not the death of the whole patient), and (2) brain stem death also suffices for the death of the brain as a whole (but not the death of the whole brain) (Pallis 1982, 1489). The first claim is plausible since, if the stem dies, spontaneous respiration and then circulation normally soon cease (Pallis 1994). The second claim is justified since, without an intact stem, some isolated parts of the rest of the brain might, for a brief time, remain alive, but the brain as a whole cannot function (Pallis 1982, 1489). Both points hinge on a version of integration death. Individuals who are sustained artificially might be considered dead when their stems die because the normal integration of their bodies' systems can no longer be restored. And their brains might be considered dead when their stems die because the normal functioning of the brain, which also depends crucially on the stem, can no longer be restored.

Revisions

Currently, then, the official criteria for death in the USA and the UK are defended as indicators of integration death. However, there are problems with this approach.

One problem is that the notion of integration death is ambiguous, and those who appeal to this notion in defense of the brain (or stem) death criterion may be exploiting the ambiguity.

We can get at the ambiguity by distinguishing between the situation in which the physiological systems of the body are integrated without the assistance of machines, on the one hand, and the situation in which they are integrated with the assistance of machines. Do human beings reach the point of integration death when their *natural* form of integration is irreversibly lost, or when integration is no longer possible even with the assistance of machines? Call the former *natural* integration death, and the latter *artificial* integration death. If the heart stops, the natural form of integration is lost, but sometimes not irreversibly so, for perhaps the heart can be restarted. This will require using a machine, but after the heart begins beating again, it functions without the assistance of machines. By contrast, if my lungs have been destroyed, and I am sustained by a machine that breathes for me, I have reached the point of natural integration death, but not the point of artificial integration death.

Now, when proponents of the brain (or stem) death criterion base their view on the concept of integration death, do they mean natural or artificial integration death? It seems fairly clear that they do not mean to appeal to artificial integration death, for two reasons. First, the main role their criterion is to play is to tell us when it is proper to turn off life support machines. It is time to turn off the machines when the patients being sustained are dead. But patients who are sustained artificially have not reached the point of artificial integration death. Second, since bodies whose brains are entirely dead can be sustained indefinitely by such machines, the brain death criterion is unacceptable as an indicator of artificial integration death.

Perhaps the proponents of the brain or stem criterion mean to appeal to the concept of natural integration death. However, the brain death criterion is a bad indicator of natural integration death too! A body whose brain is dead has indeed reached the point of natural integration death, but there are plenty of examples of people who have reached the point of natural integration death even though their brains are intact. Many such people are sustained by cardiopulmonary machinery. Arguably, some of the people equipped with artificial hearts have reached natural integration death, too.

The upshot is this: given present technology, brain death invariably results from artificial integration death, but artificial integration death does not always accompany brain death. By contrast, brain death is sufficient but not necessary for natural integration death. Only if we run the two notions together will we think that integration death is well indicated by brain death.

Of course, artificial assistance comes in degrees. Let us say that human beings reach the point of *approximate* natural integration death when integration is possible only with relatively substantial sorts of artificial assistance, such as life support machines. However, the brain (or stem) criterion is not a good indicator of this sort of 'death' either. Many of the people who cannot ever be removed from life support machines have brains that are entirely intact.

It is time to abandon the effort to justify the brain death criterion as an indicator of integration death. Is there any other reason to think that it is a good indicator of the death of a human being? It obviously does not suffice for the cessation of all of the vital processes of a human being. But might it be a good indicator of threshold death – the

comatose patient will not recover is provided by tests of brain stem reflexes, the absence of which indicate that the brain stem is dead. A light is shone into the eyes in an attempt to elicit movement of the pupils; the corneas of the eyes are touched in an attempt to elicit blinking; ice water is squirted into the ear canal to elicit turning of the head; a tube is inserted into the trachea in an attempt to elicit coughing; and the head is turned in order to see whether the eyes change their position (normally the eyes move, as if watching a stationary object, rather than remaining in the same position relative to the head, like a doll).

I have mentioned injuries that can undermine cognitive function without destroying the brain or preventing the lower brain from integrating the body's functions. A more disturbing combination is also possible: some injuries may destroy the brain's integrative functions without destroying the capacity for consciousness. This would be uncommon, since loss of bodily control will be fatal without intervention. But some patients who are rescued with the help of respirators develop a condition called "locked-in syndrome." It is usually caused by injury to the brain stem and is sometimes mistaken for coma. People who are "locked in" remain self-aware but are either completely paralyzed, or nearly so – their ability to move may be limited to their eyelids or parts of their faces. Jean-Dominique Bauby, a victim of locked-in syndrome, described his experiences in *The Diving Bell and the Butterfly* (1997); he dictated his story one letter at a time by blinking his eyes in certain sequences signifying each letter. In typical cases of lock-in, the victim's brain will retain some degree of control over the body's physiological systems. However, it is possible that its degree of control is trivial. In a condition called Guillain-Barré syndrome, various autoimmune diseases damage the central nervous system in such a way as to leave it entirely cut off from the rest of the body (Shewmon 1997). The condition may be irreversible. Individuals in this condition seem comatose, yet their brains are intact. They are completely conscious, like Jean-Dominique Bauby, but their brains are entirely unable to integrate the physiological systems of their bodies.

It is now clear that while brain death or stem death suffices for the loss of the capacity for consciousness, neither is necessary. You and I could irretrievably lose the capacity for consciousness even though neither stem death nor the death of the whole brain occurs. This occurs when the cerebrum does not function, leaving a body in a persistent vegetative state. It might also occur if the thalamus ceases to function.

So neither brain nor stem death is an accurate criterion for the death of a person or mind.

There may be a more accurate criterion for the loss of the capacity for consciousness, and hence for the death of a mind. The following is one possibility; it is often called the "higher brain criterion" (Veatch 1975):

Cerebral death criterion: Subject S is dead just in case S's cerebrum has irreversibly ceased to function.

If other parts of the brain, such as the thalamus, prove to be necessary for the capacity for consciousness, we might revise the criterion accordingly:

Cerebral-thalamic death criterion: S is dead just in case S's cerebrum or thalamus has irreversibly ceased to function.

And since consciousness is not possible without a functioning brainstem, we should adjust the criterion accordingly:

Cerebral-thalamic-stem death criterion: S is dead just in case S's cerebrum or thalamus or brainstem has irreversibly ceased to function.

But the usefulness of a criterion for death depends not just on its accuracy in marking death, but also on its verifiability, and it may prove to be difficult to determine whether a person's thalamus has ceased to function.

Even if something like the cerebral-thalamic-stem death criterion proves acceptable as the mark of the death of a mind, it will not be acceptable to proponents of the psychological account of persistence and of person essentialism. The former would seek criteria marking the irretrievable disruption of psychological continuity, while the latter would want criteria marking the loss of the capacity for self-awareness. Such criteria will be difficult to provide. As things stand, the destruction of the stem, cerebrum, or thalamus suffices for the loss of psychological continuity and the capacity for self-awareness, but the destruction of none of them is necessary. Extreme dementia or related psychological dysfunction can destroy the brains' ability to maintain psychological continuity or its capacity for self-awareness, or both, while leaving all parts of the brain alive (see the exchange between Green and Wikler 1980 and Agich and Jones 1986).

SUMMARY

Despite the oft-heard saying that we are "always dying," death should be distinguished from aging. Aging is the process by which the body's capacity to renew and maintain itself declines. It is partly (but not solely) the result of cellular senescence: for most of our cells, there is a genetically pre-programmed limit to how many times they can replace themselves, and when this, Hayflick's, limit is reached, the body is far less able to repair and maintain itself. Aging cells are more prone to die. Typically they die by necrosis, a messy process in which cells break apart and spew their contents onto other cells, or apoptosis, a tidy process by which cells self-destruct. Apoptosis is part of the regular routine by which the body develops and maintains itself.

Must death be permanent? Well, our lives do not end if our vital processes are restarted after they have halted for a time. The possibility of suspending and then reviving these processes requires that we be kept intact. However, even if we are not kept intact, and our bodies decompose, our lives could be restored, at least in theory, say by a futuristic machine that could take our atoms (or cells) apart and put them back together, just as they were before our bodies disintegrated. During the time when our bodies' atoms were dispersed, clearly we did not exist. So restoration is very different from revival. Since restoration seems conceivable, death, it seems, need not be permanent. Death is the destruction of our vital processes, and that can happen even if later our bodies are re-created, atom by atom, and our lives restored thereby.

Although some argue that we exist after devolving into corpses, I have assumed that death entails annihilation, the end of our existence. However, some ways of ending our existence do not seem to entail death. If, like amoebas, we Divide (and if, contrary to Lewis's view, Division ends the existence of those who Divide), it seems that our existence ends deathlessly, as the vital processes that sustain us do not cease.

Death might be understood in various ways, as 'death' is ambiguous. It might mean something better captured by the term 'dying,' which is the process whereby a life ends. It might also mean the condition or state of affairs of life's being over. And it might refer to certain events during the dying process: *threshold* death, which occurs when the dying process reaches the point of irreversibility; *integration* death, which occurs when an organism's physiological systems can no longer function as an integrated whole (but integration death seems to be a variety of threshold death); or *denouement* death, which occurs when the dying process completes itself.

Are there criteria by which death for human beings can be readily identified? As things stand, the criterion applied in the USA is the brain death criterion, according to which people die just when their brains as wholes irreversibly cease to function, and the criterion applied in the UK is the stem criterion, by which people die just when their brain stems irreversibly cease to function. But neither criterion is accurate, assuming that human beings can be kept alive artificially even after their brains are completely destroyed. Accurate criteria have not yet been proposed.

Nor is brain or stem death an accurate indicator of the death of a mind or person. Brain or stem death suffices for the death of a mind and for the death of a person, but neither is necessary. Minds might be irretrievably destroyed, when the cerebrum or other components of the brain other than its stem are destroyed, leaving behind a body in a persistent vegetative state. A better criterion for the death of a mind is that it occurs just when the cerebrum (or thalamus) irreversibly ceases to function. Criteria for the death of a person are also elusive.

CHAPTER 4

Challenges

While life is good, it seems more would be better (even if each additional year is less valuable than its predecessor), and the better more life would be, the worse death is. This reasoning commits us to the *harm thesis*: death is, at least sometimes, bad for those who die, and in this sense something that 'harms' them. Even after our lives are over, it seems that we have a stake in what happens in the world, for posthumous events can advance (and others can impede) the projects we undertook while alive or our directives concerning what will be done with our property after we are dead. If this view is correct, we must accept the *posthumous harm thesis*, according to which events occurring after we die can harm us.

In this chapter I will set out challenges to both of the harm theses. The best of them are very old, dating back at least to the ancient Greek philosopher Epicurus and his follower Lucretius. I will show that some of these objections can be met, but most I will confront in the next two chapters.

THE SYMMETRY ARGUMENT

Epicurus and Lucretius posed challenges to the harm theses that have been discussed ever since (Furley 1986, Rosenbaum 1986, Segal 1990, Sedley 1998, Mitsis 1988, J. Warren 2001). In this section I consider Lucretius' famous symmetry argument, and some modern variations of it. Lucretius is famous for arguing that we ought not to be concerned about death despite the nonexistence it brings upon us, since before we were born we endured a similar period of nonexistence, and no one thinks it is bad for them that they endured this period of nonexistence. Epicurus' own objections are rather different. I get to them in the next section.

Nonexistence

Lucretius' symmetry argument is suggested in the following passages from his *On the Nature of Things*:

> In days of old, we felt no disquiet … So, when we shall be no more – when the union of body and spirit that engenders us has been disrupted – to us, who shall then be nothing, nothing by any hazard will happen any more at all. (Lucretius 1951, 121 [3.832–842])

> Look back at the eternity that passed before we were born, and mark how utterly it counts to us as nothing. This is a mirror that Nature holds up to us, in which we may see the time that shall be after we are dead. (Lucretius 1951, 125 [3.972–975])

The argument concerns the state that death puts you in, which is non-existence. Lucretius asks you to consider that, before you were born, you did not exist. What exactly he wants to say about this time in which you did not exist is not entirely clear. Here is a suggestion: In all likelihood, you do not now, and never will, find it objectionable that you failed to exist during that time. Now compare the state you were in before you existed with the state in which you will be after you die. The two states are alike in all relevant ways. During your pre-vital nonexistence as well as your posthumous nonexistence, you fail to exist for an eternity. If one were unobjectionable, the other would be too. Hence, if your pre-vital nonexistence is a matter of indifference, so is your posthumous nonexistence. Recapping:

1. It is not bad for us that we once failed to exist.
2. Our posthumous nonexistence is like our pre-vital nonexistence in all relevant respects.
3. If two things are alike in all relevant respects, and one of them is not bad for us, then the second is not bad for us either.
4. So it is not bad for us that we will fail to exist once more.

(J. Warren 2004 says Lucretius meant to argue this way: *that we once failed to exist* was not bad for us while we failed to exist, so, since posthumous nonexistence is like pre-vital nonexistence in all relevant respects, then *that we will fail to exist* will not be bad for us while we fail to exist. Maybe he is correct, but this argument is not worth discussing.)

According to some commentators (e.g., Rosenbaum 1989a), Lucretius' argument turns on the observation that no one fears pre-vital nonexistence; this is taken to be grounds for concluding that we ought not to fear posthumous nonexistence. However, this interpretation is not charitable to Lucretius. It would be like arguing that we ought not to fear upcoming tooth extractions since we do not now fear the extractions that were performed on us in the past. The fact that dangers are not frightening in retrospect does not imply that it is unwise to fear dangers we anticipate. Nor is fearfulness an accurate indicator of whether we think something is bad for us, as is obvious in the case of evils now past. Our failure to fear past states of affairs does not show that we do not consider them bad for us. In what follows, let us assume that Lucretius (and Epicurus) meant to convince us that death is not bad for us, and for *that* reason death is not to be feared.

We have seen that 'death' has more than one meaning, and it is one thing to say that the state of death is harmless, and quite another to say that the dying process (or reaching its point of no return or denouement) is harmless. It is not clear whether the symmetry argument is an attempt to show that the state of death is harmless or that the process of death is harmless, or both. We will face a similar problem in interpreting the arguments of Epicurus as well.

On the reading captured in 1–4 above, Lucretius means to suggest that the state of death is not bad. But there is good reason to think that he meant to allay our concerns about both the state of death and the process of death. The stated goal of Epicureanism is *ataraxia*, or tranquility of mind; this goal is thought to be attainable because, for the enlightened, nothing in life is especially harmful. From this perspective, it would not be useful for Epicurus and Lucretius to show that the state of death is of no concern while leaving us terrified at the process of death.

Capturing this second reading will require speculation about why Lucretius might have thought that the death process shares the innocuousness of the death state. Here is a suggestion: to the argument 1–4, perhaps Lucretius would add the following:

5. If the significant effect of a process is to place us into a state that is not bad for us, then that process is not bad for us either.
6. Therefore the process of death is not bad for us.

How strong is the symmetry argument, with or without the addition of 5 and 6?

Let us start with the argument consisting of 1–4. Does our indifference about our nonexistence prior to birth show that the state of death is not bad? It is true that most of us do not bemoan our pre-vital nonexistence. We do not consider it bad that we once failed to exist. Lucretius' point is complicated by the future-directedness of many of our emotions, such as fear; however, we may experience some sort of revulsion at past events that were bad for us (if only that negative judgment itself), and even this negative attitude seems missing in the case of our pre-vital nonexistence. Our nonchalance may be due to the fact that we know what it felt like to not exist. We know that it did not feel dreadful. In fact, it did not feel any way at all, as we did not exist at the time. As Lucretius and his mentor Epicurus suggested, fearing what it will be like to not exist after we die is as silly as revulsion at the thought of what it *was* like to not exist before we were born.

However, we might have a different reason for not objecting to our pre-vital nonexistence: it was followed by our existence! Nor would we worry overly about post-vital nonexistence if it, too, were followed by existence. If we could move in and out of existence, say with the help of the Disassembler-Reassembler imagined in chapter 3, which dismantles us, then rebuilds us, bit by bit, after a period of nonexistence, we would not be overly upset about the intervening gaps, and, rather like hibernating bears, we might prefer taking occasional breaks from life until the world gets more interesting, or while horrible disasters take place. But temporary nonexistence is not the same as permanent nonexistence; it becomes permanent by virtue of what happens (or not) in the future; since non-existence might be temporary, the prospect of nonexistence *per se* is not upsetting. It is the permanence of nonexistence that worries us. Unlike the temporary nonexistence that is now behind us, the death before us is likely to make us nonexistent permanently.

Now consider the view that the process of death is nothing to be concerned about, since its most salient effect is to leave us nonexistent, and nonexistence itself is nothing to us. On this way of understanding Lucretius, he encourages us to look at the condition in which dying leaves us, and to deplore dying only if that condition is horrible. But the ghastliness of nonexistence need not be our complaint about dying. Dying might be objectionable even though being dead is not unpleasant. One complaint which has yet to be discussed is that dying might be painful. This concern will be raised later in this chapter. Another complaint, which will be discussed in the next chapter, is that dying brings a good life to an end, and, other things being equal, what ends good things is bad. Notice that the mirror image of death is birth (or, more precisely, our coming to be alive), and the two affect us in very different ways: birth initiates life; it starts a good thing going. Death ends life; it brings a good thing to a close.

Life extension

Lucretius attempted to align our attitudes about pre-vital and posthumous nonexistence so as to defeat the harm thesis. His case was not convincing.

However, our attitudes about our pasts and our futures may be significantly different in ways that do not concern nonexistence itself. It may be possible to use these other differences against the harm thesis. For example, we do not have the same attitude about extending our lives into the past as we do about extending them into the future; perhaps this inconsistency can be used to show that death is harmless.

The argument would go as follows: We prefer to die later than we will, or not at all, since postponing death extends our lives. This attitude is irrational, because few of us want to have been born earlier, or to have always existed, yet this is also a way to extend our lives. It extends our lives even to the point of making them infinitely long, even though it leaves us mortal. Since we do not want to extend our lives into the past, we should not want to extend them into the future. Actually, upon reflection, some of us might welcome the prospect of having lived a life stretching indefinitely into the past, given fortuitous circumstances. However, we would still prefer a life stretching indefinitely into the future, and that preference is irrational; we should no more wish for an indefinitely extended future life than we do an indefinitely extended past life.

As this argument suggests, we are more concerned about the indefinite *continuation* of our lives than about their indefinite *extension*. (Be careful when you rub the magic lamp: if you wish that your life be extended, the genie might make you older!) In theory, life can be extended by adding to its future *or* to its past. Is it irrational to want future life more than past life?

Not if we simply cannot extend our lives into the past. Consider that we cannot leap from the Earth into space under our own power; it is likely we have no desire to. Similarly, in practice we cannot add time to the beginning of our lives, so it is not surprising to find ourselves with no desire to do so. The structure of the world permits life extension only into the future, and that is good enough.

While leaping into space is out of the question, it is still conceptually possible. Thinking it over, we might well find the idea attractive (if we are properly equipped with an air supply – and if we can get back). However, coming to exist earlier might be literally impossible. Famously, Thomas Nagel (1993), probably drawing on Saul Kripke's (1980, 112) view that a person could only have resulted from the combination of the particular egg and sperm that gave rise to her, attempted to rebut Lucretius' asymmetry argument by claiming that while a person could have lived later than she did, she could not have lived appreciably earlier than she did. She could be a person who lived until later, but anyone who lived earlier would be someone else. Nagel's argument has proven to be unconvincing;

even if we could only have sprung from the particular gametes that shaped our genome, we can imagine coming to exist earlier, by imagining scenarios in which these gametes (and our parents) came together earlier (for further discussion, see Haji 1991, Kaufman 1996, Brueckner and Fischer 1998, Belshaw 2000).

Even if Nagel is wrong about the conceptual impossibility of being born earlier than we were, there is nothing we can do to change when our lives began. But what if life extension were possible in either direction? Would we be indifferent about a lengthier past? And should our attitude about future life match our attitude about past life?

Our attitude about future life should match our attitude about past life if our interests and attitudes are limited in certain ways. If quantity of life is the only concern, a preference for additional future life over additional past life is irrational. Similarly, the preference is irrational if our only concern is to maximize how much pleasure we experience over the course of our lives without regard to its temporal distribution. But our attitude is not that of the life- or pleasure-maximizer.

According to Derek Parfit, we have a far-reaching bias extending to goods in general: we prefer that any good things, not just pleasures, be in our future, and that bad things, if they happen at all, be in our past. To illustrate his claim, he offers the following example (1984, 165):

My Past or Future Operations: I am in some hospital, to have some kind of surgery … Because the operation is so painful, patients are now afterwards made to forget it. Some drug removes their memories of the last few hours.

I have just woken up. I ask my nurse if it has been decided when my operation is to be … She can tell me only that the following is true. I may be the patient who had his operation yesterday. In that case, my operation was the longest ever performed, lasting ten hours. I may instead be the patient who is to have a short operation later today. It is either true that I did suffer for ten hours, or true that I shall suffer for one hour.

I ask the nurse to find out which is true. While she is away, it is clear to me which I prefer to be true. If I learn that the first is true, I shall be greatly relieved.

According to Parfit, our bias is revealed in our reluctance to reduce the amount of bad experiences in our lives by locating some of these in the future.

Parfit argues (1984, 175) that if we take this bias for granted, we can refute the Lucretian argument: the fact that we can remain serene while recalling a state of affairs in our past does not show that it was not bad, since our bias leaves us indifferent about bad things in our past; hence, the fact that we contemplate our past nonexistence with serenity does not show that it was not bad. Using similar reasoning, one might argue that it is rational to deplore death more than we do our not having always existed: the former, not the latter, deprives us of good things in the future, whereas the latter would only supply good things in our pasts (compare Brueckner and Fischer 1986). This preference for future goods is unfortunate, however, according to Parfit. If cultivated, the temporal insensitivity of the life- or pleasure-gourmand could lower our sensitivity to death: towards the end of life, we would find it unsettling that our supply of pleasures cannot be increased in the future, but we would be comforted by the pleasures we have accumulated.

Some of Parfit's critics (e.g., Mitsis 1988) have claimed that our bias does not extend to all goods and evils, but only to ones we experience. For example, being secretly betrayed or insulted appears to be bad for us, but it is not clear that we would prefer it to happen in our past. Contrariwise, being secretly admired or honored seems equally welcome whether it happens in the future or past. This exception to our bias seems to weaken Parfit's response to Lucretius, assuming we are indifferent about extending life into the past as a means of gaining goods we do not experience. However, the criticism is not strong, since few if any of us would extend our lives into the *future* solely for the sake of goods we never experience.

Whether or not we have the extensive bias described by Parfit, it is true that the accumulation of life and pleasure, and the passive contemplation thereof, are not our only interests. We also have active, forward-looking goals and concerns. Engaging in such pursuits has its own value; for many of us, these pursuits, and not passive interests, are central to our identities. However, we cannot make and pursue plans for our past. We must project our plans, and pursue self-realization, towards the future, which explains our forward bias. (We could *have been* devising and pursuing plans in the past, but these plans will not, I assume, be extensions of our present concerns.) It is not irrational to prefer that our lives be extended into the future rather than the past, if for no other reason than this: only the former makes our existing forward-looking pursuits possible. It is not irrational to prefer not to be at the end of our lives, unable to shape them further, and limited to reminiscing about days gone by. As Frances Kamm (1988, 1998) emphasizes, we do not want our lives to be all over with.

Nevertheless, it does not follow that we should be *indifferent* about the extent of our pasts. Being in the grip of forward-looking pursuits is important, but we have passive interests as well, which make a more extensive past preferable. Moreover, *having been* devising and pursuing plans in the past is worthwhile. If fated to die tomorrow, it would be better to have a thousand years of glory behind us rather than fifty.

THE TIMING PUZZLE

Next we can consider Epicurus' own objections to the harm theses. As he notes in his *Letter to Menoeceus*, Epicurus (341–270 BCE) is inclined to think that death is harmless because there is no time when we undergo the harm that death supposedly brings upon us:

> Death ... the most awful of evils, is nothing to us, seeing that, when we are, death is not come, and, when death is come, we are not.

We might restate Epicurus' argument as follows: if death harms the individual who dies, there must be a *subject* who is harmed by death, a clear *harm* that is received, and a *time* when that harm is received. As to the timing issue, there seem to be two possible solutions, given that death follows immediately upon life: either death harms its victims while they are alive, or it harms them later. If we opt for the second solution we appear to run head-on into the problem of finding a subject who is harmed, for assuming that we do not exist after we are alive, no one is left to incur harm. We also encounter the problem of specifying a harm that might be accrued by a nonexistent person. If we opt for the first solution – death harms its victims while they are alive – we have a ready solution to the problem of the subject but we face the problem of supplying a clear way in which death is bad: death seems unable to have *any* ill effect on us while we are living, since it will not yet have occurred. Seeing that there is no coherent solution to all three issues, Epicurus rejects the harm thesis.

Epicurus focuses on death, but if his argument is good, it applies more generally, to include all events that follow death. If it shows that death is harmless to us (so that the harm thesis is false), it also shows that posthumous events are harmless to us (so that the posthumous harm thesis is false). I will discuss the case against both theses, but for simplicity I usually will not mention posthumous events.

Epicurus' argument can be interpreted in more than one way. First, as will be discussed in due time, it is not clear what he means by 'death.' For now I will assume that he means to refer to the process of death, whereby our lives are entirely extinguished. Second, his intent might be to show that neither death nor any posthumous event can *affect* us *at all*. It would follow that death is harmless, assuming that an event (or the occurrence of a process: I assume that the occurrence of a process can be viewed as a lengthy event) harms us only if it somehow affects us at some time (perhaps well after it occurs). Let us see if it is possible to show that death does not affect us. Then we can try out a weaker thesis: that death cannot affect us *in a way that matters*. This weaker claim is easier to defend; in all likelihood, it is what Epicurus had in mind, but the stronger claim is worth exploring.

Death cannot affect us

To proceed, we need to make some assumptions about when an event can affect us. First, it is reasonable to assume that the past cannot be causally affected by the future, so a person cannot be causally affected by an event before that event occurs. For example, what will occur tomorrow cannot have any impact on me today. Second, people can be causally affected by an event only while they exist. What occurs before I exist might well affect me, but only while I myself exist. For example, say my father's sister leaves money to his children before I am born; this money might well improve my life, but the money can affect me only while I am alive. We will need one more assumption, namely that the only way something can affect people is by having a causal impact on them. Suppose that upon anticipating what I will eat tomorrow, my mouth waters. My future meal has not made me salivate; instead, it is anticipating a good meal that has done that. I can be affected by thinking about a meal when or after I have that thought. But thinking about eating a meal is not the same thing as eating it (otherwise reading recipe books would make us fat).

Together, these three assumptions constitute the *causal account of responsibility*:

(a) An event (or state of affairs) can affect some subject (person or thing) S only by having a causal effect on S.
(b) A subject S cannot be causally affected by an event (or state of affairs) while S is nonexistent.
(c) A subject S cannot be causally affected by an event before the event occurs.

From the causal account, together with some plausible assumptions, it follows that a *post*-mortem event, such as the burning of one's corpse, cannot affect us after we are dead, since, by (a), to be affected is to be causally affected, but, by (b), nonexistent people cannot be causally affected by anything. It also follows that the state of being dead cannot affect us while we are dead. Here we are assuming that people cease to exist when they die (this claim was called the termination thesis in chapter 3):

1. An event (or state of affairs) can affect us only by causally affecting us.
2. We cannot be causally affected by an event (or state of affairs) while we are nonexistent.
3. We do not exist while dead (the termination thesis).
4. So neither being dead, nor any posthumous event, can affect us while we are dead.

From the causal account it also follows that a post-mortem event, and the state of being dead, cannot affect us while we are alive, given the ban on backwards causation imposed by (c), and hence no posthumous events can affect us at all:

5. We cannot be causally affected by an event (or state of affairs) before the event occurs (or before a state of affairs holds) (the ban on backwards causation).
6. So neither being dead, nor any posthumous event, can affect us while we are alive (by 1 and 5).
7. So neither being dead, nor any posthumous event, can ever affect us (by 4 and 6).

So far so good: Epicureans have a case against the posthumous harm thesis and a case for denying that we are harmed by the state of being dead. However, they still need to convince us that the dying process cannot affect us.

Of course, the thesis that in order to be affected we must exist, together with the termination thesis, rule out the possibility that death affects us *after* it occurs (after we are nonexistent). And the ban on backwards causation rules out the possibility that death affects us before it occurs. Thus:

8. Death cannot affect us after it occurs (by 1–3).
9. Death cannot affect us before it occurs (by 1 and 5).
10. So death can affect us, if at all, only when it occurs (by 8 and 9).

But nothing said so far rules out the possibility that death affects us exactly *when* it occurs. In particular, the problem of the subject does not arise, since it is a living, existing person who is harmed by death while it occurs. Is there any way to establish that death cannot affect us even at the time it occurs?

There might be two ways. First, we might claim that death occurs only after we are nonexistent. This assumption has the odd consequence that death can affect us only if posthumous events can, since death will itself occur after we are nonexistent. It will follow from 7 that death cannot ever affect us. Second, like a great many contemporary theorists (e.g., Grey 1999, Rosenbaum 1986), we might claim that death happens too quickly to affect us.

The first approach might seem preposterous; how could death occur only after it has made us cease to exist? Recall (from chapter 3) that death may be a state or process or a point reached during that process. Yet some theorists have indeed defined 'death' – the ending of life – in such a way as to imply that it occurs only after we are nonexistent. For example, Joel Feinberg (1984), following Barbara Levenbook (1984), defines death as "the first moment of the subject's nonexistence." Perhaps this definition is motivated by the awkwardness of attaching 'death' to a moment in the dying process when a spark of life persists. However, it is at least as awkward to attach 'death' to a moment after the dying process is over – to suggest that the ending of life occurs while we are in a state of death.

What about the suggestion that death happens too quickly to affect us? Perhaps the thought is that death is truly instantaneous, so that, after the period of time when we are wholly alive, and before the period of time when we are not at all alive, no time passes. Hence, everything that happens to us must occur either while we are alive or after we have ceased to be, and there is just no time for death to affect us.

I am not entirely sure what to say about an instantaneous death. On the one hand it is obvious that the process whereby our vital processes are completely ended affects us. On the other hand it is hard to see how a process *can* affect anything if it literally takes place in no time at all. So I am inclined to conclude that processes that are literally instantaneous, including deaths, are impossible.

In any case, no actual deaths *are* ever literally instantaneous. In the process sense, death unfolds over a period of time, and it obviously can affect us while it occurs. Any death involves the decline of the processes that constitute life; a speedier death destroys our vital capacities just as thoroughly as (albeit less painfully than) a slower one; it simply does so faster.

What if we opt for the denouement sense of 'death'? Is it plausible to say that losing the very last of life can have no effect on us? Once again, it is difficult to see why. If we were correct when we said that the complete destruction of our vital capacities affects us, surely we are also affected, albeit less, by losing the very last of the vital capacities that sustain us.

Let's review. Granting him some leeway, Epicurus can show:

11. Neither being dead, nor any posthumous event, can ever affect us, and the dying process itself can affect us, if at all, only while it occurs (by 7 and 10).

He can then reach conclusions about the harmfulness of death and posthumous events:

12. An event harms us only if it somehow affects us at some time.
13. So neither being dead, nor any posthumous event, can harm us, and the dying process can harm us, if at all, only while it occurs (by 11 and 12).

But Epicurus lacks a convincing argument against the possibility that the dying process and some of its effects overlap in time; hence he cannot displace the harm thesis. We have a subject who endures death and a time when that subject incurs the effects of death: the subject of death is a live creature, who endures its effects at the very time the creature dies.

Death cannot harm us

Instead of trying to establish that death cannot affect us at all, Epicurus might argue that death cannot affect us *in a way that is bad for us*. To that end, he will need to supply a necessary condition for something's being bad for us and convince us that death fails to meet it.

The condition Epicurus supplies is this: an event (or state of affairs) harms us only if it causes in us the presence of some condition we find unpleasant. For simplicity, we can call all such conditions pain or suffering. That condition, the suffering, need not occur at the same time as the event that causes its presence in us. An event may occur long before it has any direct impact on us; it may occur even before we exist, as when someone times a bomb to go off 150 years later, killing everyone around. Epicurus himself did not spell out a complete view of welfare. He did not make it entirely clear when things are, overall, beneficial or harmful to a person. But he surely did think that something harms us only if it causes us to suffer. In the remainder of this section, I will assume that Epicurus is correct to limit harmful things to those that cause us pain. I want to see how far Epicurus can get if we allow him this assumption. In the next chapter I will question it.

On Epicurus' criterion for harm, clearly neither the state nor the process of death is *inherently* harmful – it is, in itself, not bad for us. For death need not make us suffer. One can die painlessly, as when one dies while unconscious, and thus, according to Epicurus, harmlessly. However, in claiming that death is nothing to us, Epicurus is not saying merely that death *need* not be harmful. He is suggesting that it never is; on his criterion, this means that it never causes the subject to suffer.

To show that death can have no salient effect on us, Epicurus might argue that death cannot be responsible for *any* condition's presence in us, unpleasant or otherwise. It can only be responsible for our *ceasing* to be in a condition. However, this thesis is clearly false on the process sense of 'death': moving from being wholly alive to completely lacking life might well involve pain.

An option is to retreat to the denouement sense of death, since the ending of the final trace of life might occur extremely quickly, perhaps so quickly that it has no salient effect on us while it happens. Epicurus might argue, with some degree of plausibility, that denouement death cannot harm us:

14. Denouement death occurs too quickly to be responsible for the presence of any unpleasant condition in us at the time it occurs.
15. Only something responsible for the presence of an unpleasant condition in us is harmful to us.
16. So denouement death cannot harm us at the time it occurs (by 14 and 15).

By combining 16 with 13, established earlier, Epicureans may conclude that

17. Neither posthumous events nor the state of being dead nor denouement death may ever harm us, and process death may harm us only while it occurs.

However, this conclusion leaves in place our concern about dying, and this concern will not be relieved by the suggestion that denouement death will zip by before you know it. We are worried about whether losing our lives is bad for us, not just whether, having nearly completely lost life, it is bad to lose the very last of it (Luper 2004). Even for Epicurus himself this conclusion is not adequate, for it leaves in place the possibility that the dying process will be harmful.

Why did Epicurus say that death is nothing to us, knowing, as he must have, that dying clearly can be harmful? Possibly, he never intended to show that death is nothing to us. As many commentators have insisted, his intent may have been to show that being dead – the state of death – is nothing to us, unlike dying, which is a misfortune for many people. Alternatively, Epicurus accepted a position that several contemporary theorists have defended: that what we have called 'process death' is not part of death; instead, 'process death' is just the continuation of the events leading up to death, and death itself is what we have called 'denouement death.' This line of thought would position him to admit that 'process death' is bad for us, but it is the precursor to death. It is not (denouement) death.

However, while there is no sharp line between the events leading to death and the onset of the process of death, there is a difference between these two. When Socrates drank hemlock, the poison paralyzed his heart or lungs, causing him to begin dying. His drinking hemlock certainly was among the events that initiated his death, but he was not dying when he drank the hemlock, nor while the poison spread.

There is a far more important point to make about the attempt to rescue Epicurus and his followers by interpreting his use of the term 'death' in some narrow way. If Epicurus meant to show only that denouement death is harmless, or that the state of being dead is harmless, his efforts are disappointing, given his wider concerns. Epicurus' goal was to enable us to achieve *ataraxia*; our tranquility cannot be complete if Epicurus removes our concern about denouement death and its aftermath only to leave in place our concern about the dying process or even the events leading up to the dying process.

Given his goal, and his criterion for harm, Epicurus' best strategy is probably to downplay the painfulness (hence harmfulness) of both process death and its cause, and this he appears to do, by appealing to the dubious claim that serious afflictions are not very painful:

Continuous pain does not last long in the flesh; on the contrary, pain, if extreme, is present a very short time ... Illnesses of long duration even permit of an excess of pleasure over pain in the flesh. (1966a, Doctrine 4)

This is disappointing, since the dying process and its cause can be excruciating, but Epicurus can do no better.

Besides death, there are things that are associated with death that seem bad for us, and that might disturb us. Epicurus would need to address them, given his goal. Let us consider some examples, and what Epicurus might say about them.

Here is one example: I might suffer when I anticipate my own death. Epicurus would probably admit that *anticipating* death can be a bad thing to the extent that it upsets us. But he emphasizes that our (present) anticipatory fear is not caused by our (future) death, since future events are powerless to affect the past. Hence, by the painfulness criterion, the fear of death is not grounds for saying that death is harmful. Moreover, fear is irrational unless its object is genuinely evil in some way, which death is not:

He speaks idly who says that he fears death, not because it will be painful when present but because it is painful in anticipation. For if something causes no distress when present, it is fruitless to be pained by the expectation of it. (1966b)

Here is something else related to death that seems bad for us: our death might cause others to grieve. But Epicurus would urge us to distinguish what is bad for us from what is bad for others. At most, the fact that your family grieves at your death supports the claim that your demise harms *them*, not that it harms you. (Too, your distress at anticipating your family's grief over your death is not grounds for you to regard your death as a bad thing: the suffering your death brings them cannot affect you, and your anticipatory grief is irrational.) Furthermore, their grief should be mitigated by the fact that your death is not bad for *you*. Their grief is entirely self-centered, exactly like the self-pity a stamp collector might feel at the destruction of a treasured stamp, in that the stamp is not harmed by its own destruction.

As these examples show, Epicurus can address some death-related concerns by showing that they are misguided, if we grant him his claim that we can be harmed only by what causes us to suffer. However, this strategy has significant limitations. Consider *the fact that everyone dies*, or even *the fact that you will die*: your belief that everyone dies (and that you will die) is caused, in part, by the fact that everyone dies. Suppose that your belief, in turn, causes you distress. Then the fact that everyone dies has harmed you (as Curtis Brown pointed out to me). Hence the conclusion that your mortality is bad for you is untouched by Epicurus' claim that "if something causes no distress when present, it is fruitless to be pained by the expectation of it." Your mortality is distressing *now*.

In response, we might imagine Epicurus arguing this way: dying will not be bad for you so it is not bad for you that you will die. But it is not clear why this cannot be turned around: why not say that dying will be bad for you on the grounds that it is bad for you that you will die? Epicurus' best strategy is probably to say that mortality *need* not be bad for you; it is not bad for you if it does not distress you, as it usually does not, and perhaps you can prevent it from ever distressing you again by convincing yourself that dying will not be bad for you.

We can conclude that even if we grant him his narrow criterion for harm, Epicurus cannot show that the dying process cannot harm us. Nevertheless, if Epicurus were able to show that being dead cannot be bad for us, and that dying can harm us only insofar as it is painful, his accomplishment would be profound. Those who may expect a painless death would have nothing to fear from their demise. That they would have led a rich and extraordinary life had they not died would be immaterial; no matter when it comes, and no matter what sort of life it precludes, a painless death would be nothing to them. It is questionable that Epicurus accomplished even this much, however, as I will suggest in the next chapter, where his criterion for harm will come under scrutiny.

TRANQUILITY

What I would like to do in the remainder of this chapter is to discuss, in somewhat greater detail, Epicurus' wider project, which was to provide us with ways to achieve *ataraxia*, or equanimity.

As we have seen, Epicurus tried to help us to achieve tranquility by convincing us that death, and certain things related to death, are harmless. But there was another approach which he recommended, namely, altering our desires in certain ways that will reduce our exposure to suffering. A third strategy, not discussed by Epicurus, is also worth considering, namely adopting the view that only our present welfare matters to us now, freeing us of any fear we might have for the future.

Desire adaptation

Like several other theorists in the ancient world, including some, such as Gautama, in Asia, Epicurus recommended that we modify our desires in ways that minimize our vulnerability to suffering, which entails paring them down drastically (Luper 1985, Nussbaum 1996, J. Warren 2004). By adapting our desires, we can secure complete tranquility for ourselves, or at least come very close.

Epicurus thought that we can be harmed only by (what gives us) pain in one of its various forms. Hence the thwarting of a desire is not bad in itself; it is bad for us only if, and to the extent that, it makes us suffer. However, typically we are distressed when our desires are thwarted, and often we can avoid distress by giving up the troublesome desires. For example, I will not be unhappy about being unable to live on the moon if I do not want to live there. Since I must live on Earth, it would harm me to have the desire to live on the moon. I am better off without it. We should rid ourselves of any desire that may be thwarted, unless giving it up would cause us to suffer. For example, we should give up the desire to eat exotic and expensive food, which we may be unable to satisfy, but not the desire to eat when we have an appetite, since without the latter we would soon suffer from hunger.

One principal reason why our desires might be thwarted is that we are mortal, and may die at any time. Hence, in adapting our desires, we should pay special attention to their vulnerability to our death. We should attempt to *thanatize* them; that is, we should adapt our scheme of desires, abandoning some and modifying others, so that none of them would be thwarted if we were to die.

Consider the desire not to die: *having* this preference can harm us by making us sad when we realize our desire will be thwarted, but the *thwarting* of that desire is harmless since (Epicurus thought) it cannot cause us pain. Nor can we be harmed by the thwarting of any desire concerning what will happen after we are dead. Yet most such desires can make us unhappy, as we will worry that they might go unfulfilled. The exceptional cases are preferences concerning states of affairs that are inevitable, such as that physical matter continues to exist – it makes no sense to worry about such things. But excepting only such cases, we should cultivate indifference about our mortality and about posthumous events. At least that is the strategy, although Epicurus reportedly did not keep to it; as Cicero emphasized, Epicurus apparently did care about what would happen after his death, as he wrote a will (Cicero, *De finibus* 2.101). (Desires concerning posthumous events will be discussed further in chapter 6. See also Gosling 1969 and Scarre 2007, ch. 6.)

It is possible to have some desires that cannot be thwarted by our deaths. An obvious example is the desire to die, or to die if some condition is met. Another is a desire I can do nothing to fulfill: whether it is fulfilled does not depend on how my life goes or on what I do. Call this an *independent desire.* We may fully thanatize our desire schemes by limiting ourselves to such desires. However, thanatizing is consistent with allowing ourselves another sort of desire. Suppose we have a desire that is not independent – its fulfillment depends on how our lives go – and we realize that it may well be thwarted, since we may die at any time. Yet giving it up would make us suffer. Perhaps, for example, we would suffer boredom without some desires about how to occupy our time, and in that way are benefited by (say) wanting to spend time studying philosophy. It is an agreeable way to pass the time. We can replace such desires with counterparts that cannot be thwarted by death. The counterparts are like the originals, except that they are contingent on our continued existence (or on something itself contingent on our existence). For example, the desire to spend time studying philosophy gives way to the desire to spend time studying philosophy *unless we die first,* and the desire to eat gives way to the desire to eat *when we have an appetite.* Having an appetite is contingent on our existence. Call these *conditional desires.* Those that are not in this way contingent on our survival call *unconditional desires.*

By choosing our fundamental projects, you and I can actually shape our own interests. It is sensible to take advantage of this freedom. We are alive for less than a century; that may change one day, but until it does we can make our lives better by adopting central projects that fit within the confines of a normal lifetime. So the adaptation of desires has its uses. However, while thanatizing reduces our exposure to pain, it is surely not a strategy you or I would want to adopt. It would leave us with a greatly impoverished set of interests. Instead of wanting, unconditionally, that our life's work should succeed, or that our friends and loved ones should flourish, we would have to drop such desires altogether, or rest content with their conditional counterparts: our concern about our projects and friends would have to be contingent on our continued existence. Our attitude would be this: let my projects succeed and let the people I care about flourish unless I die, at which time it does not matter what happens to them.

This attitude is incompatible with genuine love for another; I do not love my wife if I am indifferent to what will happen to her should I die, or if I do not care how an event such as a car crash will affect her so long as I do not live through it. The consistent Epicurean can value his acquaintances for instrumental reasons only: perhaps they are entertaining, or they are generous with their money, or they enhance his security. That is very different from considering someone's well-being important for its own sake, which is at the heart of genuine love and friendship. If I really love my wife, I cannot possibly think that her fate in a car crash does not matter so long as I do not live through it.

Fully thanatizing our desires not only precludes our forming genuinely loving relationships, it can also undermine our motivation for living. Independent desires are motivationally inert. Conditional desires can provide us with ways of passing the time. They can supply reasons to act in certain ways. For example, the desire to be well fed or free of painful illnesses or entertained, should we live on, can prompt us to secure a food supply, or take vitamins. But conditional desires do not prompt us to continue our lives. Desires prompt us to live on only when they are unconditional (B. Williams 1973).

It seems possible to attain a good life even if we altogether lack unconditional desires (Rosenbaum 1989b, 302). Suppose that I judiciously select conditional desires, such as the following: *to pass the time enjoyably should I live on at all.* And suppose I will in fact enjoy myself for many years. It is possible that my life, at least during that stretch of time, is good for me. But in that case what precludes my having that stretch of good life is bad for me, even though it does not thwart my conditional desire. The very goodness of that life provides grounds for regretting anything that precludes it. Hence, other things being equal, dying just prior to that stretch of time would be bad for me. To prevent death from ever being bad for me, I must avoid having a life that is good for me.

Epicurus himself probably would have rejected this reasoning. For him, it is not necessarily bad for us when something prevents our lives from being good, or better than they would otherwise have been. However, he could sustain this view only by appealing to an implausible way of understanding harm and benefit, as I will argue in the next chapter (see the discussion of bifurcated comparativism).

The upshot is that Epicureans must set their sights low; they must not seek a life that is good, so that its loss would be bad for them. And they must avoid unconditional desires that would prompt them to live on. They will live solely out of inertia – not because life is good for them, but because it has not (yet) become bad enough to opt out of.

Present egoism

There is another strategy which Epicureans might find useful. Contrast two ways we might assess whether something is in our interests. On the first, we assess in a *temporally relative* way. We focus on the time we are assessing some action or event, or the time that the action or event itself will take place, or some other time, and assume that our interests are fixed relative to that time. For example, *present egoism* (as Parfit [1984, 143] calls the view) says that whether an event is in our interests depends on how it affects our welfare now, and that we have most reason to do whatever will promote our welfare now, regardless of how our actions will affect our welfare at other times. On the second approach, we assess in a *temporally neutral* way. We take it that something is in our interests to the extent that it boosts our welfare, no matter when the boost takes place. How well off we are at each time matters the same to us at all times. And at each time, we consider ourselves to have most reason to do what will most enhance our lives in their entirety. There might be strategic reasons for me to focus on boosting my welfare in the near future (for example, I have more control over what is near), but, all things being equal, I am as much benefited by an action that adds to my welfare in the distant future as I am by an action that adds the same amount to my welfare in the present. For example, giving myself one unit of pleasure now is no better and no worse than giving myself one unit of pleasure a week from now.

Given their causal account of responsibility, Epicureans must say that what benefits them in the future cannot benefit them now. Despite this, Epicureans could assess their interests in a temporally neutral or relative way. They can emphasize that they are the same person now and later, and say that it is important to concern themselves now with their later welfare because this will benefit them *later*. I-now am not affected by my being benefited later, but *I* am affected, since I am benefited later. Epicureans also have the option of adopting some form of temporal relativism. For example, they could accept present egoism. Together with the position that we are harmed only by what makes us suffer, present egoism implies that I-now am harmed only by what makes me suffer now; I-yesterday and I-tomorrow am harmed by what makes me suffer then, but I-now do not care about this. I am aloof from my past and present suffering; suffering at these other times is not bad for me now. Judging in a temporally neutral way, my attitude is quite different: anytime I think about my past or future suffering, it will bother me; I want my life as a whole to go well.

It can seem that Epicureans *should* accept present egoism. As present egoists, Epicureans can remain tranquil in the face of the direst future, and undaunted by a horrendous past. It can help Epicureans where they are most in need of help: in confronting the prospect of a painful death. Even if their eventual deaths will be painful, that does not matter to them now.

By the same token, however, as they approach the end of life Epicureans cannot take consolation in having lived well. And of course a painful death will matter to them once it is upon them. However, the main problem with combining present egoism with hedonism is that it eliminates our incentive to provide for our future welfare. For example, it says I should press the button described in the following case (Parfit 1984, 134):

> *The Minor Sacrifice*: "Suppose that I am in pain. If I endure this pain for another minute, it will cease forever. If I press a button, my pain will instantly cease, but will return within a few minutes, and will continue for another fifty years."

As Parfit says, any view that entails that the best thing to do is to press the button is absurd. Consider, too, that, given the combination of hedonism and present egoism, my welfare as it is at a particular time is something I shaped almost entirely in the past when I was indifferent about it. When I do care about my welfare, it is too late to do much about it. Even while caring only about my present welfare, I will wish I had not taken that attitude in the past. At nearly any time in my life I would be best off if I always concerned myself with how my life will unfold *from now on*. (This is true even though I now will be best off if I take myself to have reason to do only what boosts my welfare now.)

Instead of being indifferent about their futures, Epicureans would be better off if they took a guarded interest in them, as we noted earlier. What they might want is to have as little pain and as much pleasure as possible at a future time *unless they die first*. This attitude leaves them indifferent about living on, but prompts them to plan to avoid pain. They will still fear a painful death, just as they fear anything painful, but at least they will not care about the fact that their lives will end.

SUMMARY

We do not have the same attitude about pre-vital nonexistence, our state during the period that stretches into the past before our lives began, and posthumous nonexistence, our state during the time that follows our demise. But Lucretius was mistaken when he claimed that our attitude about the latter should match our attitude about the former, so that we are not concerned about either. One reason is that, unlike post-vital nonexistence, pre-vital nonexistence is followed by our existence. If we could exist again, we would not be as concerned about going out of existence. Another reason is that we are not merely interested in boosting the overall duration of our lives. We want more time in our futures, in part, because we have forward-looking pursuits.

Epicurus argued against the harm thesis, which says that death can be bad for us, and the posthumous harm thesis, which says that posthumous events can harm us, on the grounds that a thing can harm someone only if that harm has a clear subject who is harmed, a clear harm that is received by that subject, and a clear time when that subject receives that harm. His challenge to anyone who deplores death or any posthumous events is to supply these three items. Posthumous events seem harmless since we no longer exist when they occur, and nothing can affect the past. For the same reason, death, which ends our existence, cannot affect us after it occurs. But why say it cannot affect us at the time it occurs? For some theorists, the answer is that death is a posthumous event. For others, the answer is that it is an instantaneous event; it is over before it can affect us in any truly objectionable way. Both approaches are based on misconceptions about death. Death cannot be a posthumous event. Nor is it truly instantaneous. As we have seen, it is a process that stretches over time. And even if that process is speeded up, it is hard to see why it should be considered harmless: a terribly harmful process that stretches over a long period is no less terribly harmful if it happens quickly, except in one respect: it is less painful.

Epicurus meant to teach us how to achieve an invulnerable form of happiness, consisting in *ataraxia*, or tranquility; indifference to death was only one part of his strategy. On his approach, we should pare down our desires, since the thwarting of a desire is not bad in itself, and having them makes us apprehensive, in advance, when we think they will not be fulfilled, or regretful, in retrospect, when we see that they have not been fulfilled. Unfortunately, this strategy leaves us greatly impoverished; we lack any reason to live at all. Present egoism, which says that whether an event is in our interests depends wholly on how it affects our welfare now, would also appear to promote the Epicurean goal of tranquility, since it would free us of any worries about the deaths looming before us. However, in the long run present egoism would make us less happy, principally by undermining our motivation to promote our own future happiness.

CHAPTER 5

Mortal harm

Epicurus thought that death and posthumous events cannot harm those who die. In part, he based his argument on the view that death leaves us immune to any genuine harm. In this chapter I will argue that he was incorrect. There is a straightforward kind of *mortal harm*: misfortune for which a person's death is responsible. Posthumous events, too, can be bad for people.

The first order of business will be to explain, in the first section, when things are in or against our personal interests. With this account in hand, I will show, in the second section, that death can harm those who die. Doubts will arise; I will sketch some of these, and see if they can be put away. Not until the next chapter will I consider Epicurus' timing puzzle – the challenge of finding a time when death's victim incurs mortal harm.

PRUDENTIAL VALUE

Yesterday I got stuck in traffic on my drive home. Did this event harm me, benefit me, or neither? To answer this question, we will need a theory of prudential value: an analysis of *welfare* and of personal *interests* and how the one relates to the other. An account of welfare is an analysis of well-being; it tells us what well-being consists in, and how well off we are during a period of time or in some set of circumstances. An account of personal interests tells us what it is for something to be in our interests or against our interests.

Let us now consider an account of our interests which I will call *comparativism*.

Comparativism

Let us begin by distinguishing different senses in which an event can have value.

One way an event can have value for me is by being *intrinsically* good for me, or good for its own sake and not in virtue of its contingent effects. I assume that one thing that is intrinsically good for me is experiencing pleasure (of course, Kant and others dispute this assumption). Things can be intrinsically bad for me as well; my experiencing pain is an example. Something's being intrinsically good or bad for me contrasts with its being *extrinsically* good or bad for me. For example, events that are instrumentally good for me, such as my taking aspirin, are extrinsic goods. They are good because of their contingent effects. Similarly, instrumental evils, such as catching cold, are extrinsic evils.

There is another way an event can have value for me: it might be *overall* good or bad for me: good or bad for me *all things considered*. Roughly, an event is overall good for me if it makes my life better than it would have been had the event not occurred. And an event is overall bad for me if it makes my life worse than it would have been had the event not occurred. What is overall good or bad for me might be contrasted with what is partially good or bad for me. An example of the latter might be my drinking salt water when I am shipwrecked and in need of hydration; it might relieve some of my pain, but on the whole it is bad for me. Anything that boosts our sum of intrinsic goods (or lowers our sum of intrinsic evils) might be said to partially benefit us, but partial goods are not what is really important to us. Partial goods can be overall bad for us.

By way of illustration, let us ask whether my delay in traffic was overall good or bad for me. To assess it, we ask how my life would have gone had the traffic jam not occurred, and compare it to my life as it in fact was. As things turned out, the delay was not bad in itself (not intrinsically bad for me), but it caused me to miss my daily stroll down to the river. If not delayed, I would have enjoyed my walk. Since the delay made my life worse than it would have been had I not been delayed, this event was bad for me. Since the difference the delay made is small, it was only slightly bad for me.

Let us sharpen this rough characterization of the overall value an event has for me. To assess an event like my delay, we must examine two possible situations, or possible worlds, and determine my welfare in each. One possible world is the actual world itself. It is described by a very lengthy declarative sentence (consisting of many shorter sentences joined together with the word 'and') that sets out everything that is actually the case, including the entire story of my life, past, present, and future. But there are many other possible worlds as well – one for each set of mutually consistent sentences. In the actual world, I got stuck in traffic. There are many possible worlds in which this event does not occur, and various other things occur which also did not actually happen. I assume for simplicity that for each event E that actually occurs we can pick out the possible world that is the way things would be if E had not occurred. On one view, this would be the world that is as similar to the actual world as possible, and in that sense "closest" to it, except that E does not occur, and E's nonoccurrence cascades into other changes. (For further clarification see Lewis 1973, Stalnaker 1968.)

Referring to possible worlds makes it easier to state what is involved in assessing whether an event E is overall good for me. We begin by examining (my life in) the actual world, in which E occurs. We can call this world *WE*, to remind us that E actually occurred. We then assign a value to the intrinsic goods I possess during my life, whether in the past, present, or future, as well as to the intrinsic evils I possess during my life. Some of these were goods I enjoyed before E occurred, but that is all right – we will include them anyway. Then we sum these values; the goods will have a positive value, and the evils a negative value; the latter lowers the sum while the former boosts it. This gives us the intrinsic value for me of (my life in) the actual world. It is my actual lifetime welfare level. (Some goods might be difficult to compare meaningfully to others; this is a thorny problem which can limit the precision of value judgments. [For a good discussion, see Griffin 1986, ch. 5.] I will set it aside; we will not need the details to show that death can be bad for us. For simplicity, I will assume that all intrinsic goods are *commensurate* in the sense that a unit of one sort of good can be equated meaningfully with a unit of another sort.)

Some symbolization will clarify these ideas (compare Feldman 1991). Let G(S,W) be the sum of the values of the things that are intrinsically good for subject S in world W, and let B(S,W) be the sum of the values of the things that are intrinsically bad for S in W. Finally, let IV(S,W) be the intrinsic value of world W for subject S. Then:

$$IV(S, W) = G(S, W) + B(S, W)$$

As an illustration, let us suppose that the values of my intrinsic goods in WE, the actual world in which I am delayed in traffic, sum to 20, and the values of my intrinsic evils sum to −10; then IV(Luper, WE) = 10. (I am pulling these numbers out of my hat, of course.) Next we ask how things would have been had E not occurred; that is, we examine the closest possible world in which E does not occur, and calculate the value for me of (my life in) this world. We can call this world *W∼E*, using the tilde (i.e., "∼") to symbolize 'not'. Finally, we subtract this second sum from the first: we subtract the value for me of (my life in) W∼E from the value for me of (my life in) the actual world. This gives us E's value for me. If we symbolize the value of E for subject S as V(S,E), then:

$$V(S, E) = IV(S, WE) - IV(S, W{\sim}E)$$

That is, E's value for subject S is S's welfare level in WE, the actual world (in which E occurs), minus S's welfare level in W∼E, the closest world in which E fails to occur. Back to our illustration: we said that my welfare level in WE is 10. Now, presumably my welfare level in W∼E is greater than 10, since I would enjoy my walk. Let us say that my welfare level in W∼E is 11. Then the value for me of getting stuck in traffic is −1.

We can now specify what it is for an event to be overall bad (good) for a subject S:

An event E is bad for S just in case E's value for S is negative; that is, V(S,E) < 0; E is good for S just in case E's value for S is positive; that is, V(S,E) > 0. The more negative (positive) E's value is, the worse (better) E is for S.

Getting stuck in traffic was bad for me, since its value is negative, but it was not as bad for me as an event with an even greater negative value. Similarly, an event is good for me just in case its value is positive. (For simplicity I have taken events to be good or bad, but I think that states of affairs can be good or bad too, and that the analysis, slightly altered, can be applied to them.)

Before I state the comparativist account of interests I must clarify some things.

The first concerns an ambiguity that can arise in talk about events. Event *types* are abstract entities. They differ from event *tokens*, which are concrete entities. One *type* of event is the striking of a key on a keyboard; many tokens of this type are occurring right now, as I type these words. Each of these tokens is a concrete, particular striking of a key. The distinction between types and tokens applies to things other than events as well. For example, it applies to letters. There are both letter types and letter tokens. Many such tokens are present on the piece of paper you are looking at now. Each consists of dried ink. But not all tokens of letters do. We could construct a token of a letter by carving our initials into a tree.

The distinction is important because the events I have been discussing up until now are event tokens. I have been using the letter 'E' to refer to them, and I have described their value for us. However, it is also important to know how bad or good for us it would be if an event of some type *were* to occur, or *had* occurred. When we ask how good or bad for us it would be if an event of some *type* were to occur, often we will not have any specific event *token* in mind.

How should we handle an occurrence of some type of event? We can understand its value in much the same way as we understand the value of an event token. The occurrence of an E-type event would be good (bad) for S if and only if S's life was worse (better) than it would have been if an E-type event had occurred. To assess whether the occurrence of an E-type event would be good or bad for S, we work out S's welfare level in the actual world (in which an E-type event did not occur), then S's welfare level in the closest world in which an E-type event occurs, and subtract the former from the latter. This gives us the value for S of the occurrence of an E-type event. If that value is positive (negative), the occurrence would be good (bad) for S.

Next I want to draw attention to a subtle matter: the occurrences of some event type need not be actual to have positive value for us, but they must be actual to benefit us. Take, for example, an occurrence of the following event type: your giving me $50. Such an occurrence has positive value for me (my life is not as good as it would have been had you given me $50), and it *would* benefit me, but since it will not happen, it never actually *does* benefit me.

Now for a really subtle matter: it is appropriate to say that something is *in our interests* if it has positive value for us. It need not actually benefit us to be in our interests. It is reasonable to talk this way since things with positive value for us matter to us: it is rational to bring them about if we can.

These points about 'interests' and 'benefit' help us to reveal an ambiguity in the use of the term 'good.' When we say that something is good for us, we might well mean that it is in our interests. But we might also mean that it benefits us. Either way of using the term 'good' is proper, so long as we are clear about what we are doing. In what follows I will equate something's being *good for* us with that thing's *benefiting* us. So I will say that only actual occurrences of E-type events are good for us. Nevertheless, things that benefit us and things that would benefit us if they were actual are both in our interests.

We can now state an account of interests.

Comparativism:
1. An event E is *in* S's interests just in case E overall benefits (is good for) S, making S's life better than it would have been if E did not occur, which E does just when its value for S is positive.

2. An event E is *against* S's interests just in case E overall harms (is bad for) S, making S's life worse than it would have been if E did not occur, which E does just when its value for S is negative.

3. The occurrence of an E-type event is *in* S's interests just in case it *would* overall benefit (be good for) S. The occurrence of an E-type event would benefit S if and only if its value for S is positive.

4. The occurrence of an E-type event is *against* S's interests just in case it *would* overall harm (be bad for) S. The occurrence of an E-type event would harm S if and only if its value for S is negative.

5. How much E benefits (harms) S depends on how much better (worse) S's life is in the actual world than it would have been if E had not occurred: the better (worse) S's life is, the more beneficial (harmful) E is. Similarly, how much the occurrence of an E-type event *would* benefit (harm) S depends on how much worse (better) S's life is in the actual world than it would have been if an E-type event had occurred: the worse (better) S's life is, the more beneficial (harmful) the occurrence of an E-type event would have been.

There is a further ambiguity in ordinary discourse which should be cleared up before we move on. People sometimes say things like 'It was in my interests to fill my gas tank,' or 'It was once in my interests to collect art, but now it is not,' or 'Smoking cigarettes was in my short-term interests.' These ways of speaking suggest that we can have interests at particular times which we lack at others. We can make sense of this suggestion. Roughly, the idea is that what makes a subject S better off *at time T* is in S's *interests-at-time-T*. (We can spell this out more carefully: Instead of concerning ourselves with a subject's lifetime welfare level in a world W we can instead consider a subject's welfare level as it is in W at a particular time T – call this subject S's *welfare-at-time-T-in-W*. We can then say that some event E *benefits (harms) S-at-T* just in case S's welfare-at-T in-WE is higher (lower) than S's welfare-at-T-in-W~E, where WE is the actual world and W~E is the closest world in which E does not occur. And, finally, we can add that E is in (against) S's *interests-at-T* just in case E benefits (harms) S-at-T.) Our interests-*at-T* should be distinguished from our *interests*. Depending on the nature of welfare, which we will discuss next, our interests-at-T may vary over time: what is in our interests-at-time-1 need not be in our interests-at-time-2. This is not true of our interests. Whatever interests we have we have at all times. If something is in our interests, it is timelessly in our interests. If, today, I can do something that would greatly benefit-me-tomorrow, it is in my interests today to do it (other things being equal), even though it may not be in-my-interests-today. Comparativism, as stated above, is an account of interests, not an account of interests-at-T.

Comparativism defines our interests in terms of our welfare. But what is welfare? There are three main views: positive hedonism, preferentialism, and pluralism. Comparativism is compatible with all three, as we shall now see.

Positive hedonism

Positive hedonism analyzes welfare in terms of pleasure and pain, as follows:

> *Positive hedonism*: For any subject S, S's experiencing pleasure at T is the one and only thing that is intrinsically good for S at T, and S's experiencing pain at T is the one and only thing that is intrinsically bad for S at T. The more pleasure S experiences at T (the amount depends on its intensity and duration), the greater the intrinsic good for S at T; the more pain S experiences at T, the greater the intrinsic bad for S at T.

As an account of welfare, positive hedonism has significant virtues. Chief among these is its simplicity. Combined with comparativism it gives us a powerful theory, according to which the value of an event is determined solely by the difference it makes in the hedonic quality of our experiences. For example, if, over my lifetime, I will experience a total of 10 units of pleasure, and a total of 5 units of pain, then my lifetime welfare level is 5. Furthermore, if, had I not been stuck in traffic, I would have had a lifetime welfare level of 6, then, given positive hedonism, the value for me of getting stuck in traffic is −1.

Positive hedonism has a second excellence: it helps resolve the problem of commensurability (Mill 1863). Each of us can assess our own welfare, and the values of the things that happen to us, without working out how to equate one unit of one sort of good with one unit of another. For each of us, the only intrinsic good is our pleasure, and every other apparent good is actually an instrumental good, which we can rank in terms of how pleasing we find it. Or rather this is true if pleasures are comparable in terms of something quantifiable that is present in all pleasures. Matters will be stickier if we attempt to make interpersonal comparisons of welfare, however. It is not obvious how one unit of my pleasure relates to one unit of someone else's.

Simple views are often overly narrow. Unfortunately, positive hedonism is flawed in this way.

To see that it is an overly narrow view of welfare, consider that in some cases things are good or bad for us for reasons that have nothing to do with pain and pleasure. Consider two examples, the first set out by Thomas Nagel (1993) and the other two by Robert Nozick (1971, 1974):

The Contented Infantile Man: While you are sleeping, I pour into your ear a potion that painlessly reduces your mental capacities to those of an infant while also giving you great pleasure for the rest of your life. Suppose, too, that the life you would have led was one in which you would have had far less pleasure, but you would have developed friendships and written a few good books.

The Deceived Man: "Suppose we read the biography of a man who felt happy, took pride in his work, family life, etc. But we also read that his children, secretly, despised him; his wife, secretly, scorned him, having innumerable affairs; his work was a subject of ridicule among all others, who kept their opinion from him; every source of satisfaction in this man's life was built upon a falsehood, a deception. Do you, in reading about this man's life, think: 'What a wonderful life. I wish I, or my children, could lead it'? And don't say that you wouldn't want to lead the life because all the deceptions and falsehoods might come out, making the man unhappy. They didn't."

The Experience Machine: "Suppose there were an experience machine that would give you any experience you desired. Superduper neuro-psychologists could stimulate your brain so that you would think and feel you were writing a great novel, or making a friend, or reading an interesting book. All the time you would be floating in a tank, with electrodes attached to your brain."

Clearly I harm you by putting you into a pleasant infantile state for the rest of your life, but I have caused you to have much more pleasure and much less pain than you would have had. By hedonist lights, I have not harmed you at all. I have benefited you. In fact, due to me, you could not be better off. The Deceived Man is also harmed, although he never finds out, since for some reason he is kept in the dark. Perhaps it is part of a plot instigated by his worse enemy. To gain revenge for some unknown slight, his enemy has convinced his wife and children that he is evil, and convinced them to feign love so as to be positioned to keep tabs on him for the rest of his life. He has lost what he cherishes most – the love of his partner and children – yet retains the appearance of love. He has been harmed grievously yet in a way that causes him no troubling experiences and that does not reduce the amount of pleasure he will enjoy over his life. And Nozick's Experience Machine lets you max out on pleasure; if pleasure is all that matters, and we can choose whether or not to plug in based solely on whether we believe it is in our interests, we would plug in. Yet none of us would want to spend our lives floating in the tank. Obviously we think that pleasure is not the only thing that is good for us.

Hedonists might respond to Nagel's case by saying that upon becoming infantile you cease to exist, and some other individual, a contented infant, takes over. Since the infant gets the pleasure and you are deprived of it, you are harmed by the potion. However, this response cannot be made to a modified version of the case in which the potion just makes you far less intelligent while still giving you great pleasure for the rest of your life. And this way of resisting is futile anyway; it does not help with the other cases.

Fred Feldman (2004) suggests ways for hedonists to handle Nagel's and Nozick's cases. He begins by distinguishing (2004, 55) between sensory pleasures, which are just sensations, and something he calls "attitudinal pleasures":

Attitudinal pleasures are different. A person takes attitudinal pleasure in some state or affairs if he enjoys it, is pleased about it, is glad that it is happening, is delighted by it . . . Attitudinal pleasures are always directed onto objects, just as beliefs and hopes and fears are directed onto objects. This is one respect in which they are different from sensory pleasures. Another difference is that attitudinal pleasures need not have any 'feel.' We know we have them not by sensation, but in the same way (whatever it may be) that we know when we believe something, or hope for it, or fear that it might happen.

As an example of an attitudinal pleasure without any 'feel,' Feldman suggests the 'pleasure' taken by an accident victim in the fact that she was not killed. If she is completely numbed by anesthesia, and therefore lacks sensations of pleasure, she cannot have sensory pleasure, but this does not prevent her from having attitudinal pleasure. Feldman adds that we may take attitudinal pleasure in states of affairs that do not actually hold, and in past or future states of affairs, but only if we believe that they do hold (or have held or will hold) (2004, 60–61). He then suggests an idea, which he later rejects, which could help hedonists to handle cases like the Contented Infantile Man (2004, 73–74):

Every potential object of intrinsic attitudinal pleasure can be ranked on a scale according to its suitability to serve as an object of pleasure. We can say that the scale positions such objects according to their 'altitude'. Mental, moral, and aesthetic objects have high altitude. Physical, bodily objects have low altitude.

... Every episode of intrinsic attitudinal pleasure is good in itself; but we can add that the intrinsic value of such a pleasure is not simply a matter of quantity of pleasure taken. Rather, to find the intrinsic value of an episode of pleasure, we multiply the amount of pleasure in that episode by the altitude of the object of the pleasure.

Thus one attitudinal pleasure may not differ from a second in terms of quantity, but if the first has an object that is positioned at a higher 'altitude' than the second, then the first is more valuable than the second. If we could make clear sense of 'altitude,' we could say that the reason you are worse off as a Contented Infantile Man is that your pleasures have dropped precipitously in altitude: had I not slipped you the potion, you would have delighted in philosophy and fine art; because of the potion, you are delighted only by such things as a warm bed, milk, and a good tickle. As Feldman points out (2004, 77–78), this response to Nagel's case is unconvincing since the notion of altitude is troublesome.

Nor does the concept of altitude give us resources to explain why you are worse off Deceived or connected to the Experience Machine. In these cases, your pleasures are not low in altitude. But Feldman does think he can reconcile such cases with hedonism. He says that attitudinal pleasures are directed at propositions, and he suggests that we discount pleasures directed at false propositions. For example, we can take it that the pleasure you attain while Deceived is directed at the proposition that you have the love of your partner and children, and discount it on the grounds that the proposition is false. Being pleased at gaining love is better when one actually is gaining love than when one is not. Similarly, when connected to the Experience Machine, your pleasures are directed mostly at propositions that do not obtain. The story does not apply to Nagel's case, since the Contented Infantile Man does not have misdirected attitudinal pleasures.

I will not discuss Feldman's suggestions in any detail (for a good discussion, see Katz 2006). They raise a great many questions which he himself points out. However, my own impression is that the resources he develops do not enable hedonists to adequately explain what is bothersome about being made Infantile or spending life Deceived or attached to the Experience Machine. What is bothersome is not that we will have been deprived of a better sort of *pleasure* than we might otherwise have had, but rather that we will have been deprived of *other* things that are good in themselves, such as love, friendship, accomplishments, and so forth.

Preferentialism

Let us see if we can explain the harm involved in Nagel's and Nozick's cases using a different conception of welfare, namely *preferentialism*. According to preferentialism (which is also known as the *desire fulfillment theory*) we assess welfare in terms of desire fulfillment; fulfilling a desire benefits us in proportion to the strength of that desire; similarly, the thwarting of a desire harms us in proportion to its strength. I harm you when lying to your lover because I thwart your desire for this person's love, and I harm you when I place you into an infantile state in that I thwart the ambitions you had for your life. Preferentialists can also say that, in making you infantile, I harm you further: I prevent you from forming and satisfying the desires you would have formed had I not acted as I did. But before we can decide whether preferentialism is plausible we will need to formulate it more clearly.

To desire is to desire *that* some proposition P hold. We can call this proposition the object of the desire; thus the desire for P has the proposition P as its object. Your desire for P is fulfilled at a time just in case P holds at that time. That P holds will not necessarily result in your gaining any pleasure or gratification, hence 'satisfying' or 'fulfilling' a desire may or may not involve gratification. Preferentialism does not say that fulfilling desires is good for you because you derive pleasure thereby. It says *nothing* about gratification. Preferentialism says that fulfilling desires is *intrinsically* good for you: it is intrinsically good for you at time T that, at T, you desire P and P holds. Consider some examples.

I want to eat. Here P, the object of my desire, is that I am at a time when I am eating. P is made true by my being at a time at which I am eating. Suppose I begin eating at noon; it is intrinsically good for me that I desire to be and am eating at noon. I do not accrue this good until noon.

I want to marry some day. The desire is not to *be* married; P is not that I am *at* a time when I am married. Instead, P is that I am married eventually. P is made true by my being married at some time. But if P will ever be made true, it is true timelessly, and my desire is fulfilled now. Hence I need not wait to accrue the salient intrinsic good: it is intrinsically good for me that I desire to and will be married, and I accrue this good now. Of course, I do not now know that my desire is fulfilled, and I probably want that, too; for that, unfortunately, I will have to wait.

I want to be remembered after I am dead. P is that there is a time after I am dead at which someone remembers me. This desire is made true by someone remembering me at a time following my death. As before, if

P will ever be made true, it is true timelessly, and hence true now. If it is true now, my desire is fulfilled now, and intrinsically good for me now, whether I know it or not.

These three examples are obviously simplified. What people want is complicated, and the complication is rarely explicit in the way people express their preferences. One complication is that many desires are conditional on various things. For example, when hungry I will say things like 'I want to eat,' but my desire for food is conditional on my hunger, so what I want is more like this: I want to eat *if I remain hungry*, I want to eat *or not be hungry*. Some desires are conditional on their own persistence. For example, instead of saying I want to watch television it would be more accurate to say that I want to watch television or not desire to watch television. The desire to marry is not usually conditional on its persistence. It is complicated in a different way: I not only want to marry someday, I want to *want* to be married while I am married. Since this is what I want, I will not benefit from a marriage I find I do not want. My desire to be remembered after I am dead seems to be complicated in neither of these ways: even though, when the time arrives, I will not want to be remembered, I now want to be remembered after I am dead.

Preferentialism says not only that it is intrinsically good for you that your desires are fulfilled, but also that it is intrinsically bad for you that the objects of your desires fail to hold: it is bad for you at time T that, at T, you desire P yet ~P holds. Let us say that your desire for P is thwarted by conditions that falsify P, and that your desire is thwarted at the time these falsifying conditions hold. Then your desire for P may be unfulfilled before it is thwarted. Consider the examples once again. *I want to eat*: it is bad for me, now, that I want to be at a time when I am eating, yet am not. Ten minutes from now, if I am not eating, and still want to, this will still be bad for me. *I want to marry some day*: this desire is not yet thwarted, and will never be if I ever marry. If I never marry because every woman dies tomorrow, then my desire is thwarted tomorrow, yet it is bad for me, now, that I want to marry someday and won't. *I want to be remembered after I am dead*: in all likelihood, this desire will be thwarted, if at all, only after I am dead. If *everyone* dies tomorrow, my desire is thwarted tomorrow (since no one is left to remember me), but it is bad for me now that I desire to be remembered and won't be.

In sum, preferentialism may be stated as follows:

Preferentialism: For any subject S, it is intrinsically good for S at T that, at T, P holds and S desires P; it is intrinsically bad for S at T that, at

T, ∼P holds and S desires P. The stronger S's desire for P is, the better (worse) it is for S that P holds (∼P holds).

Few if any theorists accept this unrefined version of preferentialism, since many of the things we desire will not contribute to our well-being (Rawls 1971, Adams 1999, Kraut 1994, Carson 2000). For example, John Rawls adduced the case of a man whose main desire is to count blades of grass; satisfying this desire does not appear to benefit him. In response to examples such as Rawls's, some theorists, including Rawls himself, adopt *critical preferentialism*, the view that welfare is advanced by the fulfillment of rational aims. According to Rawls (1971, ch. 7), our desires are shown to be irrational by demonstrating that we would not have them if we were fully aware of our situation. For example, knowledge of the circumstances under which I came to want body piercing might extinguish my desire. Full knowledge of the future might prompt me to change my plan to book a passage to the Moon. Perhaps the desire to count grass would not survive my awareness of its utter pointlessness.

Even rational desires may not be relevant to our welfare, however. Parfit (1984) offered the example in which you desire that a stranger's disease be overcome. This desire is rational, but its fulfillment does not advance *your* welfare. To accommodate this kind of example, some theorists (among others, Overvold 1980, 1982) say that a salient desire makes essential reference to the self; it is a desire like "Let me, John Doe, live on a Caribbean island," and not "Let someone or other live on a Caribbean island." This view we might call *egocentric preferentialism*.

Some theorists claim that what is plausible about preferentialism is better captured if we focus on the contributions we make towards the achievement of our goals or ends. Simon Keller (2004) and other pro-ponents of *achievement preferentialism* suggest that 'goals' and 'ends' are not mere desires: we take on a goal only if we intend to put effort into its achievement. Accomplishing a goal constitutes a *prima facie* contribution to one's welfare (although other things bear on one's welfare too), while its nonfulfillment constitutes a *prima facie* harm. Thomas Scanlon takes a similar view (1998, 119–123). Douglas Portmore (2007) defends the related idea that meaningful efforts towards our own ends are beneficial to us, while we are harmed by events that make our efforts pointless. He and Keller both say that attaining goals through little or no contributions of our own does not redound to our welfare, and that posthumous events can harm us by interfering with the advancement of our goals or by rendering our efforts towards our ends pointless.

Pluralism

Preferentialism as well as hedonism may be criticized on further grounds. In the case of some things that are good for us, it does not seem plausible to explain their goodness in terms of their being desired or pleasing; instead, it seems more natural to explain why we desire and are pleased by certain things in terms of their goodness. For example, wisdom, friendship, and love seem to fit this description. Desiring wisdom, and finding it to be pleasing, are appropriate because wisdom is, in itself, good for us; similarly with love, or rather with loving relationships. The corresponding evils are perhaps ignorance and enmity. Such doubts can suggest that whether things are intrinsically good for us is a matter of their being *objectively* intrinsically good for us – good for us in a way that does not depend on their being pleasing or desired.

Objectivists tend to be pluralists, who think that various things are intrinsically good, not just one sort of thing, such as pleasure. And pluralism leaves us with difficult tasks. We will need to identify the list of things that are objectively good. Having done that, we face the question of how to rank the relative values of different goods. There may be little to say: perhaps some goods are more valuable than others, and some about as valuable, even though it is not possible to assess all in terms of one good, as the hedonist wishes to do, and even though there is no precise answer as to how much better one sort of good is as compared to another. Feldman (2004, 19) expresses another concern about pluralism: a life that is rich in the various intrinsic goods might lack pleasure. However, this concern is not worrisome; assuming that pleasure is one of the intrinsic goods, pluralists would say that a life that lacks pleasure but is rich in other intrinsic goods is not as good as it would be with pleasure thrown into the mix. It is true that pluralism would be threatened by the contention that my life cannot be *at all* good for me in the absence of pleasure, no matter how rich it is in other putative intrinsic goods. But this contention is dubious. (Could my life be good for me if devoid of the sort of pleasure Feldman calls sensory, even though it is rich in attitudinal pleasures that lack 'feel'?)

Preferentialists are likely to see some truth in hedonism simply because everyone wants pleasure. Pluralists will see their view overlapping with both hedonism and preferentialism, assuming they include at least some pleasures (possibly not pleasure taken in things that are intrinsically bad for us) and the satisfaction of certain desires among the things that make for well-being.

I am myself this kind of pluralist. We go too far if we deny that our desires play a role in determining our interests. Most of us construct and implement a plan for life into which final ends are embedded. Theorists who say we want to give our lives a coherent and unified story line seem to be making substantially the same point (MacIntyre 1981, Velleman 1991). We change our plan as we go, revising it in light of our experiences, setbacks, expectations, and applying rational principles of the sort Rawls and others discuss (1971, ch. 7). We augment it as our knowledge of the future improves. Eventually our plan matures, and becomes difficult to alter significantly, partly because much of our lives will be over, and new plans will not make sense given what we have done before. By adopting a rational life plan and refining it to maturity, we shape our own interests; we *make* it the case that fulfilling the final aims embedded in our plan is, objectively, intrinsically good for us, and that failing is intrinsically bad for us. If we do not plan our lives, we lose out on this sort of good. We all know people whose lives are impoverished in this way – people who care little about the shape of their lives as wholes. They passively accept what life offers them; typically, they are hedonists by default, by indifference. According to some writers (e.g., Royce 1908), we understand who we are, the self we are striving to actualize, in terms of our life plan. If this is correct, then a human being who does not strive to shape her life over time is nobody (cf. the position defended by Kierkegaard's character Judge William in *Either/Or*, 1843). Frankfurt (1971) says, in effect, that our final aims, whose fulfillment is what we most care about, constitute our wills; they give rise to a set of desires about our desires: we desire not to have desires that are inconsistent with our aims. If he is right, then people with no life plans would tend to be will-less beings – "wantons," he calls them.

Choosing, revising, and executing a life plan are modes of self-determination, as are identifying, and holding ourselves to, moral values. The point is worth mentioning here for, while *fulfilling* a life plan matters, engaging in self-determination itself is intrinsically good for us. An example will help make this claim plausible.

> *Desire Slavery*: The government wants everyone to live long, peaceful, happy lives, so it develops a new drug called Subdue. Subdue makes people want to do its bidding, and to enjoy doing so. After dispensing Subdue, the government directs people to carry out useful tasks and creates a harmonious, peaceful order. After taking Subdue, people realize that they are drugged; that when they were first given Subdue

as children, some of them did not want to be given Subdue; and that Subdue makes them want to continue to be drugged.

Desire Slaves not only enjoy themselves, they are doing exactly what they want to do. We can even suppose that they desire to desire what they do, and that, over the course of their lives, they will be much more successful in satisfying the desires they will form under the influence of Subdue than they would have been in satisfying the desires they would have formed had they not been drugged. Yet they are worse off as Desire Slaves. The harm they have been done is that they cannot choose their own values and aims. They are not self-determining. Engaging in self-determination is a valuable intrinsic good which they have been denied in this *Brave New World* scenario.

Responding to a similar case, Rosenbaum (1989b) says, in effect, that Desire Slaves are not harmed; they only appear to be, since they have been wronged. It is morally improper to Subdue people, but it is not against their interests. (Davis [2007] makes a similar distinction when he says that we can wrong the dead, but not harm them, by setting aside their preferences concerning posthumous events.) Now, it is true that people can be harmlessly wronged. You might steal my lawnmower, and return it undamaged before I notice its absence. It is also true that the Desire Slaves have been wronged. However, they have also been harmed. Suppose that the government allowed people to take Subdue voluntarily, and that we could know it would never ask its Desire Slaves to do anything objectionable in itself. You and I would not queue up for Subdue, and that is because we think we would be worse off on Subdue. Like death, it would prevent us from being self-determining.

THE HARM THESES

Most theorists who defend the harm thesis (which says that death can be bad for the one who dies) or the posthumous harm thesis (which says that posthumous events may harm those who have died) appeal to comparativism (e.g., Nagel 1993, Quinn 1984, Feldman 1991, 1992). Let's lay down the main line of defense, then consider ways Epicurus might respond.

The main defense

Consider

Fred's Fall: Fred lived the first twenty years of his life happily, then died, at age twenty, on April 1, 2005, while climbing Fool's Peak; had he not died, he would have lived just as happily for twenty-five more years, then spent the last five mostly suffering.

Suppose we accept positive hedonism as our account of welfare. To assess Fred's death on April 1, 2005 using the comparative account, we sum the pleasure and pain Fred had over his lifetime; this gives us his lifetime hedonic welfare level in the actual world. Let this value be 20. Then we sum the pleasure and pain Fred would have in the closest world in which he did not die on April 1, 2005. Assuming he would have lived as happily for 25 more years, then suffered for 5 more, then his lifetime hedonic welfare level in this world would be something like 20 + 25 − 5, or 40. Finally, we subtract 40 from 20, leaving −20 as the value for Fred of dying on April 1, 2005. Thus, on the comparativist approach, Fred's death gravely harmed him.

His death harmed him in that it *deprived* him of many things with substantial intrinsic value, and very little of intrinsic disvalue. This is true if we accept positive hedonism, and consider only the hedonic quality of Fred's experiences. But it is also true if we reject positive hedonism, and suppose that pleasure is not the only intrinsic good, nor pain the only intrinsic bad. (In speaking of Fred's being 'deprived' of goods such as pleasure, we run some risk of suggesting that he existed while pleasure was withheld from him [C. Williams 2007]. We can guard against this danger by stipulating that, as we use the terms, being *deprived of* something simply means being caused not to have it.)

Dying on April 1, 2005, harmed Fred. But what should we say about the following case?

> *Fred's Aneurysm*: Fred died on April 1, 2005, in a climbing accident; had he not, a burst blood vessel would have killed him the next day.

In this case, comparativism suggests that his death on April 1, 2005, was not very bad for him, since it only deprived him of a day's worth of goods. Can this be right? Is it plausible to say that dying in a climbing accident is not very bad for someone who is about to die from a burst blood vessel? Some, such as McMahan (2002), who calls this the "problem of over-determination," deny that it is plausible. Others (e.g., Feldman [1991]) disagree. I side with those who think that Fred's death – an event token – was not very bad for him. Consider more cases.

> *Fred's Coma*: Fred died on April 1, 2005, in a climbing accident; had he not, a burst blood vessel would have put him into a coma for his remaining thirty years.

Fred's Suspension: Fred died on April 1, 2005, in a climbing accident; had he not, he would have stumbled into a chamber at Cryogenics, Inc., where he would have been kept in suspended animation for his remaining thirty years.

Fred's Cancer: Fred died on April 1, 2005, in a climbing accident; had he not, cancer would have begun to give him unbearable pain, and continued to do so for his remaining thirty years, until it finally killed him.

In these examples, had Fred not died on April 1, 2005, he would have lived quite a while; in the first two examples that life would have been neither good nor bad; in the last, it would have been very bad indeed. It is quite plausible to say that his death in the first two cases was not especially bad for him, and that in the last his death benefited him. I see no reason to treat Fred's Aneurysm differently than his Coma and Suspension.

Matters seem more complicated if people other than Fred are thrown into the mix. Consider

Fred's Torture: Fred is tortured for ten hours on April 1, 2005, by his angry wife Bertha; if, but only if, he had not been tortured by Bertha, he would have been tortured to the same degree and for the same length of time the next day, by her jealous lover.

It is tempting to say that Bertha grievously harmed him, despite the fact that his life would not have been better if she had not tortured him, as her jealous lover would have done the job. This is because his life would have been better if *neither she nor her lover* had tortured him. In cases of causal overdetermination, we may think that it matters whether the overdetermining occurrence is due to an action of someone. I will not attempt to develop the point in any precision, but our idea may be something like this: in assessing the harmfulness to subject S of person P's action A, we compare S's actual welfare level to S's welfare level in the closest world in which neither P *nor anyone else* does anything comparable to A. If the former is worse than the latter (if P's action made S's life worse than it would have been had no one acted in a comparable way), then P's action harmed S.

However, cases like the following suggest a different way to deal with overdetermination:

Fred's Persistent Aneurysm: Fred died on April 1, 2005, when a blood vessel in his brain burst. Had he not died, the bursting of a different blood vessel would have killed him the next day (if not, the bursting of a third vessel would have done the job soon after).

Since Fred's aneurysm was not harmless, we should say something like this:

> An event E harms S just when S's life is worse than it would have been had neither E nor any event comparable to E occurred.

On this account Fred's aneurysm harmed Fred grievously. Fred's Torture can be handled the same way, since the overdetermining event was torture by Bertha's jealous lover, and that event is comparable to the torture Fred endured at the hands of Bertha herself.

We have been asking whether a particular death in specific circumstances is bad for its victim. However, we could ask about something less specific (Feldman 1991). For example, we might ask whether dying while we are young (which would be the occurrence of an event *type*) is bad for us. We may want to know whether it is bad for us that we die at all – whether mortality is an evil.

Comparativism gives plausible answers to these questions, too. It says that dying young may or may not be bad for us. It is bad for nearly all of us since the life that would carry us past youth is good, but dying young is a blessing for someone who would spend her additional years in constant torment. What about mortality? Same approach: whether mortality is bad for us depends on whether life as an immortal would be good for us. In both cases this way of answering seems correct.

So much for mortal harm. Can we also demonstrate the possibility of posthumous harm? Not if we combine positive hedonism with comparativism. Death leaves us unable to experience anything, and posthumous events cannot reduce the amount of pleasure or pain in our lives.

However, according to preferentialism and versions of pluralism that recognize goods such as achievements, posthumous events might well harm us. They will be bad for people who have certain desires concerning what will happen after they are gone. Death itself thwarts some of these desires, making it impossible for posthumous events to do further damage. It leaves us immune to *further* harm from pleasure deprivation and from the thwarting of desires by itself being responsible for such harm. If I want to be remembered as a great sculptor, but never achieve greatness because death takes me while I am learning my trade, death itself will have thwarted my desire. However, death does not guarantee that all of our desires will go unsatisfied. Some of our desires could be fulfilled by posthumous events. For example, the desire not to be forgotten after I expire is fulfilled if a friend remembers that I died. Posthumous events might also prevent such desires from being fulfilled. Everyone I know could forget me, the very thing I feared might happen. As well, posthumous events might determine whether our goals were achieved.

Of course, Epicureans could point out that, even if preferentialism were correct, death and posthumous events *need* not harm us by causing our desires or aims to be unfulfilled. Instead, people could give up the vulnerable desires. They could try to persuade us that we are better off giving up such desires, thereby reducing our vulnerability. But this will not quite refute the harm theses. We may consider their advice bad, and reject it.

According to comparativism, Fred's death is *extrinsically* bad for him. If we overlook this, as Epicurus might have done (Quinn 1984, Feldman 1991), it will be easy to conclude, erroneously, that Fred's death could not have been bad for him. If being harmed requires incurring something intrinsically bad, it can seem that death could not harm us by depriving us of life, for being deprived of life precludes our later incurring anything intrinsically bad. The only intrinsic harm for which death can be responsible, it seems, is the pain it causes while under way. Its extrinsic harmfulness, by contrast, can be enormous.

Epicurus may have rejected the harm theses because he overlooked the possibility of extrinsic harms. However, there are other explanations. Epicurus and his followers have two ways of responding to the claim that death can harm us by depriving us of goods: they can criticize comparativism or they can defend an exotic view of welfare which we have not yet considered. Let us see if Epicurus' position can be salvaged using one of these strategies, starting with the second.

Negative hedonism

At one point Epicurus writes:

The end of all our actions is to be free from pain and fear, and, when once we have attained all this, the tempest of the soul is quieted; seeing that the living creature has no need to go in search of something that is lacking, nor to look for anything else by which the good of the soul and of the body will be fulfilled. When we are pained because of the absence of pleasure, then, and then only, do we feel the need of pleasure. (1966b, 51)

In this passage, Epicurus suggests that the good life is one as free as possible from pain, and pleasure is important only insofar as we find it painful to be without pleasure. He goes on to advocate an even stronger view, namely, that pleasure just is the lack of suffering:

By pleasure we mean the absence of pain in the body and of trouble in the soul. (1966b, 51)

These passages suggest that he accepted a view we can call *negative hedonism*:

> *Negative hedonism*: For any subject S, S's experiencing pain is the one and only thing that is intrinsically bad for S, and *nothing* is intrinsically good for S.

Paired with comparativism, negative hedonism implies that an event harms us to the extent that it boosts our pain, and benefits us to the extent that it reduces our pain.

The combined view would easily explain Epicurean *sangfroid* in the face of extinction. Death cannot harm those who die painlessly, even if it deprives them of a very long and agreeable existence, since nothing in life is intrinsically good for them! However, death can benefit those who perish, by preventing them from suffering.

However, negative hedonism has absurd consequences. Consider an example (a version of Parfit's Minor Sacrifice case):

> *The Strategic Sacrifice*: Suppose that if I press a button, I will have a little bit more pain than I would have had, but a great deal more pleasure.

Negative hedonism implies that we should not press the button; it implies that we never have reason to endure pain for the sake of pleasure (or any other putative good), no matter how great the amount of pleasure and no matter how little the pain. (Distinguish between trading pain for pleasure versus trading pain for less pain, which a sensible negative hedonist would do, as when we endure an unpleasant tooth extraction for the sake of ending toothache.)

Negative hedonism has another especially absurd consequence: since living on cannot possibly benefit us, and will inevitably harm us to some extent, it would have been better for each of us if we had never existed, and it is best that we stop living straight away! All of us should kill ourselves as painlessly as possible as soon as possible. Moreover, the best thing we can do for the sake of our children is not to have any. Assuming that implications such as these are implausible, we can conclude that the negative form of hedonism should be rejected.

The upshot is that even if we measure harm and benefit in hedonistic terms, in terms of our pain or pleasure, we should reject Epicurus' view that we may be harmed only by what causes us pain. Combining comparativism with positive hedonism is far more reasonable than combining it with negative hedonism, and the former supports the harm thesis.

Next let us examine some ways Epicurus might attack the harm theses by rejecting comparativism itself.

Bifurcated comparativism

On one reading, Epicurus rejected comparativism in favor of the view that the harmfulness of an event E is a matter of how much intrinsic harm it causes as compared to how much intrinsic harm we would have endured if E had not occurred, and the goodness of E is a matter of how much intrinsic good it causes as compared to how much we would otherwise have had. Recall that $B(S,W)$ is the sum of the values of the things which are intrinsically bad for S in W, and $G(S,W)$ is the sum of the values of the things which are intrinsically good for S in W. Then Epicurus' idea would be this:

> *Bifurcated comparativism*: E harms S if and only if $B(S,WE)$ < $B(S,W{\sim}E)$; E benefits S if and only if $G(S, WE) > G(S,W{\sim}E)$.

According to bifurcated comparativism, goods do not *offset* evils, but might eliminate them: that is, the goods E brings do not reduce the harmfulness of E unless they cause us to have less pain or less of some other evil. Similarly, evils do not offset goods. But the most striking implication of bifurcated comparativism is that harm and benefit are *positive conditions*: E does not benefit us by causing the *absence* of evils, unless this causes us pleasure or some other intrinsic good; nor does E harm us by causing the *absence* of goods, unless that gives us pain or some other intrinsic evil.

Combined with positive hedonism, bifurcated comparativism implies that we are harmed only by what increases our suffering, and benefited only by what increases our pleasure; all else is a matter of indifference: neither beneficial nor harmful. Epicurus might have been drawn to this combination because it implies that death can neither harm nor benefit us, ignoring the pain it can cause while it occurs. Death can derail a lifetime of joy or a lifetime of misery, but the former does not harm us since it does not boost our misery, and the latter does not benefit us since it does not boost our pleasure. That might have suited Epicurus, but bifurcated comparativism is open to serious objections. Some of these stem from the highly counterintuitive idea that goods and evils do not offset each other; I will ignore such worries so as to focus on objections that stem from the idea that harm and benefit are positive. For simplicity, in what follows, I will consider bifurcated comparativism paired with positive hedonism, but the criticisms apply to bifurcated comparativism paired with other accounts of welfare.

One concern is this: surely some events or states of affairs harm us without causing us pain (or some other intrinsic evil), and benefit us without giving us pleasure (or some other intrinsic good).

Let us start with benefits that produce no pleasure. Imagine the following example.

> *The Suffering Man's Coma*: While asleep, Cory slips into a coma, from which he emerges unscathed after a week. He is then given a drug that has the peculiar side effect of blocking any memories formed during the week before it is taken. This drug does nothing to his memory, since he formed no memories during the earlier week. Had he not become comatose, his injuries would have made him endure tremendous suffering, leaving him unable to think about anything else, for that week. Afterwards he still would have been given the memory-shortening drug, causing him to forget his week of suffering, and making his subsequent experiences much like they actually were after he emerges from his coma.

Becoming comatose and remaining unconscious for a week benefited Cory, yet caused him no pleasure. It benefited him by causing him to have less pain than he would have had. During the week he would have suffered, he was rendered unconscious, and thus pain-free. However, if harm and benefit are always positive, it is impossible to be benefited or harmed by becoming comatose or by being in a comatose state, since one who is comatose experiences nothing, whether pleasant or unpleasant. Similarly, being anesthetized before a limb is removed is not beneficial; it is a matter of indifference, although the pain involved in surgery without anesthetic would be quite harmful.

Now consider painless harms:

> *The Cheerful Woman's Coma*: While asleep, a woman slips into a coma, from which she emerges unscathed after a week, whereupon she is given

the memory-shortening drug that blocks any memories formed during the week before it is taken. Since she formed no memories while in a coma, the drug takes no memories from her. Had she not become comatose, she would have experienced an extremely pleasant week, unmarred by pain, at the end of which she would have been given the drug, and become unable to recall the preceding pleasant week.

The Cheerful Woman was harmed by becoming comatose (and remaining so for a week). It harmed her, not by giving her pain, but by bringing it about that, instead of the extremely pleasant and pain-free week she otherwise would have enjoyed, she spent a week unconscious and thus wholly devoid of pleasure. Her coma deprived her of pleasure.

There is another objection to bifurcated comparativism: as we just saw, it implies that *being* anesthetized before surgery is a matter of indifference, but it also implies that *not* being anesthetized is extremely harmful! Being anesthetized gives us neither pleasant nor unpleasant experiences as a consequence, but not being anesthetized gives us a great deal of pain. Similarly, according to bifurcated comparativism, becoming comatose is a matter of indifference to the Cheerful Woman, but not becoming comatose benefits her. If some event is bad for us, we are entitled to expect that the nonoccurrence of that event is good for us; failing this expectation is a strike against an account of harm, other things being equal. If we abandon the assumption that benefit and harm are always positive, as we can easily do by rejecting bifurcated comparativism in favor of standard comparativism, we can uphold our expectation. We can say that being anestheticized before surgery benefits us (by precluding pain) and not being anesthetized harms us (by allowing it), and becoming comatose harms the Cheerful Woman (by precluding pleasure) and not becoming comatose benefits her (by allowing it).

Let's bring the discussion back to death. Death is capable of benefiting people in the same way that anesthetization and unconsciousness can. Consider a further case of suffering.

The Suffering Man's Death: While asleep today, a man dies in a hospital accident; otherwise he would have endured an unwanted existence filled with unrelenting pain, wholly unrelieved by pleasure.

On bifurcated comparativism, the Suffering Man could not possibly be benefited by dying painlessly or being nonexistent, any more than he could have been benefited by becoming comatose, for benefit entails experiencing pleasure, and one who dies painlessly, or who is dead or

comatose, has no experiences. Yet the Suffering Man clearly was benefited. *He was benefited precisely in the sense that his death prevented him
from being harmed by unrelenting pain.* Even hedonists are likely to agree
with this assessment. Compare his life to the long life of suffering he
would have had had he not died when he did: the benefit consists in the
fact that his death brought about the more preferable of the two lives.

And of course death can harm us in the same way unconsciousness can,
as another example illustrates.

> *The Cheerful Woman's Death*: While sleeping today, a woman dies in a
> hospital accident. Had she not, she would have enjoyed many years
> filled with pleasure and unmarred by pain.

The Cheerful Woman was harmed by her death in the same way she was
harmed by her coma. The harm did not involve her having pain. Her
demise harmed her in that, instead of the long life of pleasure she would
have had, it caused her life to be bereft of further pleasure, which was the
worst of the two possible lives. And this would be the verdict if we pair
positive hedonism with standard comparativism. Comparativism gets
things right and bifurcated comparativism gets things wrong in all of
these examples.

Now, Epicurus was mostly concerned to deny that death can harm us;
perhaps, as at least one commentator has said (Rosenbaum 1986), he did
not mean to deny that death can benefit us. However, we can use our
examples to question the coherence of the position that death can benefit
but not harm us. Suppose Epicurus grants that we are benefited by what
prevents us from suffering, even if we experience no pleasure while not
suffering, and fail to notice that we are not suffering. Suppose that on
these grounds Epicurus grants that death can benefit us. But if we may
benefit from what prevents us from suffering despite the fact that we never
heed this benefit, surely we may also be harmed by what prevents us from
enjoying pleasure even if we neither notice nor are distressed by this harm.
If we can benefit without enjoyment, we can be harmed without suffering.
The Suffering Man's coma and death illustrate the possibility of a benefit
that is never enjoyed, while the Cheerful Woman's coma and death
illustrate the possibility of a harm that is never suffered. We should deny
the one possibility only if we deny the other; we should deny that the
Cheerful Woman was harmed by her death or coma only if we deny that
the Suffering Man was benefited by his death or coma. Denying the latter
is absurd; nearly anyone, with the possible exception of Unamuno, would

prefer unconsciousness to unrelenting pain. So we ought not to deny the former either.

The experience requirement

Next let us consider an argument against the harm thesis which *appears* to reject comparativism, but it is hard to tell whether it does.

Harry Silverstein (1980) and Stephen Rosenbaum (1986) have tried to bolster Epicurus' case against the harm thesis by replacing his requirement that harm involve suffering with a weaker requirement stated in terms of experience. By weakening Epicurus' condition, Silverstein and Rosenbaum think they can defend him against an example offered by Nagel (their position has been convincing to many commentators, such as Walter Glannon 1994, John Fischer 1997, and perhaps Stephen Hetherington 2001):

> *The Concealed Betrayal*: You are betrayed, mocked and hated by people you thought were your friends, but they are careful to prevent you from discovering this, and so you never suffer as a result.

According to Nagel, Epicurus adopted the following requirement for harm:

> H: Something harms us only if it causes us pain.

(Note that H is implied by both bifurcated comparativism and negative hedonism, but not by the combination of comparativism and positive hedonism.) Nagel's example suggests that H is false since Concealed Betrayal never causes its victim to suffer. Rosenbaum agrees in part with Nagel. Concealed Betrayal really does show that, contrary to H, we can be harmed unawares and hence without experiencing events or situations that harm us. Rosenbaum, much like Silverstein before him (1980, 107–108), then points out that betrayal (and mockery and hatred) are the sorts of thing that *can* be experienced, and he suggests replacing H with the following experience requirement:

> E: Something harms us only if we can experience it.

We can experience betrayals, so they can harm us; we cannot experience being dead, so it cannot.

Note that E does not distinguish between intrinsic and extrinsic harm. Suppose the claim is that something is *intrinsically* bad for us only if we can experience it. Nearly any hedonist (Feldman seems to be an exception) would agree; on (nearly) any version of hedonism, the only intrinsic evil, pain, can be experienced. However, accepting E as a condition for intrinsic harmfulness does not give us grounds for accepting E as a condition for extrinsic harmfulness. To counter Epicurus, Nagel had to show that death can be extrinsically bad for us. To defend Epicurus, Rosenbaum and Silverstein must show that death cannot be extrinsically bad for us, and for that it is not helpful to show that it cannot be intrinsically bad for us. Positive hedonism is compatible with the claim that death is not intrinsically bad for us, but the combination of it and comparativism implies that death is extrinsically bad for us.

Hence I will assume that Rosenbaum and Silverstein mean to offer E as a condition for *extrinsic* harmfulness. Do they have a case? To decide, let us reexamine their response to Nagel.

Suppose that, instead of H, Epicurus had claimed that:

Something is extrinsically bad for us only if it tastes bad to us,

then argued that being dead is not extrinsically bad for us since we cannot taste being dead. Next suppose that pseudo-Nagel responds by pointing out that people are sometimes harmed by things, such as malignant tumors, which they never taste. In response, pseudo-Rosenbaum points out that (a) pseudo-Nagel's counterexample is consistent with the weaker claim that

Something is extrinsically bad for us only if we can taste it.

And (b) this weaker claim still supports Epicurus' conclusion that death is harmless. Pseudo-Nagel will have to grant that tumors are not counter-examples to the weaker claim; we can in fact pop a tumor into our mouth and taste it. But no doubt he will feel that pseudo-Rosenbaum has missed the point, which was that being harmed need not *involve* the sense of taste, which, in turn, is good reason to reject any criterion that ties harm to being detectable through taste. Yet it is not a conclusive reason for denying that we are harmed only by what we can taste, since it is conceivable that, in a suitably loose sense of the term 'could,' we could taste anything that harms us.

Back to Nagel's own case against Epicurus: the Concealed Betrayal example gives Nagel ample grounds for concluding that extrinsic harm need not involve pain or any other experience. And this conclusion is good grounds for rejecting E as a condition for extrinsic harm, even though it is not conclusive grounds, since, as it turns out, all extrinsic harms, including unheeded harms, *could* be experienced. To respond convincingly to Nagel, Silverstein and Rosenbaum must explain why it is plausible to insist that the only extrinsic harms are things we *can* experience after granting that many extrinsic harms are things we *do not* experience.

Proponents of the experience requirement face another difficulty, namely a counterexample presented earlier. Just as the Suffering Man's coma shows that what we do not and cannot experience may benefit us, the Cheerful Woman's coma shows that what we do not and cannot experience can be extrinsically bad for us. Being in a coma prevents us from experiencing anything, so we do not and cannot experience being in a coma. Yet the Cheerful Woman can be and indeed is harmed by being comatose. All of this is also true of the state of nonexistence, when it causes us not to enjoy the good life we would otherwise have had.

The experience requirement could be revised to accommodate the Cheerful Woman's coma. The experiences of the Cheerful Woman are affected by her coma; instead of making her *experience* something, whether pleasant or unpleasant, her coma affects her by making her *not* experience things. It affects *whether* she experiences things. Many conditions, such as color-blindness and numbness, can do this to us. Hence we could accommodate the coma example by saying that we are harmed only by something that makes us experience or fail to experience something, or only by something that affects our experiences. However, this will not help Epicureans defeat the harm thesis, since nearly anyone's death affects her experiences: it ends them (McMahan 1988).

Temporal relativism

According to comparativism, prudential value is temporally *neutral* in the sense (mentioned in chapter 4) that, at *each* point in my life, it is in my interests that my welfare be as high as possible across my entire life. My welfare at all times matters equally. If I can do something *now* that will boost my welfare *later*, it is *now* in my interests to do so, other things being equal. Famously, Derek Parfit supplies grounds for assessing our interests in a temporally relative way instead of a temporally neutral way. Assessing our interests in a temporally neutral way may give Epicureans a way to attack the harm theses. How this might work will take some explaining.

Sometimes we have no reason whatever to satisfy a desire. Parfit gives two examples. First, a desire might be implicitly conditional on its own persistence, in the sense that we want to satisfy it only on condition that we still have it. The desire to play cards is like this. We lose all reason to satisfy such desires as soon as we cease to have them. Compare desires, mentioned earlier, that are conditional on *our* persistence. We might have reason to satisfy these right up until our last day, even if we cease to have them much earlier. Second, Parfit notes, we might change our values or ideals, which might lead us to condemn some of our desires. In this case it is reasonable to forgo any opportunity to satisfy them. When a property, such as conditionality, undermines the importance of satisfying a desire for P, so that P's holding is not intrinsically good for us (and ∼P's holding is not intrinsically bad for us), let us say that it is an *undermining feature.*

When we no longer want something, we may speak of a *past* desire. Perhaps a desire is undermined by being past, as Parfit has claimed (compare Suits 2001 and, as Warren [2004, 35] notes, Lucretius 1951, 3.9000–3). Then Epicureans may be able to revive their attack on the posthumous harm thesis: dying ensures that we cannot be harmed by posthumous events, since we are without desires long before these occur. This strategy does not seem to vindicate death itself, since death may preclude the fulfillment of some of the very desires it destroys. However, the die-hard Epicurean might suggest that a desire is undermined, in passing, at the very moment of its destruction; if it is later thwarted, no harm is done.

In order to assess Parfit's thesis that desires are undermined by being past, it might help to relate it to other claims that he makes. His thesis is one consequence of Parfit's well-known present-aim theory, according to which I now have (*prima facie*) reason to want what best fulfills desires I have now (or rather those of my present desires that are not irrational) but I now have no (*prima facie*) reason to care about the fulfillment of desires I have in the past or future. Even though a desire is past, we may still want it fulfilled. This can occur because we have certain other preferences. For example, we might want no significant periods of our lives to be spent in fruitless efforts, and this more global desire might inspire us to, say, finish solving a mathematical puzzle we worked on for a year but in which we otherwise have lost interest. Thus, as Parfit suggests (1984, 150, 498), our *global* desires, or preferences about whole stretches of life, can provide us reason to want some of our past (or future) desires fulfilled. But it is reasonable to assume that, for at least some of our past desires, we have *no* preference that they be fulfilled. We are indifferent about them. According to Parfit, we lack any prudential grounds for fulfilling past desires about which we are now indifferent – we cannot be harmed if these are unfulfilled; it is not, now, in our interest that they be fulfilled. We may call this the *indifference thesis.*

The present-aim theory does not imply that I should care now only about what is happening now. At each time I may well have reason to care about events that are temporally distant, and to want such distant events to occur. Thus I-yesterday would be benefited if I-now satisfied a desire I had yesterday (say, the desire that I now complete work I started yesterday), and this prospect gives me-yesterday reason to want me-now to act. However, the present-aim view is inconsistent with the neutralist view that, in itself, the temporal locations of my desires have no bearing on whether I have reason to fulfill them. Neutralism says that, all things being equal, I now have reason to satisfy any of my desires, whether past, present, or future; the present-aim theory says that I now have reason to satisfy my present desires only.

In support of the indifference thesis, Parfit appeals to two examples.

The Poet: "When I [Parfit] was young what I most wanted was to be a poet. This desire was not conditional on its own persistence. I did not want to be a poet only if this would later still be what I wanted. Now that I am older, I have lost this desire. I have changed my mind in the more restricted sense that I have changed my intentions. But I have not decided that poetry is in any way less important or worthwhile." (Parfit 1984, 157)

The Savior: "Suppose that, for fifty years, I not only work to try to save Venice, but also make regular payments to the Venice Preservation Fund. Throughout these fifty years my two strongest desires are that Venice be saved, and that I be one of its saviours ... Suppose next that I ... cease to have these desires ... Have I still a reason to contribute to the Venice Fund?" (1984, 152)

Writing poems (in the Poet example) or contributing to the Fund (in the Savior case) would fulfill the desire Parfit no longer has, yet it is "hard to believe" that he has a reason to write poems or to contribute. Why is it so hard to believe? The best explanation is that we have no reason (not even *prima facie* reason) to fulfill desires about which we have become indifferent. So his examples, and others like them, suggest that this explanation is true. Moreover, if we have no reason to fulfill desires after we are indifferent about them, as the indifference thesis says, this supports the present-aim theory.

As Parfit acknowledges, everyone, including neutralists, can agree that conditionality and dependence on revised values are undermining features of desires. If either were a feature of the desires involved in the Poet or Savior cases, Parfit could not adduce them in support of the indifference thesis. But the desires in the two cases do not have these features. Something else must be responsible for undermining them. Parfit's suggestion is that his indifference about his desires – their pastness – is itself the undermining feature. According to him, unless we may ignore desires specifically because we are indifferent about them, we must say that he has "strong reason to try to write poems" even in the absence of any desire whatever to do so. Yet "most of us would find this claim hard to believe" (Parfit 1984, 157).

I believe that most of us will agree with Parfit's impression that, having given up all poetic aspirations, he no longer has any reason whatever to write poetry. Remember, we are assuming that even if, in the Poet case, Parfit has a second-order desire that his life as a whole be successful, or the like (and, indeed, Parfit endorses such global desires; see, e.g., p. 497), he is still completely uninterested in poetry. We must imagine that, in designing his plan for his life as a whole, he bypasses his earlier aspirations concerning poetry. He has a plan that draws upon other ambitions to make his life an overall success. His life could easily be an overall success if he abandons his childhood aspiration to write poetry. He might instead write *Reasons and Persons.*

What Parfit says about the Savior example is less straightforward (Vorobej 1998). Parfit's life could be a success if, for a month, perhaps a year, he tries hard to save Venice, and then abandons his goal. However, Parfit's example has him spending fifty years desperately working for Venice. It is hard to see how he could make his life an overall success if he completely abandons his project. Assuming he has something like this second-order desire, he has *prima facie* reason to complete his project, as Parfit must acknowledge. He will lack all reason only if he is wholly unconcerned about the overall shape of his life. Few of us are so callous, and so few of us will take the Savior case to be an example in which there is no reason to save Venice. Parfit could salvage his example, saying that, in it, he does not care about the way his life turns out overall, but some will say he is asking us to reflect about a creature so bizarre it is hard to form a reliable intuitive response to it. No matter: Parfit can rely on the Poet example.

What should we make of the Poet case? It is plausible to say with Parfit that his poetic aspiration is undermined and that the undermining feature is not its conditionality or dependence on revised values. However, it does not follow that the undermining feature is the indifference with which

Parfit now regards his desire. The neutralist can resist Parfit's indifference thesis by pointing to some *other* undermining feature at work in the example. What would that feature be?

Most of our aims are tentative in the sense that we adopt them in the expectation that we may later revise them. An extreme way to revise a desire for P is to stop wanting P altogether – to *end* the desire for P, say on the grounds that it conflicts with other, more pressing interests. We defer to future exercises of our own autonomy, realizing that we may reassess our priorities, until our life plan matures. In particular, we are always prepared to revise desires in light of the projects and commitments with which we identify, and loath to abandon projects and commitments which have become parts of our identities. We favor some of the ways our desires change, and take what steps we can to coax them in preferred directions. As a rough approximation, we may say that, unless our desires change in ways we (do or) would oppose, the changes are voluntary (cf. Frankfurt 1971). For our purposes we can even count, as voluntary, the intentional elimination of a desire using artificial means, as when we take pills to remove the desire to smoke cigarettes. If we voluntarily stop wanting P, ~P can no longer harm us. It will not harm us during the time we wanted P, or later, when our desire is thwarted. So we undermine a desire when we *voluntarily abandon it* (Luper[-Foy] 1987).

The fact that desires are undermined when voluntarily abandoned explains our indifference in the Poet case. (It can also explain indifference in the salvaged version of the Savior case.) Parfit voluntarily abandoned his childhood ambition to be a poet. Even a neutralist will say that he subsequently had no reason to write poetry.

The claim that we have no reason to fulfill desires which we have voluntarily abandoned is similar to Parfit's claim that we have no reason to fulfill past desires. On either view we will usually lack reason to fulfill past desires. But there are two important differences between the two. First, while voluntarily ending a desire undermines it, things are quite different when our desires are removed against our wills. When this is done, fulfilling our desires can still benefit us (unless thwarted *by* being removed). The benefit might be incurred retroactively, as will be explained in the next chapter. Yet removing desires against our will does transform them into past desires. Second, the temporal distance of our past or future desires is an undermining feature only on Parfit's view, and not on the alternative view. As neutralists, we have *prima facie* reason to provide for an aim even if it is one we have only in the future. We might have grounds other than its futurity for not fulfilling it now, however.

For example, we might have reason to think that we *will* voluntarily abandon it. We might also think that strategically it is wise to pursue most of our future aims in the future, say because some aims are appropriate for older people, or perhaps because we will have more appropriate resources in the future.

Suppose that, before Parfit completed it, I destroyed the manuscript of *Reasons and Persons*, but first I gave him a drug that removed any desire (including second-order desires) he had to complete his book. Neutralists who say voluntary abandonment undermines desires can make several plausible assertions about this example that are inconsistent with Parfit's indifference thesis. First, Parfit has reason to take an elixir that would restore the desires I have taken from him, because otherwise he will have undergone the misfortune of becoming indifferent about his project. As a whole, his life would be worse if he spent the last of it indifferent to the project that inspired him throughout most of it. Second, suppose there is no such elixir. If Parfit had a backup draft of his book (perhaps one of the many manuscripts worked over by his friends), and could still finish it with little effort, he would have reason to do so. Third, the situation changes dramatically if, in a completely *voluntarily* way, Parfit ends his desire to finish his book, and does something else that fits in well with the first part of his life (perhaps he chooses to spend more time with his family). Then fulfilling it would not benefit him, and not fulfilling it would not harm him. He would have abandoned his goal midstream, which need not be a misfortune.

I suggest that desires are not undermined by being past. They appear to be, but that is because they are undermined by being voluntarily abandoned (Luper[-Foy] 1987, 2005). If this is correct, then Epicureans cannot show that desires are harmlessly thwarted by death and posthumous events on the grounds that such desires are past (or on the way to being past) at the time death or posthumous events thwart them.

Moot preclusion

Comparativism says that something harms me when it makes my life worse than it would have been. However, there seem to be events and states of affairs that do not harm me even though their value for me is negative. I am not harmed, it seems, by failing to be a genius, or rich and beautiful. But compare my life as it is, with my unimpressive IQ, income and looks, to my life as it would be were I brilliant or rich or beautiful: the former is considerably worse than the latter. By failing to be brilliant, rich, and beautiful, I am precluded from having many goods, but we might say that the preclusion is moot, in the sense that it is harmless to me. Epicureans might renew their attack on the harm thesis by exploiting examples like these. The examples appear to show that things can have enormous negative value for me without harming me. Similarly, Epicureans might insist, the preclusion of goods by death is moot: cut short, my life is worse than it would be were I not to die, but this comparative difference does not show that I am harmed.

Even if failing to be rich or beautiful and so forth is not bad for me, it does not follow that failing to have more good life is not bad for me. Nor does it follow that death is not bad for me when it takes away the good life I otherwise would have. It seems that the comparative criteria work well when we evaluate *losses*, such as the loss of my arms, and also when we evaluate some *lacks*, such as the inability to see, or to feel pleasure. But the criteria have worrisome implications when we evaluate certain other lacks, such as *my lack of genius*. It is relatively clear that a person is harmed by the inability to see but less clear that he is harmed by the lack of genius. Why is that?

It is easy to locate part of the reason. Comparativism claims that things harm us by *making* our lives worse than they would have been otherwise. It is not so clear that our lives are causally affected by 'negative events,' or events that consist in things not happening, or by 'negative states of affairs,' or states of affairs that consist in things not holding. A mother's drug addiction might have caused her son not to be a genius by damaging his brain while it was developing. But few would say that my IQ was made ordinary by my failure to be transformed into a genius by aliens who have developed a smart ray. It seems odd to say that my failure to find the pot of gold at the end of the rainbow *makes* my life worse than it would have been had I found the pot. It is true that I am not rich. But is this really *because* I have not found gold at the rainbow's end? (Here are further complications: when we discuss not finding gold at the rainbow's end, presumably we are not referring to an event token, and asking how that token's not occurring would affect us. My typing this sentence is an event token, and *it* has the property of not-being-a-finding-by-me-of-gold-at-rainbow's-end. If the token had not occurred – if I had not typed this sentence – I still would not have found gold. Suppose instead that we mean to discuss a hypothetical occurrence of an event type. In that case we need to keep in mind that, according to comparativism, a *merely hypothetical* occurrence of some type of event can have negative value for us, but it cannot harm us. Only actual occurrences harm us. Take, for example, *finding gold at the end of some rainbow*: an occurrence of this type of event has positive value for us, but, because there is no such occurrence, we are never benefited.)

There are various ways to make progress towards solving the problem of moot preclusion. One is to deny that it makes any sense to speak of 'negativities' – negative events or negative states of affairs. This does not stop us from evaluating the event or process of dying (as opposed to the state of death) which is not a 'negativity.' Comparativists are right to claim that things harm us by making our lives worse than they would have been otherwise; negativities are not counterexamples, since they do not exist. On this approach, we will need to clarify the distinction between positive events and negative ones, as it is not so clear (How should we classify my failure to meet the application deadline?), and there appear to be negative events that causally affect us (Didn't my failure to meet the deadline cause my application to be rejected?); these must be explained away.

There may be another explanation of the troublesome cases: in them the events or states of affairs that would be good for us if they held are highly improbable (Draper 1999). Since I was not born with the requisite sort of brain, and no aliens are willing to use their smart ray on me, my becoming a genius is out of the question. But aren't people harmed by not receiving an education? Even our assessment of my lack of genius could change: suppose intelligence enhancement became readily available, as in a more lasting version of the procedure imagined by Daniel Keyes in *Flowers for Algernon*. The more far-fetched a mode of benefit, the less tempting it is to speak of harmful deprivation.

Another explanation involves the relative importance of having some goods rather than others. In some moods, we may consider it harmful to be deprived of a good just when it is important for us to have it. The troublesome lacks we have been discussing might be lacks of goods it is unimportant to have; such lacks would not be harmful even though we would be better off without them. But when is it important for us to have a good? Various answers are possible. One answer might lie in the fact that it is one thing for a life to be (merely) good, and quite another for it to be the best (physically? conceptually?) possible life; some qualities are requisite for a merely good life, or a life that meets the minimal conditions for happiness, while others are essential to the ideal life, or one that provides for a degree of happiness that cannot be exceeded. Failing to have (something essential to) a good life (or minimal happiness) is a misfortune, yet failing to have (what makes for) the best possible life (or maximal happiness) surely is not. So it is plausible to say that the goods it is important to have, and whose absence constitutes a misfortune, are *essential goods*: items essential to a (merely) good life, or a life of (mere) happiness. (Of course, given the flexibility of terms such as 'misfortune,' some hedging is in order. Perhaps things need not deprive us of an essential good to be a misfortune; perhaps it is enough that they significantly impair our chances of attaining the essentials.) Genius and wealth may well bring us great goods, but the goods they bring are inessential.

The distinction in ordinary language between things that are bad for us and things that harm us is not sharp. While the term 'harm' might sometimes mark the lack or loss of essential goods, it does not always. We often equate 'harms us' with 'bad for us,' and 'bad for us' covers a lot of territory. It is natural to equate 'bad for us' with 'against our interests,' and on this usage comparativism captures 'harms us' and 'bad for us' quite well.

Suppose, now, that our reluctance to speak of harm when we lack certain goods derives from their relative unimportance or from the likeliness of our not receiving them. Neither provides Epicureans convincing grounds for indifference about lacking such benefits. Being deprived of the goods I need for a good life is much worse than being deprived of the goods I need for an ideal life, but missing out on the latter is bad for me, no matter how unlikely it is that I shall escape my limitations.

Interest actualism

According to comparativism, the value of my dying at time T depends on the intrinsic goods (and evils) I would have accrued after T had I not died, even though I am actually dead after T. Being dead, I am incapable of accruing any intrinsic goods or evils after T, and in that sense I am *unresponsive* after T. *Interest actualism* denies that the value of my dying at T can depend on these goods. It denies this on the grounds that my death ensures that accruing goods does not come *to be* in my interests after T. Since accruing them is not in my interests after T, it is never in my interests, not even before T. Hence their accrual has no bearing on the value for me of my death. Consider an example.

> *Fatal Crash*: I die when my car strikes a tree; had I not died, I would have formed and satisfied the desire to travel to Neptune, and the desire to become a philosopher. I would have been happy in both pursuits.

My death precludes my forming and satisfying these desires, but in doing so it does not harm me, according to actualism, since, because of my

harm us if they occurred; they harm us just when they make our lives worse than they otherwise would have been; and the more they worsen our lives, the more harmful they are.

This comparativist account presupposes some account of welfare, some view about what well-being consists in. There are several such views, of which, I suspect, the last is most plausible, although the least tidy. First is positive hedonism, according to which pleasure is our only intrinsic good, and pain is the only thing that is intrinsically bad for us. Next is negative hedonism, which counts suffering as the only intrinsic evil, and nothing as intrinsically good. Third is preferentialism, which says that it is intrinsically good for us at a particular time that we desire that some state of affairs P hold at that time and P does hold at that time, and intrinsically bad for us at a time that we desire that P hold at that time yet not-P holds at that time. The fourth account is pluralism, which says that various things are intrinsically good for us and intrinsically bad for us, not just pleasure or desire-fulfillment.

Unless combined with implausible views of welfare, such as the negative hedonist idea that nothing is intrinsically good, comparativism allows that we are harmed by events that make our lives worse by depriving us of intrinsic goods, not just by events that make our lives worse by causing us intrinsic evils. When death or a posthumous event harms us, typically it does so in respect of the goods it deprives us of.

Epicureans can resist, by revising comparativism.

First, they can adopt bifurcated comparativism, according to which we are benefited only by what causes us pleasure (or some other intrinsic good) and harmed only by what causes us pain (or some other intrinsic evil). They could also insist that we are not harmed by events that make our lives worse (or benefited by events that make our lives better) unless we (can) experience those events. These revisions are implausible; they imply that we could not be benefited by comas (or other unconscious states) that cause us to have less pain, or harmed by comas that cause us to have less pleasure, since comas preclude our experiencing pleasure or pain.

Second, Epicureans could say that death undermines the importance of fulfilling our desires; fulfilling them is not good for us, and not fulfilling them is not bad for us. The undermining feature might be their pastness. However, rather than their pastness, what seems to undermine desires is our voluntarily giving them up, which we do not do upon dying.

Third, Epicureans might claim that the preclusion of goods by death is moot: it is no more harmful than my failure to find Aladdin's lamp, but for which I would also enjoy many more goods than I otherwise would have enjoyed. This argument is too quick to dismiss comparativism; the problem of moot preclusion may not be real because talk of 'negative events' or 'negative states of affairs,' such as not finding Aladdin's lamp, may be confused. Moreover, the apparent harmlessness of our lacking certain goods may derive from their relative unimportance or from the unlikeliness of our ever having such goods; neither seems grounds for complete indifference about lacking such benefits.

Finally, Epicureans could adopt interest actualism, which says that an event's value for us is affected by the intrinsic goods or evils we would have accrued had the event not occurred but not if we would have accrued them after we are actually nonexistent. Perhaps dying precludes our attaining many goods, but, for the actualist, it also sees to it that this is not bad for us. Actualism appears to be based on the observation that nothing can be in our interests or against our interests at times when we do not actually exist. However, that is no reason to modify comparativism. Comparativists can and should say that nothing is in our interests after we are dead and gone.

CHAPTER 6

The timing puzzle

In chapter 4 we saw that Epicurus rejected the *harm thesis*, on which death may harm the individual who dies. Epicurus held that the harm thesis can hold true only if there is a *subject* who is harmed by death, a clear *harm* that is received, and a *time* when mortal harm is received. This triad of requirements is easily met in some cases. For example, its subject, harm, and time are clear when death hurts its victims, and destroys their identities, while it takes place. However, things are less clear in the case of deprivation harm, which we identified in chapter 5 as harm that consists in our being prevented from attaining goods we otherwise would have had. Epicureans will presume that death can harm us by depriving us of goods only if there is a particular (stretch of) time when we are harmed. Those who agree with this presumption will then want to clarify when it is that deprivation harms us. As to the timing issue, the two solutions that come most easily to mind both seem worrisome: death harms its victims either while they are alive or later. If we opt for the second solution we appear to run head-on into the problem of the subject, for assuming that we do not exist after we are alive, no one is left to incur mortal harm. If we opt for the first solution – death harms its victims while they are alive – we have a ready solution to the problem of the subject but we face the problem of supplying a clear way in which death is bad: death seems unable to have any ill effect on us while we are living, since it will not yet have occurred.

In this chapter I consider attempts to solve the timing puzzle. First, however, I will examine the presumption that motivates such attempts.

THE EPICUREAN CHALLENGE

Epicureans presume that something harms me only if there is a time when it harms me, and challenge their opponents to supply that time. If their presumption is true, it is important for opponents of Epicureans to meet the challenge. But there is more than one way to interpret their presumption, and therefore different ways to construe the Epicurean challenge. On some interpretations the presumption is trivially true, and the challenge it suggests is easily met by proponents of the harm theses. On another interpretation, the presumption gives rise to a more difficult challenge. However, as we will see, it need not be met, since on this interpretation the presumption is false.

All this will take explaining. I will start by laying out the readings of the Epicurean presumption, and the challenges they yield. The challenges suggested by the trivial readings, we will see, are easily met. In the next section I will turn to the more difficult challenge which Epicureans probably had in mind.

The trivial challenges

There is a time when an event E harms me might mean simply that E, which harms me, occurs at some time. On this interpretation, the Epicurean presumption is this:

P1   E harms me only if E, which harms me, happens at some time.

Of course, P1 is trivially true. No event may harm me unless it happens at some time. The time an event occurs (or a state of affairs holds) might have fuzzy boundaries, and it might be brief, lengthy, or eternal – all of this is consistent with its happening at some time.

On this reading, the Epicurean challenge is quite trivial; it is simply this:

C1   Supply the time when death (or some posthumous event) happens.

Now, there is no doubt that death's exact timing can be puzzling. We have wrestled with the matter in previous chapters. However, Epicureans surely do not intend that their challenge reduce to supplying the time of death. They would say that even if we are clear about when someone dies we will be hard pressed to name the time when she is harmed by death.

Here is another way to understand Epicurus' presumption and challenge. *There is a time when E harms me* might mean that there is a time when E is against my interests, so that the Epicurean presumption is this:

P2   E harms me only if there is a time when E is against my interests.

On this reading, the presumption is trivially true, but what is the challenge supposed to consist in? It is not clear, since, as noted in chapter 5, if something is ever against my interests, it is always against my interests. All it takes for an event to be against my interests is that it makes my life as a whole worse than it would have been had the event not occurred. (Recall, too, that the occurrence of some *type* of event can be against my interests even if I am never actually harmed by such an occurrence. The occurrence of an E-type event is against my interests if my life was better than it would have been had an E-type event occurred.) Suppose, for example, that I will be infected tomorrow and, because of its effects on me during next week, the infection will worsen my life as a whole. Then being infected is against my interests – period. That means it is against my interests now and at all other times I exist. That something harms me or is against my interests, according to the terms of comparativism, is itself not an event, hence not an event occurring at some time, although it can be made true by events. When something is against my interests by the terms of comparativism, we might say that it is *timelessly* against them. Thus suppose the challenge corresponding to P2 is this:

C2   If dying at T harms me, supply the time when it is against my interests.

A perfectly adequate answer is that if dying at T harms me, it is always against my interests. It is timelessly against my interests. However, this is surely not what Epicureans want to know.

The substantial challenge

To understand the challenge Epicureans have in mind, we need a better way to interpret *there is a time when E harms me*. What it means, I suggest, is that there is a time when I incur harm for which E is responsible. Recall the distinction (from chapter 5) between my interests, on the one hand, and my *interests-at-time-T*, or what makes me better or worse off *at time T*, on the other. What Epicureans mean to say is that there is a time T when I am worse off at T than I would have been had E not occurred; at some time T, E is against my interests-at-time-T.

On this interpretation, the Epicurean presumption becomes:

P3   E harms me only if there is a time when I incur harm for which E is responsible; that is, E harms me only if at some time T, E is against my interests-at-time-T.

And this substantive reading of the presumption gives rise to the following substantive challenge:

C3 Supply the time when I incur harm for which death (or some posthumous event) is responsible (supply the time T when death or a posthumous event is against my interests-at-time-T).

As Epicureans say, supplying this time is not an easy matter. I will consider some attempts later. However, it is less important to meet this challenge than Epicureans let on, since P3, the presumption giving rise to the challenge, is false. To see why, let us review some of points made in the previous chapter.

Recall that comparativism, paired with any plausible view of welfare, implies that we are harmed by events that make our lives worse than they otherwise would be, which in turn implies that the harm thesis is correct: death may harm us. Comparativism is a plausible account of our interests. But in the last chapter we considered many ways in which Epicurus might attack the harm thesis. One of these involved appealing to negative hedonism. The others involved attacking comparativism. In each case the Epicurean arguments were weak. We are therefore entitled to conclude that comparativism is well supported, and it is appropriate to appeal to comparativism to defend a view concerning whether or not P3 is correct.

But if comparativism is indeed at least roughly correct, P3 is false. To see why, let us distinguish between two ways in which something might be bad for me.

On the one hand, something might bring it about that, for a while, I am worse off than I would have been. For example, the Cheerful Woman's coma prevented her from enjoying a week's-worth of pleasant activities; while comatose, her welfare level was lower than it would have been had she not fallen into a coma. On the other hand, something might cause it to be the case that my life as a whole is worse than it would have been. Usually, things that make our lives as wholes worse do so by making us worse off for a while. This is true of the Cheerful Woman's coma. However, what makes our lives worse need not make us worse off for any period of time. The Cheerful Woman's death prevented her from enjoying years of pleasant activities, making her life as a whole worse than it would have been had she not died, but at no time *during* her life is she worse off. Unlike her coma, her death precluded her ever again being worse off. Subsequent to her death, she can have no welfare level at all. Death is an injury to our lives as wholes; for people who live in the moment, in the sense that they pay no attention to the overall shape of their lives, it will go unnoticed.

Can't we ask when the Cheerful Woman's life as a whole first began to be worse because of her early death, and when it stopped being worse? This is like asking when Lincoln's life first began (or when it ceased) to be briefer than Socrates'. If it is true at all that her life as a whole is worse because of her early death than it would have been had she not died, it is always true, just as it is always true that Socrates lived longer than Lincoln.

The upshot is that the Epicurean presumption can be sustained if reduced to the uninteresting proposition that we are harmed only if an event that is responsible for our being harmed occurs at some time. But in its intended sense, the presumption is that a death (or posthumous event) has a victim only if it makes her worse off, and the challenge is to supply the time when death makes her worse off. Since the presumption is false, proponents of the harm theses need not meet the Epicurean challenge.

Even if death can harm us without leaving us worse off, there might still be times when, due to death, we are worse off; that is, even if P3 is false, there might be ways to meet the challenge set out by C3. Many theorists have offered ways to meet the Epicurean challenge. Let us consider these now.

SOLUTIONS

If death and posthumous events make those who die worse off, conceivably the relevant harm may be incurred at any of the following times (or some combination thereof):

1. at all times (*eternalism*);
2. after they occur (*subsequentism*);
3. at the time they (death or posthumous events) occur (*concurrentism*);
4. before they occur (*priorism*); or
5. at an indeterminate time (*indefinitism*).

All of these positions have been defended in recent years. I will consider each in turn.

Eternalism

According to *eternalism*, death harms those who die at *all* times. Of all of the options we will consider, this one appears to be the most extreme: whereas Epicurus said that death never harms us, eternalists say that it *always* harms us. To help us understand eternalism, we will consider the work of Fred Feldman (1991, 1992). Feldman's solution to the timing puzzle is an offshoot of his version of comparativism.

Like other comparativists, Feldman says that death is bad for us – extrinsically bad for us – if and only if our lives would have been intrinsically better had we not died when we did. How bad death is depends on how much better our lives would have been had we lived on, so some deaths are worse than others. Feldman states his solution to the timing puzzle this way:

I have claimed that a person's death may be bad for her because it deprives her of the pleasures she would have enjoyed if she had lived. One may be puzzled about just *when* this misfortune occurs. The problem is that we may not want to say that her death is bad for her during her life, for she is not yet dead. Equally, we may not want to say that it is bad for her after her death, for she does not exist then.

In order to understand my answer to this question, we must look more closely into the question. Suppose a certain girl died in her youth. We are not concerned here about any puzzle about the date of her death. We may suppose we know that. Thus, in one sense, we know precisely when the misfortune occurred. Nor are we concerned about the dates of any pains she suffered as a result of that death. We assume there are none. The present question is rather a question about when her death is a misfortune for her. If Lindsay is the girl, and E is the state of affairs of Lindsay dying at 4:00 A.M. on December 7, 1987, then the question is this: "precisely when is E bad for Lindsay?" I have proposed an account of the evil of death. According to that account, when we say that E is bad for Lindsay, we mean that the value-for-her of the life she leads where E occurs is lower than the value-for-her of the life she would have led if E had not taken place. So our question comes to this: "Precisely *when* is it the case that the value-for-Lindsay of the life she leads in which E occurs is lower than the value-for-her of the life she leads if E does not occur?"

It seems clear to me that the answer to this question must be "eternally." For when we say that her death is bad for her, we are really expressing a complex fact about the relative values of two possible lives. It seems clear that if these possible lives stand in a certain value relation, then (given that they stand in this relation at any time) they stand in that relation not only when Lindsay exists, but at all times when she doesn't. (1992, 153–155)

Feldman here speaks of an "eternal truth." An eternal truth is simply a proposition that is always true. For example, the following two propositions are eternal truths:

Two plus two equals four.
Pearl Harbor was attacked on December 7, 1941.

Contrast the following propositions:

There are two boxes in Joe Smith's garage.
Pearl Harbor has been attacked.

These are not eternal truths. They are true only on various occasions. For example, the second, asserted prior to 1941, is false. By contrast, even if asserted prior to 1941 it would be true that Pearl Harbor was attacked on December 7, 1941.

Feldman claims that it is eternally true that Lindsay's death was bad for her, in that it is eternally true that her life would have been intrinsically better if she had we not died when she did. He suggests that death is bad when a certain relation holds between two possible lives, and that, if this relation holds, it is an eternal truth that it holds. He also suggests that this amounts to an answer to the question, "When does Lindsay incur mortal harm?" What should we make of Feldman's response?

Well, *as* a solution to the timing puzzle, as we have understood it, Feldman's suggestion is quite puzzling. It is difficult to believe that, eons before her birth, all during her life, and centuries after she died, Lindsay was worse off, because of her death, than she would have been had she not died.

Several critics (including Neil Feit 2002 and Ben Bradley 2004) have argued that Feldman's response is not an answer to Epicurus' timing puzzle at all. Suppose I stubbed my toe yesterday. If we ask when the stubbing is bad for me, what exactly do we want to know? There are two possibilities. First, we might be asking: "At which times T is it true that I incurred harm at T?" The answer to *this* question is something like: "The stubbing harms me at all and only those times it hurt." But there is something else we might be asking: "At what times is it true that the stubbing harms me?" Here the answer may well be: "Eternally." That is, perhaps "the stubbing harmed me" is true no matter when it is asserted, but I *incur* the salient harm only while my toe throbs. The same ambiguity arises when we ask about the timing of death's harmfulness. Consider the question, "When is Lincoln's death bad for him?" The question can mean: "At which times T is it true that Lincoln incurs mortal harm at T?" But Feldman seems to take the question to mean: "When is it true that Lincoln's death is bad for him?" His answer to this question makes good sense: eternally, if ever. This is to say that death is timelessly harmful. However, according to Feldman's critics it is the first version of the question that concerns us when we ask about the timing of death's harmfulness. Yet Feldman appears to have answered the second version, not the first. Perhaps the charitable reading is that Feldman did not mean to offer a solution to the timing puzzle at all; he did not accept eternalism, and meant only to assert that death may be timelessly harmful.

In any case, eternalism is not a plausible answer to the challenge set out by C3. Let us try another proposal: subsequentism, the view that death may harm its victims posthumously.

Subsequentism

To defend their view, subsequentists point to events that occur in the normal course of life, and ask when we incur any resulting harm. They say that we incur the harm after those events occur. Recall the stubbed toe example, and the question: "At which times T is it true that the stubbing is bad for me at T?" The answer is that the stubbing harms me only after it occurs. Roughly, it is bad for me only while my toe hurts. Or suppose your enemy drugs you into unconsciousness for the next month. When does your enemy's action harm you? Arguably, after it is taken: while you cannot conduct your life as usual. Such examples suggest that, in the usual course of life, events harm us only after they occur. And if this is true, the same should be true of death: if it harms us, it may do so only after it occurs. Why should death be the only exception to the rule?

However, Epicureans claim that we *cannot* incur harm while we are dead. They seem to be right about this. If subsequentists are correct that death may harm us only posthumously, and Epicureans are correct that harm cannot be incurred posthumously, then Epicurus is vindicated: death is harmless. Obviously, then, if they are to prevail, subsequentists have work to do, starting with solving the problem of the subject.

To solve the problem of the subject, subsequentists borrow an idea from Nagel (1993) and Silverstein (1980), among others: the subject who is harmed by death is the living, breathing person who later dies. Assuming that Lincoln's death harmed him, the subject of that harm is the living Lincoln.

But how can the living Lincoln be the subject of harm incurred after he died? Is it possible for Lincoln to come to have *any* properties by virtue of events occurring after he ceased to exist? Admittedly the matter is puzzling, but despite appearances, it is possible to make good sense of things coming to be true of Lincoln by virtue of events occurring after he is dead.

Here is one way we can do so. Suppose that, with Harry Silverstein (1980, 2000) and others, we adopt a metaphysical view called 'four-dimensionalism.' On this view, past, present, and future things are ontologically on a par. If we know that an object exists, we know it is *part* of space-time, but not *which* part: an existing object may be located at any time or place. Consider things in space: an object's being *here* rather than somewhere else does not imbue it with more (or less) existence. By the same token, a thing's occurring *now* rather than at some other time does not give it more existence. From the standpoint of existence, past and future objects are ontologically on a par with present objects, even though their temporal locations are different. Of each object, it is appropriate to say that it exists, where 'exists' is used tenselessly, so that 'Lincoln (tenselessly) exists' is true whether asserted in the past, present, or future.

On the four-dimensionalist view, it makes sense to say things like "Lincoln is now dead." We can refer to Lincoln even though the name 'Lincoln' refers to a man temporally located wholly in the past, and say of him that he is no longer alive. Similarly, by virtue of certain events occurring centuries after his death, it comes to be true of Lincoln that he was discussed in a philosophy class in 2006. (For further clarification of four-dimensionalism, see Rea 2005.)

Here's another means of clarification. David-Hillel Ruben (1988) suggests we may correctly attribute properties to objects or persons who have ceased (or not begun) to exist. Consider "Lincoln was discussed in a philosophy class in 2006." This statement appears to imply that Lincoln changed: he acquired the property of being discussed in class. The apparent change occurred in 2006. We can make sense of this appearance by saying that the change involved is a *Cambridge change*. This is the sort of change a thing undergoes wholly in virtue of its relationship to something else. Notice that some of a thing's properties it has wholly by virtue of the way it is in itself. Call these its *intrinsic properties*. Thus an exact copy of something would share its intrinsic properties. By contrast, a thing may have properties by virtue of the way it relates to or interacts with other things. These we may call its *extrinsic properties* (for a more careful account of the intrinsic/extrinsic distinction see Lewis 1983). Lincoln does not undergo any change in his intrinsic properties when discussed in the twenty-first century; it is we who change our intrinsic properties; but by virtue of his relation to us, he has come to be discussed. Things must exist at a particular time in order to have an intrinsic property at that time. Moreover, things must exist to undergo changes in their intrinsic properties. But they need not exist, or change intrinsically, to acquire (extrinsic) properties via Cambridge changes. (Ruben hints that Cambridge changes are not "real" changes, but he gives us no reason to follow him in this view. Why should real changes be limited to changes in intrinsic properties?)

Can we now make it clear that people may undergo harm while they are dead, as subsequentism avers? Of course, we cannot if harm consists in being in some bad condition such as pain. After Lincoln is dead, 'Lincoln' continues to refer to the living Lincoln. Hence "Lincoln was harmed at time T" can only mean that the living Lincoln is what is harmed at T. Clearly *the living Lincoln* does not undergo harm *while his life is over* if the only harms are conditions like pain. But subsequentists adopt the deprivation account of harm. Subsequentists interpret "Lincoln's death harmed him while his life was over" as "The living Lincoln lacked various salient goods, which he would have had had he not died, during a stretch of time following his death." This we could say whether we think, as four-dimensionalists, that the timelessly existing Lincoln lacks goods while he is no longer alive, or, with Ruben, that Lincoln lacks various goods while he is no longer existent.

So a solution to the problem of the subject is available to subsequentists. But what, specifically, is entailed in incurring harm posthumously? According to Bradley, "death is bad for the person who dies at all and only those times when the person would have been living well, or living a life worth living, had she not died when she did" (2004). Let us try to explain Bradley's analysis in more detail.

Bradley's view is a refinement of Feldman's comparativist analysis. Feldman's idea was to assess the badness of the death of a person, say Sal, by comparing the intrinsic value of the life she lived with the intrinsic value of the life she would have lived had she not died. Her death was bad for her if, and in the sense that, the former was worse for her than the latter. Bradley focuses on the intrinsic value of periods of time that are briefer than lifetimes. He measures the intrinsic value of a (period of) time T for Sal by adding up the values of the intrinsic goods (and subtracting the values of the intrinsic evils) which Sal has at T. And he says that an event harms Sal at T if and only if the intrinsic value of Sal's life would have been greater at T had the event not occurred.

To apply his account to death, Bradley faces a difficulty: after death we cease to exist; how do we make sense of measuring the value of times when we are nonexistent? To solve this difficulty, he stipulates that the intrinsic value of any time during which we do not exist is zero, since we have neither intrinsic goods nor intrinsic evils while we are nonexistent. Then he offers the view that Sal's death harmed her at some time T if and only if the intrinsic value of Sal's life would have been greater than zero at T had she not died.

Consider an illustration. Suppose that Lincoln would have lived ten more years had he not died on April 15, 1865. For the first five (from 1865 to 1870) he would have suffered significantly, so that the intrinsic value of his life during this time would be less than zero, but for the last five he would have thrived, so that the intrinsic value of his life during this time would be much higher than zero. Then Lincoln's death was not bad for him (in fact it was good for him) from 1865 to 1870, but bad for him from 1870 to 1875. Let us now suppose that the intrinsic value of the life Lincoln would have had for the entire ten years following his death was greater than zero (so that the badness of the first five is exceeded by the goodness of the last five). Then, all things considered, Lincoln's death simply was bad for him, period, even though it is also true that his demise was good for him from 1865 to 1870.

Let's review. Subsequentists point out that unless we incur mortal harm posthumously, mortal harm would be highly unusual, since typically harm is incurred after events that are bad for us occur. Subsequentists also provide a subject for mortal harm: the living person, who, by virtue of her relation to subsequent events, comes to incur a form of deprivation harm. Finally, they provide an account of this deprivation harm: it is extrinsic harm consisting in the fact that, for a particular period of time subsequent to death, we would have enjoyed a life whose intrinsic value is greater than the value of times we are nonexistent, which is zero.

So far so good. But have subsequentists really solved the timing problem? There are grounds for doubt.

To be capable of incurring harm, or rather harm-at-T, a thing must have certain properties at T, some of which the dead lack. In particular, the dead lack a property we may call *responsiveness*.

In an earlier essay (Luper 2007) I suggested that a creature is *responsive at* T if and only if it is so constituted that its well-being may be affected at T – rising if certain conditions are met, and falling if certain other conditions are met. A clearer, more adequate view is that a creature is responsive at T just in case it has the capacity to accrue at T the intrinsic goods or evils in which welfare consists. Thus precisely what is required for responsiveness depends on the nature of these goods and evils.

According to the hedonist, a creature's well-being at T is determined by the level of pleasure and pain it experiences at T. On this view, responsiveness at T consists in the capacity to experience pleasure or pain at T. For all known creatures, responsiveness in this sense requires having the sort of nervous system that generates pleasure or pain depending on prevailing circumstances. Hence, for example, a zygote, which entirely lacks any cognitive apparatus, is unresponsive. By contrast, normal adult human beings, even while asleep or in a reversible coma, are responsive. By contrast, preferentialists say that a subject's, S's, welfare at T is determined by the desires S has at T that are fulfilled at T, and the desires S has at T that are unfulfilled at T. They would say that responsiveness requires the capacity to desire. Here, too, a certain sort of functioning nervous system is requisite, which rules out zygotes.

I claim that, while a creature may be harmed by being made unresponsive, a creature may incur harm only while it *is* responsive. Nothing can be made worse off at time T than it might have been unless it is responsive at T. Like a crocodile, my shoe can and does fail to have friendship. Unlike the crocodile, my shoe cannot be harmed at all, no matter what goods it lacks. Its invulnerability is due to its complete unresponsiveness.

Consider the implications for the dead. It is one thing to say that Lincoln lacked various goods while dead, and another to say that his lack of goods harmed him while he was dead. Like a shoe, a corpse, and the dust left when it decomposes, lacks goods, but is not incurring harm thereby. The unborn are not harmed while lacking life. Suppose that I have one of the machines described earlier for bringing back the dead, and at any time during the last ten years I have been able to restore Socrates' life; it is silly to say that he has been incurring harm during the last ten years due to my refusal to bring him back. For a subject S to be harmed at a time T, it is not enough that S lacks a salient good G at T. S must be responsive at T. (Living) people meet the condition, and can be deprived of goods, with corresponding dips in well-being, while they are alive; shoes fail the condition and can never literally be deprived of goods. The dead fail the condition, too. No one is responsive *while* dead, and this was basically Epicurus' point all along.

Now, subsequentists do not say that deprivation harm consists in lacking some good. Roughly, they say that S is harmed while S is deprived of a salient good *which S would otherwise have had*. Shoes can never be deprived of goods they would otherwise have, for the simple reason that they cannot have any goods in the first place. However, my point is that incurring harm entails lower well-being, and that requires having the capacity for intrinsic goods or evils. It is true that shoes cannot be deprived of goods they would otherwise have had, since they cannot have goods at all. But it is also true that, *while dead*, we cannot have goods at all, and hence true that, while dead, we cannot be deprived of goods we would otherwise have had. Our responsiveness is a casualty of death. When the capacity for welfare is removed, the result is not lower welfare.

By the same token death cannot be responsible for deprivation *benefits* incurred posthumously. The Suffering Man's death precluded events that would have harmed him had he not died. But it is not literally true that 'he is better off dead.' Removing the capacity for welfare does not boost welfare. No more than a stone is benefited by its lack of pain and failure, the Suffering Man is not benefited, while dead, by his lack of suffering and failure, since the dead are not responsive.

We seem forced to conclude that, despite its resourcefulness, subsequentism falls short of solving the timing puzzle. Perhaps concurrentism will fare better.

Concurrentism

Concurrentism says we incur mortal harm precisely when death occurs. It also says that those posthumous events that are bad for us harm us precisely when they occur. One concurrentist, Julian Lamont (1998), puts the view this way: we incur deprivation harm at the time some event ensures that we will not retain or attain some good that is otherwise available. Call such an event an *ensuring event*. Death may itself be an ensuring event, so death and at least many deprivation harms may occur simultaneously. Similar reasoning might support the concurrentist story about when posthumous events harm us, for, like death, posthumous events ensure that we will not attain some goods we otherwise would have had, such as our not being slandered posthumously. The upshot is a unified story about when death and posthumous events harm us.

As a solution to the timing puzzle, concurrentism appears to face an objection: death occurs too quickly for it to harm its victim during the brief time it transpires. We faced down this objection in chapter 4. The speed of death is no obstacle to our incurring mortal harm precisely when we die. However, concurrentists face another objection. For they also want to say that those posthumous events that are bad for us harm us precisely when *they* occur. The problem, of course, is that by the time posthumous events occur nothing remaining of us is capable of incurring harm. This is the point that was just pressed against subsequentism. However, concurrentists could be correct about the timing of mortal harm even if they are wrong about the time we incur harm from posthumous events. Indeed, they could say that while death can harm us, posthumous events cannot.

Priorism

Priorism is left unscathed by the criticism I lodged against subsequentism. My claim was that lacking goods at T can be intrinsically or extrinsically bad for us at T only if we are responsive at T. But this does not rule out the possibility that, even though we are dead at T, lacking goods at T is bad for us *while we are alive*. Priorists (Pitcher 1984, Feinberg 1984, Luper 2004, and perhaps Aristotle [see Scott 2000]) say that we may be harmed by death and posthumous events while we are alive.

As we noted in chapter 4, it would be impossible to be harmed by posthumous events while we are alive if the only way an event could affect us was by having a causal effect on us, assuming we do not countenance backwards causation. But posthumous events need not change our intrinsic properties in order to contribute to the status of our well-being. If some version of preferentialism is correct, our welfare can be lower than it might have been because of facts about the future. The fact that we will lack various goods tomorrow, which is made true today by events that will not occur until tomorrow, is against our present desire to have those goods tomorrow, so that our present well-being is lower than it might have been. Slanderous claims made after I am dead make it true that my reputation is to be sullied, and this harms me all the while I want my reputation to be good after I am gone. It is while I am alive that I have such a desire; while alive, my welfare level is lower than it would have been had the slander never occurred. Suppose I die before I can complete some project; my dying ensures that it is true of me that I shall never bring my project to fruition. During such times as I have not taken on the project, and therefore do not desire to complete it, my interests are not affected by the fact that I will fail at it, so my death does not always harm me. But I am directly harmed all the while I have an interest in finishing my project, for, during this time, my welfare is lower than it would have been had I succeeded at my project. Thus death and posthumous events may harm us while we are alive in the sense that our well-being may be lower than it might have been partly as a result of these events.

On the priorist view, most events that are responsible for mortal harm fall into a group of occurrences that have two characteristics: the events occur at one time and we incur harm from them at another, and the victim is never aware of incurring the harm. This group is not really mysterious. Compare an example like that of the Deceived Man from chapter 5: I accidentally cut Spiteman off while driving, and Spiteman will get back at me next month by convincing my fiancée that I am a notorious international criminal who needs to be under constant surveillance. She will marry me in two months, but she will loathe me, pretending all the while that she loves me as much as she does now. In this example a future event greatly affects my present interests, assuming that it is *now* in my interest to have my fiancée's love two months from now, yet I do not notice the impact on my present well-being.

The priorist view cannot be the entire story concerning the harmfulness of death and posthumous events – not, at any rate, if comparativism is correct. Given the comparativist account, part of the reason death is objectionable is that it thwarts desires which we *would* have had and fulfilled had we not died. Since we never actually have such desires, their being thwarted never leaves us worse off: they cannot be associated with any harm which we incur at particular times. As well, comparativism says that death is objectionable insofar as it precludes the pleasure which we would have enjoyed had we not died, even if we never desired the pleasure of which death deprives us. However, priorism might well be the entire story concerning harm which we *incur* and for which death or posthumous events are responsible. This is compatible with the fact that the harm for which death is responsible is not limited to harm we incur. Priorism is compatible with the claim that comparativism spells out the full story concerning why death and posthumous events are bad for us.

Suppose that, after I am dead, you will do something that will thwart desires I have now. According to priorism, I incur harm now, while I have these desires. But are you now responsible for the harm I am presently incurring (Callahan 1987)? You are, in one sense of 'responsible': your act is retroactively responsible for harm I am incurring. However, it does not follow that you are now morally responsible for that harm. Presumably it is appropriate to hold someone morally responsible for harm to another only from the time she has performed the harmful action. Your action makes it true that you have done something morally inappropriate and also that I am harmed retroactively (Taylor 2008).

Apparently priorism provides one reasonable story concerning the time when death or a posthumous event might harm us. (For further criticisms of priorism, see Waluchow 1986 and the responses of Taylor 2008.) But there is one other proposal that we should examine: indefinitism.

Indefinitism

According to indefinitism, death and posthumous events harm us but not at any definite time. This is the last solution to the harm thesis we will consider, but it was the first solution to the timing puzzle to be defended by a contemporary philosopher. Thomas Nagel (1993) and Harry Silverstein (1980, 2000) both defend it.

Nagel expresses the view as follows:

It is arbitrary to restrict the goods and evils that can befall a man to nonrelational properties ascribable to him at particular times … There are goods and evils that are irreducibly relational; they are features of the relations between a person, with spatial and temporal boundaries of the usual sort, and circumstances that may not coincide with him either in space or in time. A man's life includes much that does not take place within the boundaries of his body and his mind, and what happens to him can include much that does not take place within the boundaries of his life. These boundaries are commonly crossed by the misfortunes of being deceived, or despised, or betrayed … A man is the subject of good and evil as much because he has hopes that may or may not be fulfilled, or possibilities that may or may not be realized, as because of his capacity to suffer and enjoy. If death is an evil, it must be accounted for in these terms, and the impossibility of locating it within life should not trouble us.

When a man dies … although the spatial and temporal locations of the individual who suffered the loss are clear enough, the misfortune itself cannot be so easily located. One must be content just to state that his life is over and there will never be any more of it. That fact, rather than his past or present condition, constitutes his misfortune, if it is one. Nevertheless if there is a loss, someone must suffer it, and he must have existence and specific spatial and temporal location even if the loss itself does not. (1993, 66–67)

Here Nagel points out that individuals can come to bear (extrinsic) properties by virtue of spatial relations between them and other things – for example, I am in front of my computer – and not solely by virtue of their intrinsic properties. They can also come to bear properties by virtue of their temporal relations. For example, Lincoln bears the property of being discussed in 2006 by virtue of his relation to certain events that occur long after he is dead. Nagel seems to think that mortal harm, and harm for which posthumous events are responsible, consists in a relation between a living subject and events that occur after that subject is gone, but that harm's temporal location "cannot be so easily located."

Nagel's position is criticized by Lamont (1998) and Feit (2002) on the grounds that it has absurd consequences. Allegedly, it implies that some events take place but at no time, and there are ways of being harmed such that the harm is incurred but at no time whatever. Their view is that any event that transpires does so at some time. But William Grey (1999) defends Nagel, arguing that if we understand Nagel's view properly we will see that it does not have odd consequences. Nagel's (and Grey's) indefinitist position holds that mortal harm is incurred during a stretch of time that has blurry boundaries. The time we are harmed by death is analogous to the time someone goes bald: it cannot be located precisely.

So understood, indefinitism does not compete with concurrentism, subsequentism, and priorism. Grey's brand of indefinitism is correct only if subsequentism, priorism, or possibly concurrentism is true as well (eternalism is an exception since eternity has no boundaries to blur), for even a period of time with blurry edges must occur before, after, or at the same time as a mortem event. Grey himself supplements his (blurry boundary) indefinitism with a version of subsequentism: he says we accrue death's harm during a period of time that occurs posthumously and that has blurry boundaries.

Grey's is not the only sort of indefinitism. Another type says that, while we do incur mortal harm, there is no clear answer to the question "When?" We might call this *no-answer* indefinitism. Nagel himself may have had it in mind when he proposed that mortal harm "cannot be so easily located." This sort of indefinitism is best understood as being equivalent to the position that death may timelessly harm us; its harming us is not an event occurring at some time, but a fact that may be made true by death's occurrence.

However, no-answer indefinitism is not a solution to the timing puzzle, although it is consistent with there *being* a solution (this corrects an oversimplification in Luper 2005).

Reconsiderations

The eternalist view is inspired by the promising idea that death harms us by robbing us of a life that would have been better had we not died. However, it is extremely implausible to say that we incur mortal harm at all times. Far more plausible is the subsequentist idea that we incur mortal harm during such times as we would have been enjoying a good life had we not died. But it is difficult to accept subsequentism since it is hard to make sense of the idea of incurring harm posthumously, given that we are not responsive while dead. The indefinitist view is also disappointing. The blurry boundary version tells us that the boundaries of the time when we incur mortal harm are fuzzy, but it does not tell us when this time is. And the no-answer version gives us no answer to the question before us.

We are left with concurrentism and priorism, or some combination of the two. It does seem reasonable to say that death may harm us while it occurs. It is far less plausible to say that posthumous events may harm us while *they* occur, since we are not responsive then. It is also plausible to say that both death and posthumous events may harm us while we are alive, for living people may have interests that depend on what happens in the future. Events that will not occur until much later make various facts true of us, and some of these facts may be against our present interests. In particular, the fact that we will lack various goods tomorrow (such as a good reputation) is against our present interest in having those goods tomorrow.

Fortunately, the point made at the outset still holds: proponents of the harm theses do not need a solution to the timing puzzle, for something can harm us timelessly; it can be against our interests even if there is *no* time T at which, because of it, we are worse off at T than we would have been otherwise. As comparativism says, anything that makes our lives worse than they otherwise would have been is against our interests. This death usually does. But at no time *after* death are we worse off than we would have been had we not died, for the simple reason that we do not exist. Death might make us worse off while it occurs; however, it, and a posthumous event, might also make us worse off *before* it occurs, since it may be against the interests we once had.

SUMMARY

For the proponent of the harm thesis, there is no need to provide the time T at which, because of death, we are worse off at T than we would have been had we not died. Given comparativism, death can be bad for us even if there is no such time. It is timelessly bad for us – bad for us precisely in the sense that, because of death, our lives are worse than they would have been had we not died.

Nevertheless, there is a plausible solution to the timing puzzle. Unlike eternalism, which says that we incur mortal harm eternally, or subsequentism, which says that we incur it after we are dead and gone, or blurry boundary indefinitism, which says that the time when we incur mortal harm cannot be sharply located, priorism says that we incur mortal harm while we have the interests which dying is against, and that is while we are still alive. The same goes for those posthumous events that harm us. One other possibility, concurrentism, says that we incur mortal harm while we die, which is also a reasonable position, although it cannot be the right story concerning when we incur posthumous harm.

PART 2

Killing

CHAPTER 7

Killing

When is killing morally objectionable? The answer is especially controversial in certain special cases. For example, it is not clear that abortion, which involves killing a human being during early development, is objectionable, or, if it is objectionable, *how* wrong it is. In some cases, killing ourselves, or helping others to kill themselves, may also be unobjectionable, or at least far less objectionable than killing people who want to live. In later chapters in this part of the book I will examine these special cases: suicide and euthanasia in chapter 8, and abortion in chapter 9.

Despite controversies arising in special cases, it is clear that, ordinarily, it is terribly wrong to kill people, and it is likely that killing other sorts of creatures will be objectionable, to some degree, for related reasons. In this chapter I will put aside the special cases and ask why killing is ordinarily wrong.

To make the inquiry manageable, I will need to refine the question a bit. Whether an action is wrong is a complicated matter. The presence of some features can strongly suggest that the action is wrong. But other features can strongly suggest that the action is not wrong. Whether the action is wrong all things considered depends on all such features. In other words, an action can have a wrong-making feature even though, all things considered, it is not wrong. When it has a wrong-making feature, it is *prima facie* wrong. Instead of asking why killing is wrong, I will ask what features make killing *prima facie* wrong.

Let me refine the question even more. Presumably killing is *prima facie* wrong because of the way it affects the one who dies, even if it is also *prima facie* wrong for other reasons. Killing you would greatly upset your family, and this side effect is one reason not to kill you. But obviously killing you would be *prima facie* wrong even if they considered themselves well rid of you. To signify that a killing is *prima facie* wrong because of the way it affects the one who dies, I will say that it is *prima facie directly* wrong. In this chapter I mean to ask what makes killing *prima facie* directly wrong. Unfortunately, "*prima facie* directly wrong" is cumbersome. So henceforth I will abbreviate it to "directly wrong."

There is another complication to consider: usually people distinguish between killing a creature, which is an act, and letting that creature die, which is an omission. The distinction is important, since it can be permissible to let a creature die even if it is not permissible to kill it (even though it is surely wrong to kill a being when it is wrong to let it die). It is controversial how many starving people I must assist and not allow to die, but quite clear that I may not kill any of them. In this chapter we will assume that the distinction between acts and omissions is clear enough, and proceed directly to the question of when killings, as opposed to lettings-die, are directly wrong.

There are several accounts of the direct wrongness of killing. The Harm Account explains the wrongness of killing in terms of harm to the individual who dies. The Consent Account explains it in terms of the individual's failure to consent. Finally, the Subject Value Account explains the wrongness of killing in terms of the intrinsic value of the subject who is destroyed. Each view has virtues. However, I will suggest that the best analysis is a combination of the Harm and Consent Accounts.

THE HARM ACCOUNT

Some theorists (Rachels 1986, Marquis 1989) claim that ordinarily killing is directly wrong because it harms the victim. Their view is implied by (but does not imply) the following analysis of the wrongfulness of killing, which I will call the Harm Account:

> *Harm Account*: Killing subject S is directly wrong just in case (and to the extent that) it harms S. How wrong it is to kill S depends on how harmful it is: the more harmful it is to S, the more objectionable it is.

How strong the Harm Account is will depend on the view of harm we take. Combined with comparativism (defended in chapter 5), however, the Harm Account has considerable plausibility. Of course, comparativism is compatible with various accounts of welfare (as discussed in chapter 5). In what follows I will leave open the issue of which view of welfare is correct. Nevertheless, it is instructive to glance at the implications of the Harm Account when combined with hedonism. Doing so, it seems, gives us further grounds to reject hedonism (although the determined hedonist might be more inclined to reject the Harm Account instead). Let us consider some of these implications next.

Hedonistic versions

Recall that Epicurus' own view of prudential interests was probably negative hedonism, the view that we are harmed only by what increases our suffering and benefited only by what reduces our suffering. Stated in terms of negative hedonism, the Harm Account would give us the following position:

> *Negative Hedonist Harm Account*: Killing S is directly wrong just in case (and to the extent that) it harms S, and it harms S when and only when it causes S to suffer more than S would have had S not been killed.

How plausible is this position?

We can start with the obvious: given negative hedonism, the best thing we can do for people is to take their lives as quickly as possible, assuming that we can do so in a way that is relatively painless. This is a simple consequence of the negative hedonist's claim that we can benefit only from pain reduction, together with the fact that any life will involve a significant amount of suffering. No matter what continued life would be like, it cannot be imprudent for Epicureans to opt out by killing themselves. Nor can they object, on prudential grounds, to being killed painlessly by others. Being killed is invariably beneficial for them.

Quite clearly, then, the Negative Hedonist Harm Account does not explain the direct wrongness of killing. On the contrary: it implies that killing is directly permissible.

Things get worse if we assume that people have a duty of beneficence: the duty to benefit others. On this assumption, it appears that we ought to go on a killing spree. We cannot wrong Epicureans by killing them painlessly, since this either benefits them by reducing their suffering or has no effect on their welfare at all. Perhaps we could wrong them by failing to provide them positive 'goods,' such as pleasure, or by depriving them of such 'goods,' if they are among those Epicureans who suffer from the lack of such 'goods.' But we cannot wrong them in this way if we painlessly kill them, since then they could not suffer from the lack of 'goods.' Therefore, killing Epicureans could only wrong *other* Epicureans; it could wrong only the survivors of the dead, who are left to suffer.

Would it wrong them? One answer is that since we have a duty to benefit the survivors, and they are benefited by our refraining from killing people they care about, then we have a duty not to kill. But this answer ignores the fact that the survivors have their own responsibility to provide a painless death to those about whom they care. Nor should we assist only fellow humanity; all sentient beings can suffer, so we ought to kill them too. (Don't people have the right not to be killed without permission? Granted. However, since dying painlessly is in their best interests, in an Epicurean world there would be a standing presumption of consent to being killed painlessly. Only irrational Epicureans would refuse. And those who kill might justify their actions on the parentalist [paternalist] grounds that they are only acting in the best interests of those they kill!)

What if we give up on negative hedonism, and combine the Harm Account with positive hedonism? Thus:

> *Positive Hedonist Harm Account*: Killing S is directly wrong just in case (and to the extent that) it harms S. Harm is assessed comparatively; pleasure is the only intrinsic good for S while pain is the only intrinsic evil for S.

Certainly this view is far more reasonable than its predecessor. This is no surprise; it relies on the positive hedonist account of welfare, which is far more plausible than negative hedonism. However, there are at least two reasons to reject it. First, it does rely on positive hedonism, which is far less plausible than other views of welfare (chapter 5). Second, the Positive Hedonist Harm Account does not explain why it is worse to kill people than it is to kill other sorts of creatures. It is not clear that people are likely to gain significantly more pleasure during their lives than comparably long-lived animals, so, measured in terms of precluded pleasure, killing the one seems as worrisome as killing the other.

The Harm Account

Next we can discuss the Harm Account without adopting any particular view of welfare. So understood, it is a relatively clear view, and it explains the wrongness of killing in relatively concrete terms.

The Harm Account has another substantial virtue. Suppose that different sorts of creatures normally benefit significantly more from their lives than other sorts benefit from theirs, and that some do not benefit from their lives at all. Then killing some sorts of living things is normally far less objectionable than killing others, and killing some is not objectionable at all. (The qualification introduced by the term 'normally' is necessary in view of the possibility that killing individual creatures might be in their interests.) Suppose, for example, that self-determining (or at least self-aware) beings typically derive a great deal from their lives, far more than merely sentient beings (which lack self-awareness) derive from theirs, and that living things that are not even sentient derive nothing from their lives. This assumption is attractive since the interests of self-determining beings are much more far-ranging and sophisticated than those of merely sentient beings, and insentient life forms such as plants do not have a standpoint from which what happens to them can matter to them. On these assumptions, the Harm Account implies that killing some sorts of creatures is normally worse than killing others even though the latter is normally directly wrong as well. Let us call this implied claim the *hierarchy thesis*. The Harm Account suggests that killing self-determining beings such as people is normally far worse than killing merely sentient beings such as dogs or cats, that killing merely sentient beings is normally worse than killing plants or other things that are not even sentient, and that killing insentient life forms is not wrong at all.

Although not without virtues, the Harm Account of killing has flaws as well. In any of its forms (even the time-relative version to be discussed later), it is open to two objections. First, the Harm Account implies that the wrongness of murder will vary with the harm done to its victims. Offhand, this seems counterintuitive: murdering an older person, who has little life to lose, seems as objectionable as murdering a younger person, with more to lose. Second, harm is neither necessary nor sufficient for the direct wrongness of killing. Let us consider each of these criticisms in turn.

The equality objection

Most of us accept some version of the *equality thesis*, which says, of creatures of some sort, such as human beings or some large subgroup of human beings, that killing one is as directly wrong as killing another (McMahan 1995, 2002). But which human beings are equal in this way? Different answers yield different versions of the equality thesis:

Extreme anthropocentric equality thesis: Killing *any* human being is as seriously wrong as killing another.

Moderate anthropocentric equality thesis: Killing any *self-determining* (or at least self-aware) human being is as seriously wrong as killing another.

Each of the above is concerned with human beings alone, but we can formulate versions of the equality thesis that are not restricted in this way; for example:

> *Extreme equality thesis*: Killing any *sentient being* is as seriously wrong as killing another. (Maximally extreme: killing *anything* is as wrong as killing anything else.)

> *Moderate equality thesis*: Killing any *self-determining* (or self-aware) being is as seriously wrong as killing another.

If any of these four versions of the equality thesis is correct, the Harm Account must be mistaken, since it implies that the wrongness of killing varies with the harm caused its victims, and that harmless killing is wholly unobjectionable.

Some version of the equality thesis might be treated as an indefensible axiom of moral theory. However, it is not self-evident which of its various forms is correct. This uncertainty need not force us to abandon the equality thesis altogether, of course, but we do seem forced into wariness about it. We will need to consider the sources of its appeal, and adjust our egalitarian intuitions accordingly.

Consider the moderate equality thesis. Even if it is correct, there is quite a bit of room in which the Harm Account can operate. Certainly the moderate equality thesis is consistent with applying the Harm Account to nonhuman animals, which, as we said before, enables us to explain the hierarchy thesis. Moreover, it is consistent with extending the Harm Account to human beings who are not self-determining. Furthermore, we can, and should, acknowledge that harm plays a role in the wrongness of killing self-determining beings even if we also condemn killing on the grounds that it violates their autonomy. Even if killing someone is a highly objectionable violation of their autonomy, killing her may be worse than killing someone else because it is more harmful. If, in killing you, I deprive you of a day or week which you wanted, I have seriously wronged you, both because I failed to respect your will, *and* because I harmed you. But the wrong would be worse if, against your will, I deprive you of many years of life. Harm is not the sole factor in the wrongness of killing self-determining beings, but it is one factor.

Permissible harms and harmless wrongs

The Harm Account can be criticized on other grounds. Harming others, it seems, may be morally permissible. This is suggested by the fact that people are not always wronged when they are harmed by consent. For example, experimental subjects might well be gravely harmed, but they may also take on the risk after proper consent. Perhaps people who are harmed when killed are nevertheless not wronged if killed by consent.

Harm may also be unnecessary for the wrongness of killing. In at least some cases, people are wronged without being harmed when they are treated in ways that benefit them against their will. For example, normally physicians may not treat people against their will even if doing so would be beneficial. Perhaps, then, people are wronged when killed against their will even if being killed does not harm them.

Apparently, then, the Harm Account faces significant difficulties. Let us see if we can supply a better analysis if we emphasize that killing destroys valuable subjects rather than that killing is harmful to them.

THE SUBJECT VALUE ACCOUNT

Some say that certain individuals have intrinsic value. According to many, the intrinsic value of human beings is especially great; in fact, it is absolute, in the sense that it cannot be outweighed by any other sort of value. Those who claim that human life is sacred seem to attribute this sort of value to human beings. It is possible that different sorts of creatures have different amounts of intrinsic value, and that their value determines how wrong it is to kill them. I will explore this idea in this section. (For discussion of the idea of sanctity, see Rachels 1983, Kuhse 1987, Singer 1994, Keown 2002, and Young 2007. According to Ronald Dworkin, the view that human beings have intrinsic value is an "essentially religious" belief [1993, 155] which "we almost all share in some form" [1993, 13] yet interpret differently; however, I will treat it as a philosophical position.)

Subject value and welfare

We might call the sort of value subjects themselves have *subject value*. It is value they have by virtue of their nature. It should be contrasted with their levels of well-being, or the values of their lives measured in terms of their well-being. How well off we are varies over time, while our value as subjects is thought to remain constant over our existence. Another difference is that subject value is agent-neutral and impersonal, whereas welfare is agent-relative and personal. If something's value is agent-relative, then it may have its value for one agent without having it for

value, and were once early fetuses, our subject value does not derive from our essential attributes.

We can accept the Subject Value Account despite transience. We might say that it is objectionable to kill subjects *while*, but only while, they are intrinsically valuable. On this approach, killing subjects later in their lives is typically worse than killing them earlier in life, and it would be a mistake to object to killing fetuses and infants on the grounds that human beings have intrinsic value. To condemn abortion, we would need to demonstrate that human beings are intrinsically valuable *while* they are fetuses or infants.

There is another response to transience. We could say that it is objectionable to kill subjects who would have been intrinsically valuable had they not been killed. The following analysis captures this idea:

> *Highest Subject Value Account*: Killing subject S is directly wrong just in case S *would have become* or continued to be an intrinsically valuable subject if not killed; how wrong it is to kill S depends on how great S's intrinsic value would have been or continued to be: the greater that value, the more objectionable it is to kill S.

Suppose that we do not attain intrinsic value until we are self-aware, or until we are self-determining. According to the Highest Subject Value Account, it is wrong to kill us even before we attain our subject value. Now suppose that we have intrinsic value as soon as we are sentient, but that our value is much less than it will be when we are self-aware. Then killing us while we are sentient but not self-aware is just as wrong as killing us after we are self-aware. The wrongness of killing does not hinge on the value of the subject when killed, but rather on the value the subject would have attained if not killed. Killing individuals is wrong because it *deprives them of subject value.*

The Highest Subject Value Account can be defended on the grounds that it is supported by a plausible general principle concerning when it is wrong to treat a subject a certain way, namely, the following:

> *Subject Value Principle*: Doing A to subject S is directly wrong if, because of A, the intrinsic subject value S will attain or retain is less than it would have been had A not been done; how objectionable it is to do A to S depends on how much subject value A deprives S of: the more the subject value S would have attained or retained (had A not been done) exceeds the subject value S will actually attain, the more objectionable it is to do A to S.

By way of illustration, suppose I destroy an infant's capacity to become self-aware, as in the following example:

> *Heedless*: I give an infant, Fred, a poison called Heedless that prevents his ever becoming self-aware, but he will have a pleasant life of normal duration.

Is what I have done permissible? Not according to the Subject Value Principle. Would it be permissible to give Heedless to Fred, thus rendering him incapable of self-awareness, and *then* kill him? No. It is true that killing a Heedless infant is not as wrong as killing a normal infant, but making a normal baby Heedless is as wrong as killing a normal infant outright (or very nearly so).

In its defense, we might cite the fact that the Highest Subject Value Account is in accord with ordinary intuitions about equality in some ways: it suggests that killing a normal human being during her early infancy is as wrong as killing her just after she gains self-awareness, and both are as wrong as killing her after she becomes self-determining. In all of these cases the killing is wrong to a degree that equals the highest subject value the victim would have attained if not killed.

It is not entirely clear what should count as ordinary intuitions about equality, but let us assume for the moment that one such intuition says that killing one human being is as directly wrong as killing any other (earlier this view was labeled the extreme anthropocentric equality thesis). Then the Highest Subject Value Account may not accord entirely with some of the intuitions some people have. For example, the account raises no objection to the killing of those in persistent vegetation, as they lack higher subject value entirely; or if they have any subject value at all, it is the value they have by virtue of being alive, which puts them at the level of plants. The account is out of line with ordinary intuitions in another way: assuming that merely sentient beings have less subject value than those who are capable of self-awareness, then killing human beings with defects that preclude their gaining the capacity for self-awareness is not as objectionable as killing normal human beings. If severe mental impairment permits an infant to be sentient, but guarantees that it will not gain the capacity for self-awareness, its way to higher subject value is blocked. Much the same can be said for killing an adult whose dementia has destroyed his capacity for self-awareness but left him sentient, or able to feel pleasure and pain: such a killing is not as wrong as killing a normal human being.

Of course, some of these concerns can be rendered moot by denying that the individuals involved really are alive, or by saying that, although alive, they are no longer human beings. If they are dead, a concern about killing them cannot arise; if they are not human beings, they are irrelevant to the point at hand. But the following claims seem overwhelmingly plausible (a) if there are living human beings whose extreme dementia has left them sentient yet irreversibly un-self-conscious, killing them is not as directly wrong as killing normal human beings, and (b) if there are human beings whose insentience and un-self-consciousness are both irreversible, killing them is not directly wrong at all. Let us dub these two claims the *inequality of the oblivious*. These implications of the Highest Subject Value Account will trouble some people, but they should probably be accepted anyway, since any basis for rejecting them is going to be *ad hoc*. Here is one place, at least, where ordinary intuitions need revision.

Now suppose that among the ordinary intuitions about equality (or perhaps inequality) is the claim that killing any human being is more objectionable than killing any nonhuman animal. Anyone who shares this intuition will consider the Highest Subject Value Account counterintuitive. It is implausible to suppose that all human beings can be expected to gain more subject value than all animals, so killing human beings will not always be more objectionable than killing nonhuman animals. Suppose that the highest subject value is attained by self-determining beings, that beings capable of self-awareness enjoy the second highest subject value, and below them are sentient beings. Then killing any creature, regardless of species, that would have become or continued to be capable of self-determination if not killed, is as wrong as killing another, and more objectionable than killing any creature that would not have developed the capacity for self-determination. Similarly, killing one creature whose potential is limited to self-awareness is as wrong as killing any other, and worse than killing a merely sentient being, and killing any merely sentient being is on a par with killing another. Thus, for example, if dolphins, or the nonhuman creatures from the planet Crouton, normally become self-determining at adulthood, then killing normal dolphins or Croutonians, whether in their infancy or adulthood, is as wrong as killing normal human beings, whether in their infancy or adulthood, and worse than killing oblivious human beings. Also, killing merely sentient animals is on a par with killing sentient human beings who are un-self-conscious due to extreme dementia.

No doubt these claims concerning the seriousness of killing different sorts of creatures could use refinement. However, I suggest we accept at least two of the things the claims imply: if there are human beings who are un-self-conscious but perhaps still sentient, then, first, killing some human beings might not be more directly objectionable than killing some merely sentient animals, and second, killing self-aware animals might be more objectionable than killing some human beings. Call these *the cross-species claims*. Rejecting these claims surely forces us into some form of chauvinism. Hence we should count it as a strength of the Highest Subject Value Account that it endorses the cross-species claims. Here too, then, ordinary intuitions should be revised.

The Subject Value Account is open to another sort of criticism (McMahan 2002, 245). Consider *merely* sentient beings, that is, sentient beings, such as dogs and cats, that are not self-determining. Suppose that these creatures are intrinsically valuable subjects. Is it *ever* reasonable to painlessly kill them for their own sakes? If not, no matter how beneficial it would be for them, let us say that their intrinsic value as subjects *trumps* their welfare. As we have stated it, the Subject Value Account entails that the wrongness of killing a creature depends entirely on the creature's subject value, and in no way on whether killing it is against its interests. Hence the Subject Value Account is correct only if subject value always trumps welfare. Yet it is clear that subject value does *not* always trump welfare. As nearly everyone will grant, it is entirely reasonable to painlessly kill our pets when it benefits them.

If the wrongness of killing merely sentient beings depends not just on their subject value but also on how it affects their welfare, the Highest Subject Value Account cannot be correct. At best, some sort of hybrid view is correct. On the hybrid view, killings can be beneficial enough to warrant sacrificing subject value. The account might be formulated in various ways, but the following seems to capture the idea well enough:

> *Hybrid Account*: Killing subject S at time T is directly wrong just in case there is a period of time beginning at or after T during which, if not killed at T, S would have been an intrinsically valuable subject and S's welfare together with S's subject value would sum to a number greater than zero; the higher the sum, the more objectionable it is to kill S.

On the hybrid view, subject value theorists will be committed to the position that subject value is commensurate with welfare, so they owe us an account of how subject value is measured, and how it is weighed against welfare.

The criticism we have been discussing goes away if merely sentient beings do not have subject value. Maybe it is not obvious that they do.

But if they do not, then the Highest Subject Value Account entails that killing them is not directly wrong. That is quite implausible. Let us add that one well-known argument for the view that you and I have value as subjects applies to animals as well. According to Velleman (1999, 611), a person's good matters only if that person herself has value. If this is true, it seems equally reasonable to say that an animal's good matters only if that animal itself has value, as Velleman admits (1999, 627). He may also think that their subject value trumps their interests, but it is difficult to tell.

Maybe I have mischaracterized what is going on when we properly euthanize a sentient being, such as a cat. Perhaps euthanizing it is acceptable because its suffering drives its subject value to zero or maybe even lower than zero. So once again subject value is the only consideration bearing on the wrongness of killing. But there are real problems with this story. First, it is pretty obviously permissible to euthanize a cat specifically in order to benefit the cat. Second, on Velleman's view, if a cat's subject value is zero, we should be indifferent about its welfare. In that case we don't have any reason to euthanize it, no matter how much it is suffering. And the related value judgment is horrendous: can it really be true that we should be indifferent about a cat whose suffering has reached the point of obliterating its value as an individual? Nor is there much to be said in favor of the baffling view that a cat might have a negative subject value. Should we be indifferent about the interests of negative-value cats, as with zero-value cats? Do negative-value cats somehow deserve to be destroyed? None of this can be right. By contrast, we can say, of any negative-value cats there might be, that they do not deserve to suffer. But that would be true of any cat.

The Hybrid Account faces further difficulties. The main problems are that it presupposes that subject value is quantifiable and commensurate with welfare. Unfortunately, however, it is difficult to see how the one is to be weighed against the other. (Let the subject value of individual S be SV(S). There are many ways to define SV(S) so that it will be commensurate with S's welfare. For example, we could say that SV(S) equals the lifetime welfare S will achieve. But that is no good; it implies that we can lower S's subject value just by killing S. Also, one sheep will have a different subject value than another. [Aren't all sheep equal?] All right, let SV(S) equal the highest lifetime welfare achievable by creatures of S's type T. [But how shall we type creatures? By species? By capacities?] On this approach it is much too difficult to justify euthanizing an animal. Euthanizing a sheep would be proper only if the intrinsic value of its remaining life is such a large negative quantity that, added to its subject value, which equals the highest welfare achievable by sheep-type creatures, the result is less than zero. It is virtually impossible for that to happen. This approach also has silly implications for the relative values of creatures of various types; for example, it will imply that one human being is equivalent to N sheep, for some value of N.) In fact, even if we do not worry about the problem of commensurability, the view that subject value is quantifiable seems to have absurd consequences. It is false (is it not?) that, from the standpoint of impersonal moral value, it is better that there should be 20 sheep rather than 10, or that more sheep are better than fewer. Morally, it is not best that we boost the sheep population as much as we can. All this goes for people and other sorts of individuals, too: it is false that, in the abstract, 20 people are better than 10, or more are better than fewer. This is quite different from saying it is worse to kill 20 sheep rather than 10 (or 20 people rather than 10), or better to save 20 rather than 10 – *that* is not absurd. If an act, like killing someone, is wrong, doing it again and again is worse and worse, and if it is morally good, repeating it is better and better. (If there is an ideal number of people, it will be determined by considerations such as the carrying capacity of Earth or the requirements of a stable, self-sufficient society, and not by their subject value. Having settled on the ideal number, it is an open question whether that number could be reached through morally permissible steps.) But how can we avoid saying things like this if we accept the position that individuals have some quantifiable subject value?

Kantianism

Many commentators think that Kant defended the absolutist version of the Subject Value Account. There may be some truth to this.

Kant's ethics focuses on moral agency, thought of as the capacity to recognize, and the inclination to acknowledge, the principles of morality (Hill 1980). Presumably, too, moral agency includes the capacity for self-determination, so that moral agents are able to act in accordance with principles which, they see, are rationally binding. However, on Kant's view moral agents do not necessarily act in accordance with moral principles; even immoral people will be moral agents.

To respect moral agency is to recognize its worth, which he called "dignity," and to respond to it appropriately. Kant seemed to think that his claims about the value of moral agency can be restated as claims about moral agents: all moral agents have dignity as subjects; they have a special worth, as subjects, which derives from their capacity to exercise moral agency. This is true even of the worst criminals. Kant also appeared to think that every human being has dignity, and he often attributed it to humanity itself. As we have seen, the view that we have subject value (dignity) because of our capacity for moral agency is problematic, since we live a good while before we become moral agents. Kant shielded himself from this difficulty by assuming that human beings are moral agents as noumenal beings. Notoriously, Kant claimed that moral agents enjoy a kind of autonomy that derives from a commitment to moral principles that is wholly uncaused and that takes place outside of space and time (Hill 1991).

Kant plainly thought that respect for the dignity of human beings sharply restricts what we may do to them, and what they may do to themselves. For example, we may not take drugs that could erode our moral capacities and thus disrupt our efforts to live morally, no matter how enjoyable the drugs would be, and no matter how great the pain they would relieve. Anything that undermines the exercise of our moral agency violates us. Slavery, too, violates people, and Kant thought we must resist it even if it means that we will be killed. Killing human beings is also directly wrong. Indeed, ordinarily harming us in any way is inconsistent with the respect we are due (Lippert-Rasmussen 2007). But Kant also thought that killing us cannot be justified even on the grounds that we will be benefited by death, and he condemned suicide, no matter how beneficial it would be for those who wish to die.

All of this suggests that Kant accepted the absolutist version of the subject value account: moral agents have a value that is absolute in the sense that it outweighs all other sorts of value.

THE CONSENT ACCOUNT

If the wrongness of killing people is not explained by the way it affects their interests or by the way it affects their subject value, how might it be explained? Perhaps the wrongness of killing people turns on whether they *choose* to be killed. We might say that people have the moral authority to kill themselves, or to have themselves killed, in at least some cases in which it would harm them, and that killing them against their wills is always directly wrong, since it does not respect their autonomy. This view favors the following analysis:

> *Simple Consent Account*: Killing subject S is directly wrong just in case it is not by her consent.

On this analysis, there is no allowance for degree of the wrongness of killing: killing subjects either is or is not objectionable, since subjects either have or have not consented. This invariance might seem problematic. However, we might also view it as a virtue, since it gives the Simple Consent Account the resources it needs to meet the equality objection. Killing one person against her will is as objectionable as killing any other.

The competent

The Consent Account is not acceptable without further refinement. We cannot escape the charge of wrongdoing if we wheedle consent from the children we kill, or if, while unable to think clearly, or on impulse, people consent to our killing them. What is decisive is consent that is *competent*, or given by someone who can grasp and rationally assess the matter at hand, and *informed*, or based on adequate information (for clarification of the notion of competence, see Faden and Childress 1986, G. Dworkin 1988). The notion of competent consent is meant to be flexible enough to allow for the possibility of competently consenting to certain things that we know are against our interests. For example, typically it is assumed that people can competently choose to smoke cigarettes, and pugilists can competently choose to box, if they know the risks. Nevertheless, it is not possible to competently consent to certain things that are egregiously irrational. These may include enslaving ourselves, or taking drugs that quickly undermine our ability to exercise self-determination.

These refinements suggest the following view:

> *Consent Account*: Killing competent subjects is directly wrong just in case they have not made an informed choice to be killed.

The Consent Account is defended by many theorists (e.g., Brock 1992, Buchanan 1989) who emphasize the importance of respecting people's self-determination. If we should respect a person's decisions about the management of her own life, we should also honor her decision about whether or not to end her life.

To be self-determining, I must possess certain capacities. Chief among these is the capacity to *will*. To will that such and such occur is not just to desire that it occur, but also to identify with that desire – to see that desire as expressing my identity (see Frankfurt 1971, G. Dworkin 1981). I exercise my will when I adopt fundamental values, goals, or commitments by which I shape my life. Another capacity I must have if I am to be self-determining is the ability to work out reasonable ways to act according to my will, and, at least to some degree, to critically revise my will and desires in ways that are rational given my circumstances and my fundamental values and commitments. I fail to be self-determining when I fail to have a will concerning my life or fail to implement that will, at least in ways my natural circumstances permit. Being self-determining also requires that I lack certain obstacles. I fail to be self-determining when others prevent me from shaping my life as I wish, or when others shape my life against my will. This is not to say that my will and the wills of others concerning my life must be at odds; that their wills concerning my life align with my own is consistent with my being self-determining.

It is one thing for others to impose their wills on us, another for them to do so permissibly, and still another for them to do so legally (Feinberg 1986, ch. 18). If a person is actually shaping her life as she wills, let us say that she is *de facto* self-determining; if it is morally wrong for others to interfere with a person's self-determination, let us say that she is *morally* self-determining; and if it is illegal for others to interfere, let us say that she is *de jure* self-determining. When consent theorists urge respect for people's self-determination, they mean to say that people who have the capacities requisite for *de facto* self-determination are morally self-determining, and that such people should also be *de jure* self-determining.

The incompetent

In stating the Consent Account, we have focused on subjects who are competent at the time they are to be killed. Closely related are subjects who make a competent decision concerning whether they should be killed at a later time when they no longer will be competent. It seems reasonable to extend the Consent Account to them. For convenience, I will call all such subjects the *competent*. All others I will call the *incompetent*. These include youngsters who will gain competence if they continue to develop under favorable circumstances, as well as subjects who can never acquire the ability to make competent choices. These would include severely impaired human beings, and nearly all nonhuman animals.

We cannot apply the Consent Account to the incompetent. However, we may be able to apply the Harm Account to them, and then we could combine the Consent Account with the Harm Account.

THE COMBINED ACCOUNT

Combining the Consent and Harm Accounts gives us the following analysis:

> *Combined Account*: If S is an incompetent subject, killing S is directly wrong just in case (and to the extent that) it harms S; if S is competent, killing S at time T is directly wrong just in case S has not made an informed choice to be killed at T.

Let us see if this Combined Account is plausible.

The Combined Account can be defended on the basis of the fact that both the interests and the choices of subjects are important from the moral point of view. Let us flesh out this defense a bit.

The fact that competent subjects choose to shape their lives in a certain way is, in itself, of moral importance; other things being equal, their choices should be respected (Quinn 1984, 49).

At the same time, the fact that subjects can be harmed or benefited, whether those subjects are competent or not, is also, in itself, of moral importance. Other things being equal, their interests should be respected.

According to Quinn, these points about what is important from the moral point of view suggest that we apply one set of moral considerations to the competent, and another to the incompetent (compare McMahan [2002, 245–265], who calls Quinn's approach the two-tiered view). That is, the proper treatment of incompetent subjects is wholly a matter of being responsive to their interests, but the proper treatment of the competent is primarily a matter of respecting their exercise of self-determination. Their interests surely are also of moral importance, but we may presume that competent subjects will give careful consideration to their interests in making their choices. Still, the very fact that a choice clearly is extremely detrimental to them may itself be grounds for concluding that it was made in a moment of incompetence; at that point it becomes reasonable to respect the choices they *would* have made had they been competent rather than the choices they actually made.

Let us add that there is an important sense in which respect for a young person's interests and respect for the same person's later exercise of self-determination overlap: if, as argued in chapter 5, exercising self-determination is intrinsically good for people, respect for a child's interests entails fostering the development in that child of the capacity to determine herself, whereupon her choices will carry moral weight, and she will be the moral equal of all other competent autonomous beings.

Consider, now, what Quinn's view suggests about the direct wrongness of killing. If the proper treatment of incompetent subjects is wholly a matter of being responsive to their interests, then it is reasonable to conclude that killing them is directly wrong just in case it is not in their interests. As for competent subjects, the view that seems most sensitive to the importance of their choices about their lives is the position that killing them is wrong just in case it is not with their competent, informed consent.

Equality

The Combined Account is egalitarian in substantial ways. For instance, it suggests that all competent subjects are on an equal footing in that their wills should be respected, and that all subjects who can be harmed or benefited, which is presumably all sentient beings, are on an equal footing in that their interests should be respected. However, if we accept the Combined Account, we will have to refine, if not revise, some of our moral intuitions about equality.

For example, it will not be true that killing any person is as seriously wrong as killing another, for some persons are not competent; how objectionable it is to kill them depends on how harmful killing them is, and killing some of them will not be directly wrong at all. Like the Highest Subject Value Account, the Combined Account commits us to the inequality of the oblivious. Accepting the Combined Account also precludes our saying that killing one competent person is as wrong as killing another, for some will consent, while others will not. What we can say is that all nonconsensual killings of competent people are alike in being extraordinarily wrong (but I presume we would allow that the wrongness of a killing is increased by its harmfulness). On certain plausible views of morality, we could add that, all things being equal, such killings violate the rights of their victims.

I would speculate that, upon reflection, most of us will accept these implications concerning people, since the differences in the wrongness of killing various people seem to rest on genuinely significant differences in the people killed. Consider, too, that in treating incompetent people differently than competent people, the Combined Account does not discount the interests of incompetent people. If a person irreversibly ceases to be competent, say because of dementia, her interests matter just as before, although they will have changed, and others must look out for them.

Should we worry about the implications which the Combined Account has concerning the importance of animals relative to human beings? Like the Highest Subject Value Account, the Combined Account implies the cross-species claims. This can be cited as a virtue of both views. However, both accounts might be worrisome for a related reason: most of us think it permissible to kill animals – or at least ones that are incapable of self-awareness – in order to benefit people. Most of us condone the killing of the animals we eat, for example, and many people kill for recreation, although many of the latter also mean to eat their prey. Yet both accounts say that killing animals is directly wrong when it harms them. If it is wrong to harm animals by killing them, isn't it wrong to kill animals for our own benefit? Actually, it is by no means clear that the one claim follows from the other. Let us consider two ways of arguing that it is permissible to kill animals for our benefit even though it is wrong to harm animals by killing them.

The first approach begins with the assumption that virtually no animals are harmed as long as they are killed painlessly. This is because animals do not benefit from longer life; they are unable to recall the good things that happen to them, and hence for animals goods are not cumulative. Hence animals cannot be harmed by being deprived of the goods they might have accrued. Call this view *animal Epicureanism*, since it suggests that the Epicurean rejection of the harm thesis is correct as applied to animals (Velleman 1991). Perhaps there are some exceptions; maybe some animals are actually self-aware, and in other respects much like people, and killing them normally harms them for the same reasons it normally harms people. Then sacrificing the exceptional animals is objectionable, but it remains possible to say that sacrificing nearly any other sort of animal is not. If animal Epicureanism is correct, proponents of the Combined Account need not condemn the killing of animals. It is permissible even if the benefits to people are not substantial.

Notice that this approach, the appeal to animal Epicureanism, is not really consistent with the Highest Subject Value Account, since, on that account, animals have subject value even if they do not benefit from not being killed; killing them is wrong since it destroys that value. In fact, the appeal to animal Epicureanism is not consistent with the Combined Account either, since that account appeals to comparativism. If animal Epicureanism is correct, comparativism will need revision, assuming that the pleasures animals enjoy over many moments may well constitute a great good cumulatively, which killing them would preclude.

However, there is no good reason to accept animal Epicureanism, so the first approach fails. It seems entirely reasonable to say a life that contains years of pleasure which an animal cannot recall is better for that animal than a life that contains only a few minutes of pleasure which the animal can recall, just as your life and mine are better for the pleasures we have forgotten.

On the second approach we admit that animals are normally harmed when killed, but we also say that even in the best of circumstances they will not benefit very much from their lives, so killing them is not a substantial harm. On this, the *diminished harm thesis*, killing typical animals is directly wrong, but it is not an especially serious direct wrong. What we gain from killing them may be important enough to outweigh the direct wrongness of killing them. Of course, this kind of argument will not succeed if our gain is frivolous, but it seems plausible if the gain is substantial – if, for example, the lives of people are saved. Surely animals benefit much less from their lives than people typically benefit from theirs. Hence the direct wrongness of killing them is outweighed by the importance of preserving the lives of people who have the potential to gain a great deal from further life. Or at least killing animals can be so justified, if certain other conditions are met; for example, they must be killed in a relatively painless way, they must be permitted to live in decent conditions, and so forth. Hence, all things considered, it is permissible to sacrifice animals.

Why say that, typically, life benefits animals less than it benefits people? The main reason is that people normally develop the capacity for self-determination, and engaging in self-determination itself is intrinsically good for us. Animals are denied this good. And there are other intrinsic goods that animals cannot have, except perhaps in some extremely quali-fied sense, and that people normally can have, such as loving relationships and wisdom. In many other ways our self-consciousness and intelligence typically make the lives of human beings richer and more rewarding than those of animals. This is true despite the fact that we are capable of receiving greater harm as well.

No doubt this appeal to the diminished harm thesis as an argument for the permissibility of killing animals needs more discussion than is pro-vided here. But let us move on to another concern: if the killing of animals admits of justification, presumably the same must be said of the killing of relevantly similar human beings. Hence either it is a mistake to say that killing animals is acceptable when the harm done is offset by a sufficiently important gain to people, so that killing animals to benefit people is not justifiable, or else we should say the same about relevantly similar human beings, so that killing both is justifiable.

This dilemma can seem much more worrisome than it really is, since it is easy to mistake which human beings are similar to animals in the relevant respects. It might seem, for example, that normal infants are included, but this is not correct. Normal infants would attain the capacity for self-determination if they were to develop further under favorable circumstances, so killing them would gravely harm them. The human beings to which the dilemma applies are actually individuals who are so severely impaired as to be unable, even with further development, to enjoy a life that is substantially better than that of animals. These would be the oblivious human beings of whom we spoke earlier – those who are irreparably incapable of self-awareness, such as anencephalic infants or individuals in a persistent vegetative state, as well as those with dementia so extreme that it destroys the capacity for self-awareness. Is killing animals acceptable for sufficiently great gains to people only if killing irreparably un-self-aware human beings is too? I suggest that an affirmative answer is at least plausible. But I would add this: the fact that either is acceptable in principle does not force us to kill human beings as well as the animals. We can have various reasons not to do things that are permissible, including sentiment and convention.

How does the Combined Account stack up against the other analyses we have considered?

Chief among the virtues of the Harm Account were its relatively clear implications concerning how objectionable particular killings are, and its support for the hierarchy thesis; chief among its vices was its unresponsiveness to the importance of respecting the choices of competent persons, and its failure to uphold common egalitarian intuitions. The Combined Account inherits the virtues of the Harm Account, while correcting some of its defects. It assigns a clear role to choice, and it has plausible egalitarian implications; while it is not entirely in line with common egalitarian intuitions, the reasons it diverges do not appear worrisome for the Combined Account; on the contrary, they seem to support revising some ordinary intuitions.

The Combined Account shares one of the advantages of the Highest Subject Value Account: both support the hierarchy thesis, at least if the diminished harm thesis is correct. As for their degrees of alignment with ordinary intuitions about equality, the two views are extremely close. In particular, both support the cross-species claims. The most substantial divergence is that the Highest Subject Value Account sees no difference whatever in the wrongness of killing normal human beings at any point prior to their loss of the capacity for self-determination, whereas the Combined Account does. Roughly speaking, on the Combined Account, the earlier incompetent subjects are killed the more objectionable it is, as they are deprived of more good. However, it is hard to see this as an advantage for the Highest Subject Value Account, since greater deprivations really do seem more objectionable.

The Combined Account has some clearer advantages over the Highest Subject Value Account. It has sharper implications concerning how wrong particular killings are. As well, advocates of the Highest Subject Value Account need some way to quantify subject value, whereas advocates of the Combined Account do not. Given these advantages, the Combined Account seems superior.

If we accept the Combined Account, we need not deny that sentient beings and competent persons have value as subjects from the moral point of view. What we should say is that they have value as subjects precisely in the sense that they *matter*, in themselves, from the moral point of view. Merely sentient beings matter by virtue of having *interests*. We acknowledge their moral status by being responsive to their interests. Competent persons matter by virtue of having interests and by virtue of being self-determining. We acknowledge their status by being responsive to their interests and by respecting their exercise of self-determination.

The Time-Relative Harm Account

There is one final matter to consider. Recently, Jeff McMahan has criticized accounts of the wrongness of killing that rely on comparativism. We should examine his reservations since, if they are merited, the Combined Account is flawed.

In his own account of the wrongness of killing, McMahan (2002, 245, 339) applies a Kantian requirement of respect to moral agents, "who are above the threshold of respect," and a different analysis to those that are beneath the threshold of respect, such as fetuses, infants, the severely deranged, and most animals. The Combined Account implies that, in the case of those who fall below the respect threshold, the direct wrongness of killing individuals is wholly a matter of how harmful it is to the one killed, and the harmfulness of death is determined by its comparativist value. McMahan disagrees with these implications, since he rejects comparativism.

Earlier, we stated comparativism as follows (compare McMahan 2002, 105):

> *Comparativism*: An event E harms (benefits) S, making S's life worse (better) than it would have been if E did not occur, just when E occurs and E's (prudential) value for S is negative (positive). E's value for S equals S's welfare level in WE, the actual world (in which E occurs), minus S's welfare level in W~E, the closest world in which E fails to occur.

McMahan thinks that this is an oversimplification of the harm death does. First, it is inconsistent with Parfit's view that prudential interests can be *detached* from identity. Parfit defended this view by citing Division. Division shows that it can be rational to view the interests of another as our own, even though that person is not us. Second, comparativism ignores the significance of declining degrees of psychological connectedness. Let us consider each of these reservations.

Comparativism implies the *attachment thesis*: the prudential value of something for me depends wholly on how it affects *my* life, and not on how it affects the lives of other people, except insofar as the latter is bound up with the former (for example, their good fortune might make me happy – or unhappy, if I am prone to *Schadenfreude*). Parfit's *detachment thesis* is the denial of the attachment thesis. Like Parfit, McMahan deploys Division against the attachment thesis. My brain is physically continuous with those of each of the people into which I Divide in the respects that are relevant to consciousness; according to McMahan, this "is both a necessary and a sufficient condition of a minimal degree of rational egoistic concern" (2002, 79). I also share strong psychological ties with each, which is necessary for a maximal degree of rational egoistic concern. Thus, like Parfit, McMahan thinks that you share the interests of the survivors of your Division in precisely the same sense that you, before a haircut, share the interests of the groomed person you will become: what benefits or harms them benefits or harms you.

This criticism of comparativism is not very strong. According to Parfit and McMahan, since, in Division, it is rational to view the interests of another as our own, we should conclude that their interests can *be* ours. As McMahan realizes (2002, 41), we can turn this argument around: a person's interests are mine only if I *am* that person, so if, as Parfit and McMahan assume, I am not the people I Divide into, it is not rational for me to take any attitude about them that is predicated upon the view that their interests are mine.

McMahan's second reservation about comparativism concerns its suggestion that, in assessing the value a period of life has for us, we should consider only the intrinsic value it has for us. McMahan thinks that we must also consider whether our degree of psychological connectedness would have fallen off by the time we live through that period (2002, 80, 105–106, 170). This gives us the time-relative value of that period. Similarly, when assessing an event, we should not only consider its impact on a particular period of our lives; we should also discount for declining connectedness.

To see, with more precision, what McMahan has in mind, it will help if we first reformulate comparativism so that it applies to periods of life. This more complex and cumbersome formulation of comparativism is given in three stages:

Comparativism:

(a) By definition, the intrinsic value for S of S's life in world W *during period P*, IV(S,W,P), equals the intrinsic value for S of S's life in W during P.

(b) The intrinsic value for S of S's life in W, IV(S,W), equals the sum of the intrinsic values for S of S's life in W during each of its periods (assuming that these do not overlap); that is, where S's life in W is exhausted by periods P_1, P_2 ... P_N, then IV(S,W) = IV(S, W,P_1) + IV(S,W,P_2) + ... + IV(S,W,P_N).

(c) E's (time-neutral) value for S, V(S,E), equals the intrinsic value for S of S's life in WE, the actual world (in which E occurs), minus the intrinsic value for S of S's life in W∼E, the closest world in which E does not occur. That is, V(S,E) = IV(S,WE) – IV(S,W∼E).

McMahan does not provide an exact formulation of his analysis. But in nonbranching cases (unlike Division) we can formulate McMahan's account in a way that parallels the cumbersome version of comparativism:

Time-Relative Account of Interests (for short: Interest Relativism):

(a) The intrinsic value for S *relative-to-time-T* of S's life in world W *during period P*, RIV (S,W,T,P), equals the intrinsic value for S of S's life during P *multiplied by a fraction representing how connected S's life at T is to S's life during P.*

(b) The intrinsic value for S *relative-to-time-T* of S's life in world W, RIV(S,W,T), equals the sum of *the intrinsic values for S relative-to-time-T* of S's life in W during each of its periods; that

is, where S's life in W is exhausted by periods P1, P2 ... PN, then
RIV(S,W,T) = RIV(S,W,T,P1) + RIV(S,W,T,P2) + ... + RIV
(S,W,T,PN).

(c) The time-relative value which E occurring at time T has for S, RV
(S,E,T), equals the intrinsic value for S *relative-to-time-T* of S's life
in WE, the actual world (where E occurs), minus the intrinsic value
for S *relative-to-time-T* of S's life in W~E, the closest world in
which E does not occur. That is, RV(S,E,T) = RIV(S,WE,T) −
RIV(S,W~E,T).

On this approach, as the degree of connectedness declines between my life
when ended and my life as it would have been at later times, my level of
welfare at those later times matters less in assessing the harmfulness
(beneficialness) of my death. So, for example, my death does not greatly
harm me if it precludes my (future self from) attaining a good at a time
when my (future self's) life would be wholly unconnected to my life when
I died. If connectedness remains strong over my life, interest relativism
and the comparative criterion coincide (McMahan 2002, 106).

McMahan draws on interest relativism in formulating his analysis of
the wrongness of killing beings who are below the threshold for respect:

> *Time Relative Account of Killing*: Killing individuals below the thresh-
> old for respect is directly wrong just in case (and to the extent that) it
> has a negative time-relative value for the individuals who die.

Thus it is not quite true that, the better an animal's or infant's life would
have been, the more objectionable killing her is; as the degree of connectedness declines between her life when ended and her life as it would have
been at later times, the less her level of welfare at those later times matters
in assessing the wrongness of killing her.

How plausible is this analysis of the wrongness of killing?

One worry concerns the way McMahan defends interest relativism. He
considers his analysis to be superior to comparativism because the latter
has unacceptable implications when applied to various cases. For example,
it suggests that "the killing of a fetus or infant is more seriously wrong
than the killing of an older child or adult, because the death of the fetus or
infant involves a greater harm – that is, the effect of the death on the value
of the life as a whole is worse" (2002, 192). There is a greater harm because
the fetus is deprived of more good life than is an older person. But it is far
from clear that McMahan's analysis is superior to comparativism. We will
consider this matter in chapter 9; there we will see that, supplemented

with assumptions that McMahan himself accepts, comparativism can handle the cases he adduces against it.

SUMMARY

When is killing directly wrong: wrong because of its effects on its victim rather than because of the side effects it does or may have? Four views vie for our allegiance. The Harm Account says that the wrongness of killing is a matter of the harm to the individual who dies; the Consent Account says it is a matter of the individual's failure to consent; and the best version of the Subject Value Account, the Highest Subject Value Account, explains the wrongness of killing in terms of the intrinsic value of the subject who is destroyed. Each of these views has its virtues. Each, in its way, supports the hierarchy thesis, which says that killing some sorts of creatures is worse than killing others even though the latter is directly wrong as well. And each gives us a way to assess how wrong killing a particular individual would be. However, the best analysis is a fourth view: the Combined Harm-Consent Account, according to which killing competent persons is directly wrong just when they have not made an informed choice to be killed, and killing incompetent persons is directly wrong just in case (and to the extent that) it harms them. It more or less matches the Highest Subject Value Account's degree of conformity to common intuitions about equality, and it is substantially clearer. In particular, it bypasses the troublesome notion of quantifiable subject value.

The Combined Account relies on comparativism, which says that the harmfulness of events depends on their value for us. Comparativism is mistaken if McMahan is right to say we should discount that value, depending on our degree of psychological connectedness over time. On his view, in assessing how harmful an event is to me, we should consider its effect on my future welfare, but my level of welfare in the future matters less if the degree of connectedness over periods of my life declines between now and then. Hence, for example, dying now does not greatly harm me insofar as it precludes my attaining a good at a time when my life would be wholly unconnected to my life now. McMahan's account of harm has flaws that will be emphasized in the last chapter.

CHAPTER 8

Suicide and euthanasia

The vast majority of us will end our lives struggling against one disease or other that ultimately kills us. Or at least this is true of people in the United States. Relatively few will be killed in accidents (5 percent) or assaults (0.7 percent). Only about 1.4 percent will take their own lives. (2004 statistics provided by the US Department of Health and Human Services [2007]).

But when, and how, *should* we die? It can be entirely reasonable to fight to the end against diseases or injuries that ultimately prove to be fatal. Since our very lives are at stake, seeking aggressive medical treatment, including drug therapy for the control of pain, is often the best choice. However, it is not always the best choice. For some of us, it will be best to decline treatment, and let ourselves die. For others, a more proactive choice can be best, especially if our well-being has been undermined by a condition that will not kill us, or that will do so very slowly.

When living on is against our interests, it can be reasonable to end our lives, preferably with the help of a medical expert. That assistance might take the form of assisting in our suicides. However, assistance in the form of euthanasia is justifiable as well, especially for people who are too incapacitated to take their own lives. The decision to end our lives, with or without assistance, is one we will want to postpone as long as we can, for when living on can still be good it is a grave misfortune to die. But for some of us that decision is prudent as well as morally permissible.

Or so I believe. However, assisting in suicide is a crime in the UK and in most US states. Active euthanasia is a crime throughout the UK and USA. And a great many people think that these things should remain crimes. Most of these people believe that suicide, assisting in suicide, and euthanasia are, without exceptions, directly wrong. In this chapter I will not directly address whether assisted suicide or euthanasia should be legalized (on that score see Gorsuch 2006 and Young 2007), but I will argue that, except in certain extreme cases, they, and suicide itself, are not directly wrong, and need not be indirectly wrong (wrong all things considered), which bears on the legal issue in a straightforward way: there are no moral obstacles to legalizing certain forms of assisted suicide and euthanasia.

I will get to my argument in the second section of this chapter. First, I will clarify how I will use the terms 'suicide' and 'euthanasia.'

'SUICIDE' AND 'EUTHANASIA'

The task in this chapter is to consider the permissibility of proactive decisions about our own deaths. I will need to distinguish among various such decisions, and will need the terms 'suicide' and 'euthanasia,' since avoiding them would be cumbersome. Unfortunately, theorists sometimes provide tendentious analyses of these terms. This is especially true of 'suicide.' Many analysts think that nothing should be called 'suicide' unless it is wrong, and this shapes the definitions they defend (O'Keeffe 1984 is refreshingly candid about this). For example, they will not count as suicides the deaths of those who sacrifice themselves for others, since such sacrifices are admirable. Some writers even use the term 'suicide' to signify self-murder, or wrongful auto-termination. Even as ordinarily used, the terms 'suicide' and 'euthanasia' tend to carry negative connotations. Hence labeling auto-termination as 'suicide' can make it difficult to answer the question 'Is auto-termination permissible?' fairly and impartially. For that reason, and for perspicacity, I will stipulate uses of the term 'suicide' and 'euthanasia' that are not true to common usage. However, I want to be perfectly clear about how my suggestions depart from ordinary language. Therefore I will clarify the ordinary uses of 'suicide' and 'euthanasia,' coin terminology, and relate the former to the latter.

'Suicide'

Let us start with 'suicide.' How might it be defined if we are to get as close to ordinary usage as possible while still avoiding the immediate implication that suicide is wrong?

A close account of ordinary usage would look like this: A suicide is someone who does something in order to die and succeeds, and who foresees, at least roughly, how her action would bring about her death. A suicide is also this act itself. This is to say that person S's act A is an act of suicide just in case three conditions are met:

(a) A brought about S's death;
(b) in doing A, S foresaw, at least roughly, how A would result in S's death; and
(c) in doing A, S intended to bring about S's death; S did A in order to die.

Some analysts (J. Margolis 1978, O'Keeffe 1984) add a fourth condition, namely:

(d) S did A in order to fulfill a noninstrumental desire for death, where a desire for an item is noninstrumental when that item is sought for its own sake.

However, this fourth condition is not widely accepted, since (as O'Keefe notes) no one has a noninstrumental desire for death. Those who take their lives intentionally do so as the means to something else, such as saving another, or escaping pain. They might want to live, even fervently, but they might also want to live only under certain circumstances. They then will try very hard both to live and to avoid those circumstances they consider unbearable. If they cannot avoid the circumstances any other way, they might do so by taking their lives. Such people never come to desire death noninstrumentally.

Acts with the requisite sort of intent, as required by (c), but not the proper result, as specified by (a), are acts of *attempted* suicide, not suicide proper. Apparently, people sometimes *pretend* to attempt suicide, too; they damage themselves in ways they do not expect to be fatal but that resemble real attempts at suicide, in order to draw attention to themselves. In practice, such *feigned* attempts might be difficult to distinguish from real attempts, especially if things do not go as expected, and damage intended as a pretense proves to be fatal, as was perhaps true of Sylvia Plath (Alvarez 1971).

Fatal acts involving the requisite intent, as (c) requires, but not the requisite foresight, as (b) demands, are not cases of suicide. Such cases are possible since our acts can bring about our deaths via wholly unexpected (deviant) causal chains (see, e.g., Goldman 1970, Bishop 1989, Mele 1997). Here is an example:

Death by Deviant Causation: A woman mixes arsenic with prune juice and drinks it in order to die. She believes she has chosen a fatal dose of poison, but it is only enough to make her slightly ill, not enough to kill her. However, earlier she took a new heart medication that was poorly tested before being released for use; as it turns out, the drug is deadly when taken with prune juice.

So, in drinking the juice, she did act in a way that caused her death, as she expected, but drinking the juice did not kill her in the manner she expected. She attempted suicide, but failed, even though she ended up dead as she intended, because she had no idea why her action would be fatal. She no more killed herself than did any of the other people on the same medication who happened to drink prune juice and died. Still, it would be a mistake to overstate the foresight requirement. Suicides do not need to know precisely how their actions will result in their death. If I shoot my gun, meaning to kill myself, and my bullet fatally wounds me in the chest, rather than in the head as I had intended, or even ricochets from the wall behind me before killing me, what I have done is suicide.

What about fatal acts involving the requisite foresight but not the requisite intent: are these cases of suicide? Some theorists leave out the intent component of the definition, and say that (a) and (b) are necessary and sufficient for an act to be an act of suicide. Durkheim is a famous example; according to him, "the term suicide is applied to all cases of death resulting directly or indirectly from a positive or negative act of the victim himself, which he knows will produce this result" (Durkheim 1952, 41; compare Brandt's definition [1975]).

But most theorists insist on the intent component (e.g., Frey 1981, Tolhurst 1983, Fairbairn 1995). According to them, if I leaped onto a grenade in order to save my comrades, and not to kill myself, my act was not suicide, even if I was well aware that my action would be fatal, and expected to die. By contrast, leaping onto a grenade in order to die is suicide.

Suicide is an act performed by someone who expects, correctly, that it will be fatal, and who does it in order to die. It is still suicide if she does something fatal in response to circumstances that greatly limit her choices; if her only options are to drink poison or die of thirst while trapped deep in a cave, drinking the poison is something she does under her own volition. If a maniac threatens to slaughter her family unless she kills herself, the latter will also be an act she performs under her own volition, and will count as suicide. Socrates had to choose between obeying the government that ordered him to kill himself and going into exile. The choice he made was suicide.

It is common to distinguish between acts and omissions, and to count a death as suicide only when it results from an act, and not when it results from an omission (see, e.g., Holland 1971). However, some omissions seem to constitute suicide. Certainly one may choose an omission as a way to die. For example, I can omit to eat, or to submit to a life-saving medical treatment, in order to die (Tolhurst 1983, 80). Most of us would say that if I stop eating in order to die, and succeed, what I have done is suicide.

Varieties of suicide

I take it that the term 'suicide' is ordinarily used much as (a)–(c) suggest. But there are ways in which its meaning can be usefully extended.

First, we might distinguish auto-destruction that relies on omissions from auto-destruction that relies on acts: person S's suicide is *active* just in case S takes some action A expecting, correctly, that it will bring about S's death, and does A for that reason; by contrast, S's suicide is *passive* just in case S omits to take some action A expecting, correctly, that death will occur sooner than it would if S did A, and omits A for that reason. That is, person S's act A constitutes active suicide just in case (a)–(c) above are met, while S's omitting to do A constitutes passive suicide just in case the following three conditions are met:

1. S's death occurred sooner than it would have had S done A;
2. in omitting to do A, S foresaw, in some detail, why death would occur sooner than it would have had S done A; and
3. in omitting to do A, S intended death to occur sooner than it would have had S done A; S omitted to do A in order to die sooner.

Second, we might coin terminology to refer to acts that meet (a) and (b), and omissions that meet 1 and 2. Let us say that S's act or omission is suicide just in case S foresees how it will bring about or allow S's death and does it anyway; that is, A meets (a) and (b) or 1 and 2. We can then say that S's act or omission is *intentional* suicide just in case it meets (a)–(c) or 1–3.

The two stipulations can be combined, of course. For example, S's action is intentional active suicide just in case S not only foresees how it will bring about death, but does it in order to die. The death of Socrates is an example of intentional active suicide, assuming that he was ordered to kill himself by the Athenian government, and killed himself in order to comply (Frey 1978). S's action is active suicide just in case S foresees how it will bring about death. Throwing oneself onto a hand grenade, expecting the death that results, is active suicide, but it is not intentional suicide if one's aim was to save others, so that, given another, nonfatal, way to save the lives of one's compatriots, one would choose it. (But see Kagan 1999, 145, who argues that the soldier did intend his death: after all, we would say that *you* intended the soldier's death if you knocked the soldier onto the grenade in order to save others.)

Again: these stipulations extend ordinary usage. The stretch beyond ordinary usage is greatest for 'unintentional passive suicide,' or cases that meet 1 and 2 but not 3. Any of us who realize that we would live longer if we exercised or ate five servings of vegetables a day, and who still choose not to do these things, meet 1 and 2, and hence engage in unintentional passive suicide, yet our omission does not constitute suicide in the ordinary sense. (Even speaking of 'passive suicide' here might strike you as silly, since our lives are shortened so little. But imagine a poison which will not kill you until two days before your life would have been over anyway: deliberately taking this poison now, whether to shave off the last few days of your life or for some other reason, would be active suicide, despite the fact that it shortens your life very little.)

Next consider some points about the motivation associated with the various sorts of suicide.

Suicide may be intended as a means to one's own welfare, or to the welfare of others (or both). We might call the former *prudential* suicide, and the latter *altruistic* suicide. Consider an example.

> *The Lunatic's Demand*: A lunatic threatens to kill thousands of people unless you kill yourself. He lets you choose the means.

If you chose to comply, you would go on to do something, such as poisoning yourself, in order to die. This is true even though you would have intended your death as a means to an end – saving others – that did not include your death. Here's an actual case of altruistic suicide:

> *Captain Oates*: Oates became disabled during Scott's polar expedition and walked into a blizzard.

Oates engaged in altruistic intentional active suicide, assuming that he meant to die so as to unburden his companions, who would not leave him behind alive, and assuming that his means, walking into a polar blizzard, is an act rather than an omission.

Our motives might also be mixed, as in the following cases:

> *Expensive Care*: You are receiving expensive treatment in a hospital and choose to end treatment. You intend your death as a means to ending your suffering and also as a way to minimize the financial burden your survivors will face.

> *Samson*: In pulling down the temple of his captors after they blinded and shackled him, Samson's suicide was intentional, judging from the words "Let me die with the Philistines" (Judges 16:30). He brought

down the temple in order to escape torment and ridicule through death and also to attack his captors.

Suicide Bomber: By setting off a bomb that kills himself and others, Fred, a suicide bomber, intends to move on to a blissful afterlife as well as to fight injustice.

Suicide can have a darker motivation as well:

Vindictive Vicky: Vicky takes her life in order to inflict pain on her former husband.

As a final preliminary matter, I will mention some ambiguities which I will leave unresolved. First, for my act to be suicide, is it enough that I had a true belief concerning how it would result in my death? If I come to believe, for no reason, that I will be struck by lightning if I step outside, and I step outside in order to die by being struck, and by sheer coincidence I am indeed struck fatally, have I committed suicide? Or do I need knowledge or at least a justified belief concerning the way my act will bring about death? Second, is it necessary that I believe my action will be fatal, or is it enough to believe that it will *probably* be fatal? And what if I am merely aware that it is dangerous? Have I committed suicide if I play Russian roulette because I want to do something that will probably kill me, and I die as a result (Windt 1980)? (Does the issue turn on how many empty chambers I leave in my gun, or on how many times I play?)

Concerning these ambiguities, perhaps the following suffices. Many people choose acts or omissions which they believe (perhaps mistakenly) to be dangerous in order to put their lives at risk. We might say that their behavior is suicidal, since it is meant to put their lives at risk, rather than suicide.

'Euthanasia'

Like 'suicide,' the term 'euthanasia' needs discussion. The conviction that euthanasia is murder can affect the way a writer analyzes euthanasia. Everyone agrees that an act is not euthanasia unless it benefits the one who dies, but writers who consider euthanasia to be murder often limit the application of 'euthanasia' to the act of intentionally killing another who is meant to benefit. Thereby, they ensure that euthanasia is always directly wrong if, as they believe, intentionally killing human beings is directly wrong.

However, usage has shifted in recent years. Many writers (such as Rachels 1975) who have wanted to reexamine the permissibility of granting others a merciful death have widened the scope of the term 'euthanasia.' It has become standard to extend the term in two ways.

First, theorists often abandon the assumption that euthanasia involves killing, and distinguish between *active* euthanasia, or killing that benefits the individual who dies, and *passive* euthanasia, or benefiting an individual by allowing her to die. Second, it is standard to distinguish varieties of active and passive euthanasia in terms of the attitude of the individual who dies. Euthanasia, whether passive or active, is *voluntary* when it is competently consented to by the one who dies, *involuntary* when competently opposed, and *nonvoluntary* when the one who dies is incompetent or cannot express an attitude about dying.

Further refinements are possible. Normally, the act A by which a person P actively euthanizes subject S would meet all of the following conditions (obviously, similar distinctions are possible in the case of passive euthanasia):

(a) A brought about S's death, and S's death via A benefited S;
(b) in doing A, P foresaw, at least roughly, how A would result in S's death, and that S's death via A would benefit S;
(c) P intended to benefit S by bringing about S's death via A.

When A meets (a) and (b), let us say that A is active euthanasia. When A meets all of these conditions, we can characterize A as *intentional* active euthanasia. For example, physicians who give patients high doses of morphine might do so to relieve their suffering and not to kill them, despite foreseeing that their patients will benefit from death and that the morphine dose will be fatal. This would be unintentional active euthanasia.

In some situations suicide and euthanasia both occur. If I discontinue medical treatment knowing it will hasten my death, my action is passive suicide; if I refuse the treatment in order to shorten my life, my action is intentional passive suicide. Either way, when a physician removes me from life support, knowing that this will benefit me by cutting my life short, it is passive euthanasia. It is intentional passive euthanasia if the physician also intends to benefit me by hastening my death.

RATIONALLY CHOOSING TO DIE

To be our best option, suicide must be something we choose rationally and morally. The same would go for having ourselves killed. In this section I will consider whether choosing to die can be rational. I will focus here on suicide, but if it were always irrational to kill ourselves, it would also be irrational to have ourselves killed. I will examine moral objections in the next section.

To show that suicide is always irrational, one might claim that dying cannot be in our interests, or that, even if it would benefit some people, no one chooses suicide through rational deliberation; instead, all or nearly all suicides are caused by mental impairment. One might take a similar approach to the decision to have oneself killed: it cannot be in our interests, and even if it could be, everyone who had himself killed would be mentally impaired. The first claim is related to the second: doing something that is extremely bad for oneself, such as cutting off one's own arm with a pocket knife, is evidence that one is mentally unbalanced. But of course what appears to harm us may be in our interests after all, and hence not evidence that we are unhinged. In 2003 Aron Ralston did cut off his arm with a pocket knife, but only after concluding it was the only way to save his life. His arm had been pinned under a massive boulder while he was hiking in a remote part of Utah.

Let us consider whether killing ourselves or having ourselves killed can be in our interests. Later we can ask whether it is always the product of mental illness.

Prudential considerations

Actually, we are already well on the way to an answer, since it has already been established that dying can be in our interests. As we have seen, we can decide whether dying at some time is better for us than living on by comparing our lives as they would be were we to die with our lives as they would be were we to live on. If the former is better for us than the latter, dying is in our interests.

Dying might benefit people for different reasons. The main beneficiaries are people who find their level of suffering unacceptable, and who have good reason to believe that even with treatment their suffering cannot be reduced to an acceptable level. For some people it is mental suffering, not pain due to injury or illness, that tips the scales, and mental suffering can have various causes, including the loss of autonomy resulting from immobility or dependence on machines or others (Gazini, Dobscha, Heintz, and Press 2003). C.G. Prado (2008, ch. 1) distinguishes between *surcease* and *preemptive* suicide; the former is suicide chosen as the means of escaping "present, intolerable circumstances," while the latter is suicide chosen "in anticipation of intolerable terminal conditions." Prado argues that both can be in our interests. For example, if we anticipate that some disease which we have will soon put us through unrelenting pain, it might well be in our interests to end our lives before the illness progresses. Obviously, however, our timing matters: if during its early stages our illness is tolerable and our lives are still good, it is best to put off ending our lives.

To show that ending our lives is prudent, it is not quite enough to demonstrate that dying is in our interests. We must also consider the means we will use. Using some methods will be a bad idea because they are slow and painful, and others because they pose too great a risk of failure, leaving us worse off than before. Passive suicide by starvation would probably fall into the first category. According to some theorists (e.g., Arras 1998), such a death need not be as horrible as it sounds, but it clearly would be harder to endure than a quick and painless death. For only a few will it be prudent to die this way. They would have to lack a quicker, less painful means of dying, and the future they seek to avoid would have to be bleak indeed. Active suicide by firearm probably falls into the second category; it, too, would rarely be prudent.

Generally, a good means of suicide would be painless, fast, and reliable. In all likelihood, it would involve some sort of drug prescribed by a physician. When dying is in a person's interests, I would say that this sort of active suicide would be prudent. However, I would not say that it is the only prudent approach to active suicide. Nor would I say that it is the very best approach. The best approach would be to take our lives under the supervision of a physician who is willing to help us, and who would step in if something unexpected happens. If something does go wrong, the physician would euthanize us. But of course this presupposes that active euthanasia is permissible and available.

As a method of ending life, the advantages of euthanasia itself are clear. It can be administered by professionals, assuming that they are willing to take part, which ensures that death will come painlessly, quickly, and reliably.

Insanity

In some suicides mental impairment of some sort is a contributing factor. No doubt mental impairment would also be a contributing factor in some decisions to request euthanasia. However, there is no reason to think that everyone who has killed or will kill herself is mentally impaired, and even if certain sorts of impairment are contributing factors in some decisions to end life, that decision can still be rational. Or so I will argue.

One early and influential empirical study of suicide was conducted by Eli Robins (1959). Robins examined 134 suicides that occurred in St. Louis over the course of a year, from May 1956 to May 1957, and reported that 94 percent were mentally ill; 45 percent were manic depressives, 23 percent were chronic alcoholics, and 19 percent had an undiagnosed mental illness. As Robins was aware, however, only about 14 percent of manic-depressives kill themselves (1959, 154), and many do it after their depression is treated and overcome. Similarly, most chronic drinkers do not kill themselves. Later suicidologists found that a much better correlation exists between suicide and "hopelessness," defined as a person's "desire to escape from what he considers an insoluble problem" (Beck, Kovacs, and Weissman 1996, 332). According to Beck, Kovacs, and Weissman, "hopelessness accounts for 96% of the association between depression and suicidal intent (1996, 336)." Something similar is true of schizophrenia: only about 10 percent of schizophrenics kill themselves (Roy 1982, 444), but hopelessness is strongly associated with suicide among schizophrenics. Beck's position is refined by Herbert Hendin (1991, 616), who argues that an even stronger correlation exists between suicide and "desperation," which involves not just hopelessness, the desire to change an insoluble problem, but also "a sense that life is impossible without such change."

Notice that people's hopelessness and desperation, as defined by Beck and Hendin, are entirely compatible with their judging, correctly and reasonably, that dying is in their interests. (It is also compatible with the possibility that many such persons will become profoundly unhappy and that many will begin to drink heavily.) If I come to believe that I cannot escape my circumstances, say because my schizophrenia or manic-depression cannot be made tolerable to me, or because I have an illness whose symptoms cannot be treated in a way I deem acceptable, and that it is better for me to die than to be in these circumstances, my condition will be "desperation"; if I also arrive at this belief after making a reasonable assessment of my situation, and opt to kill myself, I will have chosen suicide rationally. Hence the data do not support the idea that suicide cannot be chosen rationally or that it is never chosen rationally, or even that it is rarely chosen rationally. To think otherwise is to assume, on no basis, that I am irrational precisely because I have made the distressing discovery that my life is best ended.

Even if a suicidal person is not mentally ill, he might be irrational, perhaps temporarily so. Many suicidologists appear to think that the people who attempt to kill themselves are confused and ambivalent, since everyone, including those who attempt suicide, really want to live. In a famous passage, Edwin Shneidman advises healthcare workers that "a few straightforward assumptions are necessary in suicide prevention." One of these assumptions is the following:

> Individuals who are intent on killing themselves still wish very much to be rescued or to have their deaths prevented. Suicide prevention consists essentially in recognizing that the potential victim is "in balance" between his wishes to live and his wishes to die, then throwing one's efforts on the side of life. (Shneidman 1965, 154)

Here Shneidman appears to say that those who set out to kill themselves really want to be stopped because everyone wants to live. This reasoning is simplistic. The fact that we want to live does not show that we have not rationally decided to kill ourselves. Even if we badly want to live, it is likely that there are circumstances in which we do not want to live. We will do what we can to avoid these abhorrent circumstances, and others, including therapists and psychiatrists, might help us do so. However, if the only way to avoid them is through death, we might decide rationally to kill ourselves, wishing all the while that there were another means of escape.

What about the distress people are in when they contemplate self-destruction? Won't this distress prevent them from choosing suicide rationally? There is no doubt that severe mental or physical pain can prevent people from deliberating well, and cause them to overlook relevant facts (Brandt 1975, 124–126). It might lead them to make bad estimates of their chances of beating a mental or physical illness. They may not sufficiently appreciate the extent to which mental and physical pain can be reduced by psychiatric and drug therapy. I would guess that the vast majority of the young people who kill themselves have made terribly irrational judgments. They did not think past their pain, I suspect; they did not see clearly that, in time, their pain would have receded, and their interest in life would have returned. In the long run their lives would have been vastly better if they had stayed alive.

However, while distress may undermine the reasoning of some people who choose suicide, there is no reason to think that this is inevitable. Consider that people make all sorts of choices while under great mental strain, and we do not normally assume that the outcome is irrational. For example, when people become seriously ill and decide to *let* themselves die, their choice is typically considered competent and rational, even if (or perhaps especially if) they are in grave mental and physical pain. People in great misery due to terrible accidents, perhaps involving massive wounds or loss of limbs, quite often act rationally; some bind their wounds, and escape from dangerous vehicles, for example. Aron Ralston is a good case in point. His arm was crushed, yet he was able to assess his situation, and act in his own interests, taking an extremely unpleasant course of action.

A final point. Here and now you and I can get very close to a rational decision in favor of active suicide. Certainly we can come to have a well-supported belief that under certain circumstances suicide would be in our interests. In fact, I have this belief now: if I were to contract an incurable illness whose mature stages would strip me of my autonomy and cause me great pain, it would be in my interests to end my life painlessly before my disease matures. My ability to reason has not been impeded by anything involved in reaching this view. Nor is it impeded if I now take a further step, and conclude that one day I will probably come to *be* in these circumstances – dependent on machinery, and struggling to overcome some disease or other. When I dwell on it (something I rarely do), this conclusion makes me exceedingly sad, but my sadness does not undermine the rationality of this further judgment. I make all sorts of grim rational judgments that sadden me. Suppose that the day comes when I conclude that I am in the grip of a terrible disease, and I take my life before my disease matures. Isn't it wholly implausible to say that my misery will undermine the rationality of that choice?

MORALLY CHOOSING TO DIE

Some theorists object to suicide and euthanasia on the grounds that killing is itself directly wrong. Most of them think that there may be exceptions, or overriding considerations, involving the defense of the lives of innocent people, or retribution for serious acts of injustice, but these do not excuse suicide or euthanasia. However, the claim that killing is directly wrong must be defended, and, as the previous chapter established, it is quite reasonable to say that killing is very often *not* directly wrong. In this section I will consider the best argument for the view that suicide and euthanasia are always directly wrong. I leave to the side arguments appealing to such well-criticized claims as that suicide is wrong because we do not own ourselves or our lives, or because it is not natural, and so forth. (Good replies can be found in Hume 1826 and Schopenhauer 1851.)

The absolutist argument

The best way to argue that active suicide and euthanasia are always directly wrong is to assume two things: first, people have subject value that is absolute in the sense that it trumps all other sorts of value, and second, those who engage in suicide or euthanasia foresee or intend that their actions will promote the best interests of the one killed. On these assumptions suicide and euthanasia sacrifice a person's absolute subject value for the sake of her welfare, which is forbidden by the principle that absolute value trumps. I will call this the *absolutist argument* for the direct wrongness of active suicide and euthanasia.

Absolutist Argument:

1. Suicide and euthanasia sacrifice a person's subject value for the sake of her welfare.
2. It is directly wrong to sacrifice a person's subject value, which is absolute, for the sake of some other sort of value, such as her welfare.
3. Hence suicide and euthanasia are directly wrong.

Kant based his own opposition to active suicide on something like the absolutist argument. According to Kant, we must avoid all behavior, whether act or omission, that interferes with the exercise of our moral agency, which has absolute value. Any threat to our lives is a threat to our agency. Kant condemns trading away something of absolute value for something of incomparably lesser value. Hence we may not risk life simply for the sake of financial gain (1963, 155). Nor could the enjoyableness of activities such as skydiving justify endangering our lives. If we may not risk our lives for the sake of things that lack absolute value, we may not take them for the sake of such things either. It is because Kant thought that all suicides give up something of absolute value for the sake of things that lack absolute value that he condemned it (Hill 1991, 85–104). The typical suicide, Kant thought, is motivated by the desire to escape unhappiness, which lacks absolute value (1963, 152). Kant reserved the term 'suicide' for what I have called intentional active suicide (1963, 150); however, the sort of trade off which Kant abhorred is as likely to occur in passive as in active suicide (Hill 1991, Gunderson 2004), and it may be made intentionally or merely knowingly (as in unintentional suicide).

The absolutist argument faces at least two criticisms.

First, it appeals to the absolutist version of the Subject Value Account or of the Highest Subject Value Account, yet these analyses were shown to be false in the previous chapter. There it was noted that the analyses imply that killing pets in order to benefit them by eliminating their suffering is directly wrong. However, euthanizing pets is not wrong. Hence the Subject Value Accounts must be replaced with the Hybrid Account, according to which killings can be beneficial enough to warrant sacrificing subject value. And if the hybrid view is correct, the absolutist argument fails. In principle, killing ourselves, or having ourselves killed, is permissible if living on is sufficiently against our interests.

Of course, the criticisms of the Subject Value Accounts offered in chapter 7 considered merely sentient beings; perhaps the wrongness of killing such creatures as cats depends on their subject value as well as their interests, yet the same is not true of people. Perhaps for people, unlike animals, subject value trumps welfare.

But if subject value does not trump welfare in the case of merely sentient beings, why would it do so in the case of people? The answer would have to be either that it does not, or else it is because our subject value is vastly greater than that of animals. It is so great that the importance of our welfare is trivial by comparison. (Finnis 1995 and Velleman 1999 defend a view much like this.) Presumably this is the point of saying that it is 'absolute.' However, this story is implausible. Grant for the sake of argument that our subject value is much greater than that of animals. From that, maybe it follows that *our* subject value trumps the welfare of *animals*. But it certainly does not follow that our subject value trumps our *own* welfare. Presumably we are so much more valuable than animals by virtue of capacities that we have and they lack, such as the capacity for self-awareness, or maybe the capacity for rational thought or self-determination. However, presumably these capacities will enable us to benefit vastly more from our lives than animals can from theirs, and also to incur vastly greater harm than they can. So why shouldn't we think that the extra amount of subject value we enjoy can be outweighed by the extra harm we are subject to?

There is a further problem with this story: it is highly implausible to say that the subject value of people is absolute, trumping our welfare, as the following counterexamples show.

Unconsciousness: I trick Fred into drinking a magical potion that keeps him unconscious for the rest of his life and that ensures that he will live as long as he would have lived had I not drugged him. I could wake him with an antidote at any time, but I never do. He sleeps his life away.

What I have done to Fred is as objectionable as killing him would be. (Stretton [2004, 158] would presumably disagree.) But if Fred has absolute value by virtue of being a human being, or by virtue of having the capacity for self-determination, what I have done is of trivial significance compared to killing him. Now consider another example:

> *Two Spells*: I know how to cast two magical spells. One of them, which Mary wants me to use on her, would ensure that she has a life that is extremely good, and far better than the life she otherwise would have had, but the spell will also kill her painlessly in her sleep one day sooner than the day she otherwise would have died of old age. The other spell, which she has forbidden me to use, would not kill her but would ensure that she has a life that is wretched, and far worse than the life she otherwise would have had.

It seems clear that using the first spell on Mary is not objectionable at all. In any case it surely would be better from the moral point of view than using the second spell on Mary. But if we say that Mary has absolute value as a subject, we must reject both claims, since the first spell, and not the second, destroys something whose value trumps all other sorts. Her welfare, no matter how great or prolonged, cannot give us grounds for killing her even a day before she would otherwise have died.

Consider another criticism of the absolutist argument. In chapter 7 it was argued that the Combined Account is the most plausible analysis of the direct wrongness of killing. It is superior to the various versions of the Subject Value Account since it makes clearer sense of when killings are wrong and how serious they are, it compares well when scrutinized from the point of view of our intuitions about equality, and it avoids the need to make sense of quantifiable subject value. The Combined Account is even more congenial to suicide and euthanasia than the Hybrid Account. According to the Combined Account, it is not wrong to kill sentient beings when it benefits them, or competent persons when we have their informed consent.

We can add that proponents of the Combined Account have a reasonable response to the Kantian charge that suicide and euthanasia treat people as if they lacked value as subjects: they can say that the sense in which persons have value is simply that, morally, they matter in themselves. To treat them as if they lacked value is to treat them as if they did not matter from the moral point of view. But to kill someone, or for them to kill themselves, in accordance with their wills and because it is in their interests, is not to treat them as if they did not matter. They matter by virtue of having interests and by virtue of being self-determining. Killing people who wish it, or killing themselves, because it is best for them, is fully responsive to their interests and entirely in accord with their autonomous wills.

There may be another way to respond to those who condemn active suicide and euthanasia. The absolutist argument rests on the idea that absolute value trumps other sorts. But according to the *parity argument,* if their absolute value trumps any considerations there might be in favor of *killing* others, their absolute value also trumps any considerations there might be in favor of *allowing them to die.* If so, then the absolutist argument commits us to extremely dubious conclusions. Those who wield the absolutist argument mean to attack intentional active suicide and euthanasia. But their argument opposes other varieties of suicide and euthanasia as well. Consider an example:

> *Unintentional Suicide*: I have an illness that will kill me within a week if allowed to progress. There is a treatment that will extend my life by one more year but I will be in pain nearly the entire time. I weigh the extra time against the pain involved and decide to refuse the treatment. I die three days later.

What I have done is unintentional passive suicide. I did not refuse treatment with the intention of bringing about my death; I did it despite the fact that my death would result. Nevertheless, I made my decision at least in part on the basis of an assessment of the importance of further life versus the importance of pain avoidance. I knowingly traded away longer life in order to reduce my suffering; if such bargains are directly wrong, then my unintentional passive suicide is directly wrong. However, it is not at all objectionable for me to let myself die in this case, so the absolutist argument has unacceptably strong implications.

There are various reasons why killing people might have different moral significance than letting people die, even if the individuals involved are alike in their absolute value. For example, it is far easier never to kill anyone than it is never to allow anyone to die. (I assume that we can allow people to die only if we can prevent their deaths; otherwise it is impossible not to allow people to die, since they are mortal!) Each of us could spend all of our time and resources preventing others from dying, and never complete the task. I doubt that anyone believes we are morally required to do so. However, in cases like Unintentional Suicide, death is easily avoided, and the victim is clear. It will be hard to escape the conclusion that such suicides are directly wrong if we assume that absolute value trumps other considerations.

Irresponsibility

A different kind of reservation about choosing to die is that it can be irresponsible, as others might depend on us. At most this charge will show that choosing to die is wrong because of its possible side effects, not that it is directly wrong. Nevertheless, these side effects can be serious indeed.

One version of this charge is that those who choose to die neglect their duty to serve society (Thomas Aquinas 1925). However, Hume's famous response to this objection is quite convincing. Hume noted that we do not harm society when we withdraw from life, we only cease to do good. As for our duty to do good, surely it has limits. We permit people to neglect society when they become ill or when their continued service would harm them. Indeed, people are expected to serve society only if they want to. So those who opt to die should not be condemned for not serving society.

A man who retires from life does no harm to society: he only ceases to do good; which, if it is an injury, is of the lowest kind. All our obligations to do good to society seem to imply something reciprocal. I receive the benefits of society, and therefore ought to promote its interests; but when I withdraw myself altogether from society, can I be bound any longer? But allowing that our obligations to do good were perpetual, they have certainly some bounds; I am not obliged to do a small good to society at the expense of a great harm to myself: why then should I prolong a miserable existence, because of some frivolous advantage which the public may perhaps receive from me? If upon account of age and infirmities, I may lawfully resign any office, and employ my time altogether in fencing against these calamities, and alleviating as much as possible the miseries of my future life; why may I not cut short these miseries at once by an action which is no more prejudicial to society? But suppose that it is no longer in my power to promote the interests of society; suppose that I am a burden to it . . . in such cases, my resignation of life must not only be innocent, but laudable. (Hume 1826)

Another version of the charge of irresponsibility is more potent. Some of us have responsibilities to specific individuals; for instance, we might be parents, whose children will suffer if we were to die. It is conceivable that in rare circumstances our responsibilities may oblige us to live. If my children would die unless I stay alive and take care of them, I may need to live on. But many of us will not have such responsibilities, and even if we do we may transfer them to others. For example, parents may give their children up for adoption. Moreover, it might be impossible for us to carry weighty obligations if we have lost the will to live, or are immobilized by paralysis or pain. Surely it is permissible for people to do what they can to arrange for those in their care, then end their lives (Glover 1990).

A final point should go without saying: if the means by which we arrange to die endangers others it is irresponsible to proceed. This point leads back to one made before: ideally, suicide would be accomplished with the willing assistance of a medical professional in controlled circumstances.

The upshot is this: if we mean to end our lives, we must arrange, as best we can, for the welfare of those in our care, and we must find a means that will not endanger others. Failing to take these steps leaves us open to the charge of irresponsibility. But this obligation is no bar to ending our lives.

INTERVENTION, ASSISTANCE, AND EUTHANASIA

I have suggested that the strongest argument for the wrongness of active suicide and euthanasia, the absolutist argument, fails. I also pointed out that, on the most plausible account of the direct wrongness of killing, it is not wrong to kill sentient beings (or for them to kill themselves) when it benefits them, or moral agents when we have their competent, informed consent. If all this is true, how should we respond to those who wish to die or who would benefit from dying?

There are two groups to consider. The first comprises people known to have been *competent* when they chose to die; this includes those who, while competent, chose to die after ceasing to be competent. The second group comprises all others. For convenience, I will refer to individuals in this second group as the *incompetent*. Let us ask, of those in each group, whether we should ever intervene in their suicides, whether we should ever assist, and whether we should ever euthanize them.

The competent

Suppose that we decide to end our lives after making a competent, informed judgment that this, and the method we will use, are in our interests. Suppose, too, that what we are doing is not irresponsible, and that all this is known to others. Under such circumstances, suicide, whether passive or active, is clearly unobjectionable, and there are no moral grounds for others to interfere. It is also entirely permissible for them to assist us, just as they may assist us when we do other things we are entitled to do. Except in special circumstances, such as when we are contestants who must act alone, others are free to help us to do anything we ourselves may do, and that includes ending our lives.

But what if we are mistaken, despite making a competent, informed judgment that killing ourselves, using some method, is in our interests? This is certainly possible; even with the best evidence our conclusions sometimes turn out to be false. In such cases suicide and assisted suicide seem more problematic.

When others doubt that suicide, whether passive or active, is in our interests, or that our chosen method is sufficiently painless and reliable, it seems as if they should intervene, since by doing so they might prevent us from harming ourselves. However, this argument for intervention over-looks the fact that we should assist people only in ways that are consistent with respect for their self-determination. Given the importance of self-determination, we are frequently bound not to prevent people from doing things that are against their interests: we must let them destroy their lungs by smoking cigarettes, for example. We must let them be insensitive to the needs of others, even though this eventually will leave them loveless and forlorn. Nor should we intervene in the suicides of those who have made a competent, informed decision to die, whether actively or passively. This is not to say that we may do nothing, of course: we may always attempt to persuade them that they are behaving in a way that is seriously against their interests.

Isn't it reasonable for others to intervene, albeit only on a temporary basis, when they have good reason for thinking that our method of killing ourselves will harm others? In extreme cases it will be reasonable. We should be stopped if we propose to kill ourselves by crashing cars into buildings, for example, since this action places others in grave danger. Yet in less extreme cases intervention is problematic. We really ought to get our affairs in order, and do what we can to ensure that no one is harmed by our deaths, before we opt for suicide. Again, however, it is important not to underestimate the significance of self-determination. It may be important to prevent harm but it will rarely be important enough to justify the sort of intervention it would require to interrupt a suicide attempted by someone who is not directly endangering others. There are many examples of objectionable behavior we permit on the grounds that preventing it is less important than protecting individual freedom. For instance, it is wrong for people to have children they do not want or cannot support, or to abandon their friends in time of need, or to turn their backs on their parents in their old age, but no one thinks that the state should intrude into our personal lives to the extent necessary to prevent these wrongs. Consider, too, that someone who allows herself to die may be just as irresponsible as someone who kills himself, yet few of us would advocate forcing the former to undergo medical treatment which she refuses.

In sum, the following conclusion seems plausible: When an individual has made a competent, informed decision to die,

(a) we may intervene if and only if she proposes to die by an irresponsible method, and
(b) we may assist in her suicide if and only if she asks this of us and her death will be brought about responsibly.

Next let us consider the question of euthanasia. This question is especially pressing in the case of individuals for whom suicide is physically impossible or extremely difficult. Several conditions might be involved: they may be unable to swallow or to move their hands. They may lack hands, or a mouth. They may be completely paralyzed. Despite such obstacles – indeed, in view of them – they might reasonably decide that their lives should be ended. I have argued that assisting them would be permissible. But assistance does not suffice, since they are helpless.

What they need is the freedom to authorize someone to kill them, and they should have it. I have already shown that people may assist in the suicides of individuals who have made competent and rational decisions to die and whose deaths will be brought about in responsible ways; for the same reasons, people may provide active euthanasia in the very same situations. In both cases someone kills someone and the one who dies has made a competent and informed decision that the killing should take place. According to the Combined Account, the killing is permissible; killing someone is just as acceptable as killing ourselves when the person killed has made a competent, rational choice that the killing should occur.

An assistant in active suicide does not actually kill anyone, whereas the provider of active euthanasia does: this seems to be the only salient difference between the one case and the other. But isn't this difference relevant? If so, it is not because it shows that the one case involves killing and the other does not. Killing occurs in both cases. Is there some other reason to attribute moral relevance to the difference in the roles played by the assistant and the provider of active euthanasia? It is hard to see why; if we can authorize ourselves to kill ourselves, it is hard to see why we cannot authorize others to kill us.

Apparently, then, assisted suicide and active euthanasia are permissible in precisely the same sorts of situations. That means that paralyzed people are not the only ones who may authorize someone to kill them. Anyone who competently and rationally chooses to die may do so. I think, then, that we can augment our earlier conclusion as follows: When an individual has made a competent, informed decision to die,

(a) we may intervene if and only if she proposes to die by an irresponsible method, and
(b) we may assist in her suicide *or kill her* if and only if she asks this of us and her death will be brought about responsibly.

Now suppose that we are aware ahead of the time that we might lose the ability to reason, and we make a competent, informed choice about what should happen to us. For example, we might agree to a course of treatment that, for a time, would leave us unable to make good decisions. Or perhaps we are in the grip of an illness that is likely to rob us of our faculties and leave us severely demented or in a persistent vegetative state. Realizing what might be in store for us, we leave instructions about the circumstances in which treatment should cease and we should be allowed to die. We decide, in advance, in favor of passive suicide, and we authorize others to passively euthanize us.

In such cases others should normally defer to our decisions, as has become standard practice in healthcare facilities. For if moral agents may decide their immediate fates, under the conditions I suggested earlier, they may also decide what should happen to them even at times when they will no longer be able to reason. Needless to say, they may also change their minds.

What is more, just as moral agents may insist that others should let them die under certain sorts of future circumstances, they may also authorize others to kill them in those circumstances. The argument is this. I have already argued that competent people may authorize others to kill them immediately, and I just suggested that what they may authorize immediately they may authorize in anticipation of future contingencies. It follows that when we decide, competently and with adequate information, that we should be killed should future contingencies arise, others may euthanize us.

Hence the following additional conclusions are warranted:

(a) If, competently and with adequate information, an individual decides that he should be allowed to die if and when certain contingencies arise, we must comply unless he changes his mind.

(b) If, competently and with adequate information, an individual decides to ask us to kill him if and when certain contingencies arise, we may comply unless he changes his mind.

The incompetent

We come finally to persons who have not competently chosen to die or who have not made their preferences known to others. Some of these are people who are only temporarily incompetent, and can be expected to recover. Some of them are now permanently incompetent. And some have never been competent. These latter might be self-aware individuals who never possessed the ability to reason, or individuals who have never been more than sentient.

How should we respond to people who decide to kill themselves (or have themselves killed) while temporarily incompetent? In such cases it is unreasonable to help bring about their deaths. In fact, it is reasonable to intervene, both to save their lives, and to help them to regain competence. A clear example is a man who is temporarily extremely distraught because he has been jilted. It is obvious to everyone except him that his suicide would gravely harm him. Others should restrain him; if he were thinking clearly, he would want them to, and in time, he will be grateful that they did. The grounds for interference are parentalistic: measured restrictions on a person's freedom are warranted while he is not fully competent if they are likely to benefit him.

Now consider persons who have never been competent or who have become incompetent without making known their preferences concerning their fates. In these cases, the burden of decision rests entirely on our shoulders. We cannot defer to individuals who are incapable of deciding what is best for themselves. What we can and should do, however, is base our decisions on their best interests. Usually this will mean preserving and enhancing their lives as best we can. Sometimes it will mean allowing them to die from terminal illness. But sometimes it will mean making a far more difficult decision. There are people so deluded or demented that they simply cannot make rational choices; some of them live in mental anguish or outright terror, or extreme physical misery, which cannot be relieved without leaving them in a permanent stupor. The fact that they are not able to ask, rationally, that we kill them when it is in their interests should not prevent us from coming to their assistance, any more than it precludes our coming to the assistance of a miserable beast lying broken by the road.

Robert Young (2007) defends euthanasia in many of the same cases as I have done. The main exceptions are these last cases, involving persons who have never been competent, or who became incompetent without making it known whether they wished to be killed upon becoming incompetent. Young thinks it permissible to allow an incompetent individual to die when any preferences he might have had at one time are unknown and "there is no realistic prospect of him recovering to lead a worthwhile life in the time that remains" (2007, 217), as indeed happens in hospitals routinely. He also thinks that "if it is justifiable to allow no longer competent, terminally ill patients to die when nothing further can be done for them . . . it should equally be justifiable to assist such people to die" – that is, to kill them. Yet he is reluctant to *say* that killing them is permissible, and it is not altogether clear why. He says his reservations are solely "strategic": he does not want to give anyone "cause to claim that the legalization of voluntary medically assisted death will lead inevitably to terminally ill incompetent persons being killed." However, he also says that there is a "crucial difference" between terminally ill incompetent individuals and people who choose death for themselves: assisting the latter "merely ensures that effect is given to their choices. It is they who act, albeit with assistance . . . Since the competent are differently situated from the incompetent as regards their capacity to request assisted death, only the former may properly be afforded it" (2007, 218). No doubt Young would also resist saying it is ever permissible to kill no longer competent individuals who are not terminally ill, and for the same reasons.

I doubt that Young's stratagem will cause the foes of active euthanasia to worry any less about how far euthanasia will be carried. In any case, the claim that active euthanasia is always improper except by request should not go unchallenged. Actively euthanizing an individual who is permanently unable to choose for herself is not directly wrong when it is in her best interests. In some cases it might still be objectionable, all things considered; perhaps she is pregnant, for example, and the baby can be saved if she is kept alive. But unless special considerations arise, such as pregnancy, there are no moral grounds for condemning the killing of incompetent persons who benefit thereby.

SUMMARY

Suicide and euthanasia can be chosen rationally and morally, and so assisting in suicides, as well as performing euthanasia, are morally permissible. To be in our interests, suicide normally would need to be performed using a means that is painless, fast, and reliable; ideally, it would employ a drug prescribed by a physician for the purpose. Euthanasia often will be a superior option, especially for those who cannot take their own lives, since it can be performed by professionals who would ensure that death will come painlessly, quickly, and reliably.

Many suicidologists have argued that suicide and suicide attempts are caused by mental impairment, and not chosen rationally. However, it is very difficult to see why this must be the case. There is little correlation between mental illness and suicide, and while there is no doubt that anyone who opts to take her life is likely to be in great distress, it does not follow that her choice is unreasonable. People make a great many reasonable choices under great mental strain.

The best argument against suicide and euthanasia appeals to the absolutist version of the Subject Value Account. But the Subject Value Account is implausible unless qualified to allow for the possibility that some killings are beneficial enough to outweigh lost subject value. Yet precisely this qualification is ruled out by absolutism. On the most plausible account of the wrongness of killing, the Combined Account, suicide and euthanasia are permissible if dying and our mode of dying benefit us, and if no moral agent is killed without her informed consent.

Given that suicide and euthanasia are permissible, the following policies are reasonable:

1. When people choose, competently and with adequate information, to kill themselves using some responsible method, they may proceed, and others may assist, at their request.
2. When people decide, competently and with adequate information, that they should be allowed to die, whether immediately or when some future contingency arises, and do not change their minds, others must comply.
3. When people decide, competently and with adequate information, that they should be killed using some responsible method, whether immediately or when some future contingency arises, and do not change their minds, others may comply.
4. When people are temporarily irrational when they choose to kill themselves or when they ask to be killed, others may not assist (unless palliation is appropriate); instead, they may interfere, and help them to regain their competence.

5. We should act in the best interests of those who cease to be competent without making known their preferences concerning their fates; we should also act in the best interests of those who have never been competent. Acting in their best interests may mean preserving their lives; however, in some cases it will mean passively or actively euthanizing them.

CHAPTER 9

Abortion

As a rule, killing people is terribly wrong. However, as noted in the last chapter, there are exceptions to the rule. Perhaps abortions that involve killing human beings who have not fully developed are among the exceptions. But aborting pregnancies does not always involve killings. In some abortions developing human beings are allowed to die, not killed. And some abortions occur before an individual is even partially developed. In such abortions, an individual is prevented from coming into existence, and what is killed is the tissue from which it is being formed.

I will not address many of the questions involved in the abortion controversy. If 'abortion' means the removal of a zygote, embryo, or early stage fetus from the uterus, my question only indirectly concerns abortion, since, in theory, these could be removed without killing them (if frozen or placed in an artificial womb), or killed without removing them from the uterus (which might occur when embryos developed *in vitro* are destroyed). My question concerns the killing itself (although, for convenience, I will use the term 'abortion' for the killing of developing human beings). Moreover, I will narrow my question in another way: the question I will attempt to answer in this chapter is whether killing a zygote, embryo, or fetus is *prima facie* directly wrong – *prima facie* wrong because of its effects on the subject who is killed, rather than because of its side effects. (As in previous chapters I will abbreviate '*prima facie* directly wrong' as 'directly wrong.') Thus, for example, I will not consider whether women have a right to abort their pregnancies regardless of the moral status of the developing human being (on that issue, see Thomson [1971] and Boonin [1997, 2002]).

ARGUMENTS AGAINST ABORTION

There are two main arguments for the view that killing human beings at the early stages of life is directly wrong. The first adopts the Subject Value

Account of the wrongness of killing, or some modification thereof, and condemns abortion on the grounds that fetuses (and perhaps embryos and zygotes) are intrinsically valuable subjects. The second assumes the Harm Account, or some modification thereof, and condemns abortion on the grounds that killing fetuses is extremely harmful to them, as it deprives them of lives that would have been of great value to them.

In this section I will review both arguments. Since the first argument appeals to the Subject Value Account, which was criticized in chapter 7, I will merely sketch the argument and its shortcomings. Then I will turn to the second, stronger, argument against abortion. Its own shortcomings I will consider later in the chapter.

The subject value approach

Some theorists reject abortion because they accept some version of the Subject Value Account of the wrongness of killing. On their view, it is wrong to destroy individuals who have substantial subject value or who would attain substantial subject value if not killed. We might call their argument the *subject value argument* against abortion; it can be formulated as follows:

1. It is directly wrong to kill any individual who would have gained or retained substantial intrinsic value as a subject if not killed, especially an individual whose subject value would have been absolute.
2. Human beings have substantial (and perhaps absolute) intrinsic value as subjects (or would if not killed).
3. Since abortion entails killing human beings, it is wrong.

However, as noted in chapters 7 and 8, the Subject Value Account (especially the version of it formulated in terms of absolute value) is vulnerable to powerful objections, even when reformulated as the Highest Subject Value Account, or when revised as the Hybrid Account. Hence the first premise of the subject value argument should be rejected, and the argument fails.

Let us see if we can find a better basis for objecting to abortion.

The harm approach

Are fetuses seriously harmed when killed? Marquis thinks so, and in a well known essay he objects to abortion precisely because it is bad for the fetus:

When I am killed, I am deprived both of what I now value which would have been part of my future personal life, but also what I would come to value. Therefore, when I die, I am deprived of all of the value of my future. Inflicting this loss on me is ultimately what makes killing me wrong. This being the case, it would seem that what makes killing any adult human being prima facie seriously wrong is the loss of his or her future ...

The claim that the primary wrong-making feature of a killing is the loss to the victim of the value of its future has obvious consequences for the ethics of abortion. The future of a standard fetus includes a set of experiences, projects, activities, and such which are identical with the futures of adult human beings and are identical with the futures of young children. Since the reason that is sufficient to explain why it is wrong to kill human beings after the time of birth is a reason that also applies to fetuses, it follows that abortion is prima facie seriously morally wrong. (1989, 190–192; compare 1994, 1995)

Killing fetuses harms them for the same reason killing mature human beings harms them: in both cases we *deprive individuals of good lives.* All things being equal, the earlier in life we kill an individual, the more we harm her, since the earlier in life her death comes, the greater the quantity of life, and goods it brings, which she loses. Hence, according to Marquis, killing fetuses is a grave wrong indeed. The claim that killing fetuses deprives them of lives like ours I will call the *comparable lives thesis.* The argument Marquis builds around this claim can be stated as follows:

1. Killing individuals is a serious direct wrong if it deprives them of lives like ours (Marquis's partial account of the wrongness of killing).
2. Killing fetuses typically deprives them of lives like ours (comparable lives thesis).
3. So killing fetuses is typically a serious direct wrong.

Call this the *comparable lives argument* against abortion. (Quinn 1984 considers it well before Marquis, see pp. 40–41; similar arguments are given by Feezell 1987, Stone 1987, 1994, and Schwarz 1990.) I will assess its premises shortly. First, however, let me make a few remarks in order to clarify Marquis's argument.

First, it may appear that premise 1 misstates Marquis's idea of harm. In speaking of what we value, as opposed to what is valuable *for* us, he leaves himself open to an alternative interpretation, namely that killing individuals is a serious direct wrong if it deprives them of a life they value or desire. However he explicitly rules out this interpretation: "it is the loss of the goods of one's future, not the interference with the fulfillment of a strong desire to live, which accounts ultimately for the wrongness of killing" (1989, 196).

Premise 2 includes the qualifier "typically" (corresponding to Marquis's term "standard" in "standard fetus") because not all fetuses come to have lives like yours and mine. Some die, and others develop into children with anencephaly (they lack a cerebrum or an entire brain), Tay-Sachs disease, and other grave conditions.

Many theorists criticize abortion on the grounds that fetuses are *potential* people whom it is wrong to kill. This criticism is often rejected, since the notion of a potential person is unclear (for discussion, see M.A. Warren 1973; Tooley 1983, ch. 6; and Pahel 1987). Notice, however, that the criticism can be restated so as to avoid this difficulty. The first step is to replace the claim

Abortion is objectionable because it sacrifices potential people

with the claim

Abortion is objectionable because it sacrifices the potential *lives* of fetuses.

The latter can then be restated in Marquis's way:

Abortion is objectionable because it deprives fetuses of the lives they would enjoy if not killed.

Hence it seems likely that critics who object to aborting potential people probably have the comparative lives argument in mind.

Critics of Marquis's comparable lives argument may attack its first or second premise. Let us consider both strategies, beginning with the second. We can discuss the first strategy later.

COMPARABLE LIVES THESIS

Let us assume, for now, that Marquis is right to condemn killing whenever it deprives individuals of lives like ours. Abortion will still be defensible if fetuses do not *have* lives like ours, for then they cannot be deprived of lives like ours. *Do* fetuses have the same sort of lives as us?

The personist and mindist responses

Not according to person and mind essentialists (discussed in chapter 2). Personists and mindists will argue that you and I are one sort of being with one sort of life, while fetuses are another, with a different sort of life, so that killing fetuses deprives them of lives that are not like ours. Let us see if this way of attacking the comparative lives thesis is plausible.

If mind essentialism is true, my life began when I was a mind within a late fetus's body. A late fetus is one that has acquired the capacity for consciousness; an early fetus lacks this capacity. If person essentialism is true, then my life began when I was a person occupying an infant body, and the relevant psychological connections were first laid down. Before that, there was a creature with a mind who lived briefly and was not able to lay down connections to me.

On certain assumptions, either view can be pressed against the comparable lives thesis. Suppose that everything with the property of mindedness has it as an essential property, so that, not just you and I, but anything minded has its mindedness as an essential attribute. It follows that although minded creatures may come to exist, nothing mindless can *become* minded (and that nothing mindless has the *potential* to be minded), assuming this entails that the mindless being is one and the same as the thing that is later minded, for if something is ever mindless, its mindedness would not be essential to it. Given that a creature needs a mind to enjoy a future like ours, then nothing unminded can enjoy such a future. So the comparable lives thesis is false (DeGrazia 2003, 427). Recapping:

1. Mindedness is essential to everything that has it.
2. So nothing mindless can become minded.
3. To enjoy lives like ours, early fetuses, which lack minds, must become minded.
4. So early fetuses can never enjoy lives like ours.
5. Hence killing them does not deprive them of lives like ours.

Call this the *mindist's reply*.

A similar argument is available to person essentialists. Suppose that the property of personhood is essential to everything that bears it. Then nothing can become a person, and no nonpersons can enjoy a future like ours. Spelled out, the argument is this:

1. Personhood is essential to everything that has it.
2. So no nonperson can become a person.
3. To enjoy lives like ours, early fetuses and early infants must become persons.
4. So early fetuses and early infants can never enjoy lives like ours.
5. Hence killing them does not deprive them of lives like ours.

Call this the *personist's reply* to the comparable lives thesis.

Of course, killing fetuses does have important consequences. Sometimes, for example, it will prevent a person from existing. But that is permissible. Another consequence is that it harms the fetus. But personists and mindists will say that the harm done to fetuses cannot be serious. Killing them is no more harmful than killing any other mindless nonpersons, and the latter, in turn, is far less harmful and therefore far less objectionable than killing beings like us.

Consider the following response to the personist's reply: If personhood is essential to everything that has it, then neither early fetuses nor infants can become persons. Yet eventually there are infant persons. That leaves a difficult question unanswered: What happens to the infant nonperson who is replaced by an infant person, and what sort of creature is it? If the infant nonperson is an animal, does it cease to exist with the arrival of the infant person? That is implausible; it is hard to see why gaining self-awareness ends an animal's existence. So does the infant nonperson continue to exist as an animal when the infant person arrives? If so, it would have to be an animal that is never self-aware, assuming that something is self-aware just in case it is a person, and personhood is essential to whatever has it.

Conceivably, mind essentialists could invoke this line of thought in order to show that their position is superior to person essentialism. Unlike person essentialists, they can say that late fetuses and infant nonpersons become persons, in the same sense that caterpillars are insects that become butterflies. However, animal essentialists will be ready to use a similar line of thought against mind essentialism. They will ask: What happens to the mindless fetus that is replaced by a minded fetus, and what sort of creature is it? If it is an animal, does it cease to exist when the fetus acquires a mind? Can gaining a mind really end an animal's existence? But it is also implausible to say that fetuses continue to exist as mindless animals with lives of their own. If we are not them, each of us shares his body with one of these dull-witted, oblivious beings. This is implausible on its face, and it leaves us with the odd task of justifying ourselves when we act against the interests of the human beings with whom we cohabit. Abortion may be harmless to creatures like us, but it is fatal to our human intimates. Shouldn't we refrain from aborting fetuses unless something very important is at stake, not because it could harm the likes of us, but because it would harm human beings?

Rather than accept these dubious consequences, perhaps it is better to accept animal essentialism, and say that fetuses are animals that acquire minds and eventually develop into persons. Yet this supports the comparable lives thesis: if fetuses are human beings like us, killing them deprives them of lives like ours. Marquis is back in business.

There may be another problem with the mindist and personist replies: it is not obvious why we should accept their first premises, the claims that mindedness and personhood are essential to every creature that bears these properties. Denying these claims is fatal to the mindist and personist replies; without their first premises, the replies are open to the objection that early fetuses can acquire mindedness and then personhood. Fetuses would come to possess these properties contingently rather than essentially. But they would possess them nonetheless, and in that case it seems plausible to say that killing them would deprive them of lives like ours.

However, the most likely route to mind essentialism is the combination of mindism and the assumption that anything minded is essentially minded (similarly, the likely route to person essentialism is the combination of personism and the assumption that anything that is a person is essentially a person). Still, mind essentialism does not entail that everything minded is essentially minded. (Nor does person essentialism entail that every person is essentially a person.) Mind essentialism is consistent with the possibility that some things have mindedness, or will come to have it, as a contingent feature. Nothing can acquire a property as an essential feature, but that does not preclude the acquisition, as a contingent feature, of a property that is essential to something else. Perhaps the capacity for photosynthesis is essential to trees and other plants; but even if it is, it is entirely conceivable that I might be genetically altered so as to gain this capacity as a contingent property.

The gradualist response

We just saw that mind and person essentialists have trouble explaining what early fetuses are, and what happens to them when minds develop. Critics of abortion can fill that gap; appealing to animal essentialism, they can defend the comparable lives thesis on the following basis:

(a) You and I are the same animals as the fetuses we once were.
(b) So the fetuses we were have the same lives as we do.
(c) So killing fetuses typically deprives them of lives like ours (the comparable lives thesis).

However, this argument is not decisive. Even if we accept animal essentialism, we can resist the comparable lives thesis on the basis of *metaphysical gradualism*, which says that fetuses are not *fully* human beings, and hence not fully subjects who may or may not be harmed. Warren Quinn puts the view this way:

The fetus is a human being in the making, a partly but not fully real individual human being. However, the fetus is also a full-fledged fetus, fully satisfying the appropriate criteria ... While it is correct to see a full-fledged biological organism from conception on, it is wrong to interpret "biological organism," in this sense, as a substance sortal. It is more naturally seen, the process theory will insist, as a mock-generic sortal that stands to "human being" in the way that "construction" stands to "house." A fetus is indeed a full-fledged organism, but this is quite consistent with the claim that such a full-fledged organism is not a fully real individual. (1984, 39–40)

Although fetuses are human beings, like you and me, this property is acquired gradually. Compare the property of being a house or bridge: for a period of time certain materials are gathered, and some of them are attached to others; eventually a house-in-progress emerges; only later is there a house (full stop). Like houses, human beings come into existence progressively. At one point a sperm enters an egg, and their genetic materials are combined. The resulting zygote splits, and splits again, eventually forming a mass of eight cells, each of which, if separated from the others, could itself begin the process of forming a human being. If instead the mass continues to develop, eventually it forms an embryo, which, until roughly two weeks, will sometimes divide into two embryos, producing twins. If instead the embryo continues to develop, it eventually forms the fetus. Until week two it is an indeterminate matter how many human beings are developing. But not until late in the life of the fetus does a fully formed human being emerge, according to Quinn.

Since human-beings-in-progress, like other animals-in-progress, are not yet individuals whose existence can be ended, they cannot yet be harmed by being deprived of their lives. Metaphysical gradualism supports *value gradualism*: the harmfulness of interrupting the development of a human being depends on its degree of completion; precluding the developmental process before it has even begun is entirely harmless; ending that process soon after it gets under way is negligibly harmful; but ending it when it is nearly complete is just about as harmful as ending it after its completion.

The gradualist view is consistent with a range of ideas about when fully formed human beings come to exist. Presumably, human beings are fully formed before self-awareness begins; neonates are capable of self-awareness probably no earlier than 15 months of age, which is when they can pass Gallup's (1970) test: they can use a mirror to locate marks on their nose (Butterworth 1992). Quinn suggests that "the becoming process is over when the higher nervous system is developed enough for the organism to start learning, in the fashion of the normal neonate, the ways of the world." It is not easy to say when normal human learning becomes possible, since learning begins gradually, too. Neonate learning depends on the elaboration of the dendrites of cortical neurons, which is greatly accelerated during the third trimester of gestation (Super, Soriano, and Uylings 1998, Eyre, Miller, Clowry, Conway, and Watts 2000) and most substantial during the first six months after birth (Rakic 2002, Nimchinsky, Sabatini, and Svoboda 2002). Hence we can give only a rough answer to the question of when normal neonate learning becomes possible: towards the end of the third trimester.

It seems reasonable to suppose that human beings are fully formed when they develop minds, and that fetuses develop minds roughly towards the end of the third trimester, too. It is no coincidence that minds develop about the same time learning begins: the sort of learning that is relevant to the advent of fully formed human beings is possible only when the mind develops.

Suppose that a fetus can be deprived of a human life only after it is a fully formed human being. Then if gradualism and animal essentialism are correct, killing fetuses does not deprive them of lives like ours.

THE COMPARABLE LIVES ARGUMENT

Recall that the comparable lives argument against abortion is this:

1. Killing individuals is a serious direct wrong if it deprives them of lives like ours (Marquis's partial account of killing).
2. Killing fetuses typically deprives them of lives like ours (comparable lives thesis).
3. So killing fetuses is typically a serious direct wrong.

In this part of the chapter I will consider the plausibility of its first premise, which endorses Marquis's account of killing.

Marquis's account of killing rests on the following argument:

(a) Killing individuals is a serious direct wrong when it seriously harms them.
(b) Killing individuals seriously harms them when it deprives them of lives like ours.

(c) So killing individuals is a serious direct wrong when it deprives them of lives like ours.

In chapter 7 we rejected premise (a), which is implied by the Harm Account of killing, roughly on the grounds that the wrongness of killing competent subjects depends not just on the harm it does them, but also on whether they consent to being killed. The view we defended in chapter 7 is as follows:

> *Combined Account*: If S is an incompetent subject, killing S is directly wrong just in case (and to the extent that) it harms S; if S is competent, killing S at time T is directly wrong just in case S has not made an informed choice to be killed at T.

On this approach, an acceptable alteration of (a) is available; namely, that killing individuals is a serious direct wrong when it seriously harms them unless it is with their competent, informed consent, which fetuses cannot provide. This assumption then positions Marquis to revise his argument against abortion, as follows:

1′. Killing individuals is a serious direct wrong when it deprives them of lives like ours unless it is with their competent, informed consent (revision of Marquis's account of killing).
2′. Killing fetuses typically deprives them of lives like ours, and does so without their consent (which of course they cannot give).
3′. So killing fetuses is typically a serious direct wrong.

Critics attack Marquis's account of killing by rejecting the most vulnerable assumption upon which it rests, which is (b), the generalization that individuals are seriously harmed when deprived of lives like ours. Anyone who agrees with comparativism will accept this generalization, but Marquis's critics argue that comparativism must be modified. I will consider various modifications which would be damaging for Marquis's position. The first is based on interest actualism.

Actualist comparativism

According to interest actualism (discussed in chapter 5), our welfare is affected only by the intrinsic values for us which our lives would have during periods of time when we are *actually* capable of incurring harm or benefit. Since we actually have this capacity only while we exist, what advances desires we would have developed if not killed has no bearing on our welfare.

If correct, interest actualism forces us to modify comparativism. Earlier (in chapter 5) we formulated the modified view this way:

Actualist comparativism: E's value for S equals the intrinsic value for S of S's life in WE, the actual world (in which E occurs), minus the intrinsic value for S of S's life in the closest world, W~E, in which E does not occur excluding any intrinsic value S would accrue in W~E after S ceases to be responsive in WE.

As an illustration, suppose that you are killed today, and that you would have lived during period PT had you not been killed. According to interest actualism, when we assess the value being killed has for you, we are to ignore the value for you of your life during PT. Whether killing you would cause you great losses or great gains during PT has no bearing on the value of killing you. By contrast, winning the lottery would be very good for you, since the sum of the values each period of your life would have if you won greatly exceeds the sum of the values each period would have if you did not win.

Even if metaphysical gradualism is false, and early and late term fetuses alike have futures like ours, actualists can acknowledge that killing fetuses typically deprives them of lives like ours yet deny that they are substantially harmed. Killed, fetuses never actually develop desires like ours; impediments to these (merely hypothetical) desires is harmless. Assessed solely in terms of the desires such fetuses actually develop, their deaths are only slightly bad for them. This gives us a reply to Marquis: despite the fact that killing fetuses precludes their enjoying lives like ours, killing them is not seriously bad for them, and hence not a serious direct wrong.

By the same token, impediments to desires which death prevents you and me from developing are harmless. Doesn't this show that killing *us* is not seriously bad for us, and that killing normal adult human beings is not significantly worse than killing fetuses? Not if priorism (chapter 6) is correct; even if impediments to our hypothetical desires are not bad for us, killing us harms us far more than killing fetuses harms fetuses. For we develop far more sophisticated desires before we are killed than do fetuses; given our greater stake in survival, dying is a greater blow to us.

Since it implies that aborting fetuses is always quite harmless, actualism seems to constitute strong grounds for permitting abortion. However, we saw earlier (in chapter 5) that actualism is subject to serious doubts. Still, if actualists can find ways around the objections, they can reject Marquis's account of harm on the grounds that fetuses may be harmlessly deprived of lives like ours.

Interest relativism

There may be other grounds for modifying comparativism. Recall that in chapter 4 we contrasted temporally relative assessments of well-being, which emphasize our welfare as it is at some particular time, with temporally neutral assessments, which weighs our welfare at each time equally. Perhaps we should assess our welfare in a temporally relative way. If so, we may conclude that the loss of a life like ours is not very bad for us.

This is precisely what McMahan proposes. As we mentioned in chapter 7, McMahan recommends weighing the harmfulness of being killed in terms of its effect on our *time-relative* interests, which are assessed using interest relativism, and not in terms of its effect on our *interests*, which are assessed using the comparativist account. (McInerney [1990] and Stretton [2004] also appeal to interest relativism.) In turn, he builds this idea into his account of the wrongness of killing subjects like fetuses that fall below the threshold of respect, as follows:

> *Time Relative Account of Killing*: Killing subjects that are beneath the threshold of respect is directly wrong just in case (and to the extent that) it has a negative time-relative value for them.

On this approach, we assess the wrongness of killing fetuses and infants from their standpoint at the time we perform the action that is fatal to them. We make our assessment in two stages. First we examine the value of the life they would have had; if positive, we can tentatively conclude that depriving them of this life is harmful and hence objectionable, as comparativism suggests. But our tentative conclusion is subject to revision at the second stage. Here we discount for lack of connectedness.

McMahan's account allows us to admit that killing late fetuses generally deprives them of valuable lives, yet deny that it is a serious direct wrong. Since minded fetuses have few connections to the persons they might become, depriving them of lives like ours is not nearly as harmful to them as depriving us of our lives harms us. (Stretton [2004] defends abortion on similar grounds.)

McMahan defends his analysis of killing partly on the grounds that his account of harm, interest relativism, is more plausible than the comparativist account of harm. This latter claim, in turn, is based on the grounds that it is the best explanation of various intuitive claims, including the view that it is reasonable to reject the following Cure (2002, 77):

> *The Cure*: "Imagine that you are twenty years old and are diagnosed with a disease that, if untreated, invariably causes death (though not pain or disability) within five years. There is a treatment that reliably cures the disease but also, as a side effect, causes total retrograde amnesia and radical personality change. Long-term studies of others who have had the treatment show that they almost always go on to have long and happy lives, though these lives are informed by desires and values that differ profoundly from those that the person had prior to treatment. You can therefore reasonably expect that, if you take the treatment, you will live for roughly sixty more years, though the life you will have will be utterly discontinuous with your life as it has been. You will remember nothing of your past and your character and values will be radically altered. Suppose, however, that this can be reliably predicted: that the future you would have between the ages of twenty and eighty if you were to take the treatment would, by itself, be better, as a whole, than your entire life will be if you do not take the treatment."

As McMahan says, if we assess welfare in accordance with time-relative interests, not interests, dying is worse for a child or adult than for a fetus, and the Cure would not benefit you.

However, assessing welfare McMahan's way has highly counterintuitive consequences. To see why, let us adjust the Cure example a bit:

> *Post-Cure Killing*: While you were incapacitated, concerned relatives authorized your physician to Cure you, and you were given the treatment on Saturday. The effects on your memory and personality will occur next Tuesday, after which point your life as a profoundly different but happy person is expected to begin. On Monday, however, I kill you in your sleep.

I have precluded your enjoying nearly sixty years of happiness. Surely that is very bad for you. But the harm is negligible if we measure in terms of your time-relative interests, since one day after I kill you the Cure would have drastically changed your personality.

Consider another modification of the Post-Cure Killing example:

> *Post-Cure Poisoning*: This example is like the Post-Cure Killing case, except that instead of killing you, I poison you in your sleep. In the

immediate future, the poison I use will cause you to have fewer headaches, and no other perceptible symptoms, but later, after your personality is completely transformed, it will kill you.

Did I harm you? If we assess your interests relative to the time I slip you the poison, McMahan's account says, once again, that what I have done is not very bad for you. That cannot be right.

Would it help McMahan if we assessed your interests relative to the time the poison kills you? That would undermine McMahan's position that your welfare *then* should be sharply discounted *now*.

McMahan's analysis of the *wrongness* (versus the harmfulness) of killing seems flawed, too. Consider an example:

> *Poisoned Fetus*: I give the fetus you carry a poison that will have no noticeable effect until the fetus develops into a three year old child or an adult, at which time the poison will be fatal.

I end the life of a three-year-old child by giving it a slow-acting poison while it is a fetus. That is both a grave harm and a grave wrong, but it has little impact on the time-relative interests of the fetus. Doesn't the child's lost life count fully against my killing the fetus? Apparently it will not – if we accept McMahan's Time-Relative Account of Killing.

There is a way to argue for neglecting the harm to the child. The argument starts with the following principle, which nearly anyone will accept:

> *Prevention Principle*: In itself, acting in such a way as to prevent someone from coming into existence, or failing to act in a way that would bring him into existence, is never wrong.

Unless this principle is true, it would be wrong not to have as many kids as we can. We accept the Prevention Principle at least in part because we accept the following principle as well:

> Subjects who never exist cannot be harmed.

Suppose that the child is not the same person as the fetus. Given the Prevention Principle, harm to the child drops out of the picture. While killing the fetus is objectionable in view of the harm it does the fetus, the killing prevents the child from existing, or being harmed. However, this argument is not available to McMahan or anyone else who thinks that the fetus and child are one and the *same*.

Actualist interest relativism

McMahan offers a response to examples like Fetal Poisoning. He considers the following case:

> *Prenatal Injury*: A pregnant woman chooses to take a mood-altering drug, knowing that this will damage the reproductive system of the fetus she is carrying in a way that will cause it to be sterile later in life.

He notes that the time-relative interests of the fetus are little affected by the drug, and that his Time-Relative Account of Killing might therefore suggest that the woman's action is not seriously wrong. Quite reasonably, he admits that her actions *would* be seriously wrong, and says that, in moral assessments, we must fully weigh all of the effects of our actions, and not discount for lack of connectedness. The full harmfulness of damaging her fetus counts against the pregnant woman's decision to use drugs. He goes on to ask: "How, then could it be morally permissible to kill a developed fetus but not to cause it some nonlethal harm?" (2002, 280). Here is his answer:

> Whereas abortion affects its victim only when the victim is a fetus with weak time-relative interests, prenatal harm affects its victim later, when the victim is a person whose time-relative interests are much stronger. In the case of a late abortion, the only time-relative interest that can be satisfied or frustrated by one's action is the comparatively weak time-relative interest the developed fetus has now in continuing to live. For if an abortion is performed, the fetus will not have any future time-relative interests …
>
> In the case of prenatal injury, by contrast, one's action affects not only the weaker time-relative interests concerning its own future that the developed fetus has now, but also the stronger time-relative interests it will have later as an older child or adult. If our concern is with individuals' time-relative interests, we must take account of all the time-relative interests affected by our action. (2002, 282–283)

On the next page he adds:

> The defense of abortion does not depend on discounting the fetus's future interests. It appeals only to the fact that the fetus's present time-relative interest in continuing to live is weak. Abortion cannot be contrary to the fetus's future interests because it effectively prevents them from ever arising. (2002, 284)

McMahan is saying two things. First, in moral assessments, we must give full weight to all of the effects our action has on a subject, including its future effects, without discounting for psychological disconnection.

Second, in moral assessments, we should ignore the effects our treatment would have had on a person at times when she will not actually exist, since she lacks interests at those times, and no one is harmed (benefited) by what advances (impedes) interests she will not actually have. Hence abortion "cannot be contrary to the fetus's future interests." If we abort a fetus, we can ignore the fact that the fetus would have developed into someone with various interests which the killing would have been against, since the fetus never will develop those interests. The salient principle here is interest actualism: our welfare is not affected by what advances (impedes) interests we will not actually have but would have had if we had existed.

To accommodate interest actualism, we would need to restate McMahan's account. As it stands, his account can be formulated as follows (in nonbranching cases):

> *Interest Relativism*: The time-relative value which E occurring at time T has for S, $RV(S,E,T)$, equals the intrinsic value for S relative-to-time-T of S's life in WE, the actual world (in which E occurs), minus the intrinsic value for S relative-to-time-T of S's life in the closest world, $W{\sim}E$, in which E does not occur.

Restated, it would look something like this:

> *Actualist Interest Relativism*: The actualist time-relative value which E occurring at time T has for S, $ARV(S,E,T)$, equals the intrinsic value for S relative-to-time-T of S's life in WE, the actual world (in which E occurs), minus the intrinsic value for S relative-to-time-T of S's life in the closest world, $W{\sim}E$, in which E does not occur *excluding* any intrinsic value S accrues in $W{\sim}E$ after S is no longer responsive in WE. That is, if $T(S,W)$ is the last time S is responsive in world W, and $RIV[S,W,T,T(S,W)]$ is the intrinsic value for S relative-to-time-T of S's life in world W *excluding* any intrinsic value S accrues in W after $T(S,W)$, then $ARV(S,E,T) = RIV(S,WE,T) - RIV[S,W{\sim}E,T,T(S,W)]$.

On this analysis, we are not harmed by what would deprive us of goods (nor benefited by what would preclude our suffering evils) during a period of time if we are actually dead during that time. Nevertheless, dying can harm me by impeding desires I now have (given priorism). The same goes for fetuses, but we can assume that their present desires are insubstantial. Moreover, the Prenatal Injury would seriously harm the fetus in its future. Assuming all of its interests matter from the moral point of view, the Prenatal Injury is seriously objectionable.

McMahan seems to accept interest actualism because examples like Prenatal Injury force him to say that "morality requires us to show the same respect for an individual's future time-relative interests as we must show for his present ones" (2002, 193). Given this view, the unmodified form of his interest-relative account of harm implies that abortion is seriously wrong. Interest actualism gets him back into the fray.

That said, McMahan's appeal to interest actualism is surprising for several reasons (and not just because, as we saw in chapter 5, interest actualism has counterintuitive consequences).

First, McMahan does not seem to notice that interest actualism is inconsistent with his interest-relativist view (the view he calls the "Time-Relative Interest Account"), which says that the harmfulness of death *is* largely determined by its effect on interests we would have had had we not died. He illustrates his interest-relativist view with the following example:

Young Cancer Patient: A man dies of cancer at the age of twenty.

According to McMahan, "to determine how bad death is for the Young Cancer Patient, one must compare his death with what would have happened to him had he not died when he did; assuming he would have had a long, rich life, the later bits well connected to the earlier bits, his death harmed him grievously" (2002, 106; compare what he says on p. 165: "it is worse for one person to die at thirty than it is for another to die at eighty: the one suffers a greater loss or misfortune than the other," and on p. 182: "the loss of future goods that are undesired at the time of death can contribute to the badness of death"). All of this is correct if we accept his original interest-relativist view of interests, but not if we replace it with actualist interest relativism. According to interest actualism, the Patient's death cannot be contrary to his future interests, "because it effectively prevents them from ever arising."

Not only is interest actualism inconsistent with his view that the Young Cancer Patient's loss of many good years of life adds to the harmfulness of his death, it is also in tension with his claim that "even if an animal would be slightly more closely related in the ways that matter to itself in the future than an infant would be, the amount of good that an infant or fetus loses by dying is vastly greater" (2002, 199). The tension exists if we assume that killing either precludes it from having future interests.

Third, if interest actualism is correct, there are no good grounds for accepting McMahan's interest relativist view: the combination of interest actualism and comparativism is at least as plausible as the actualist version of interest relativism. Combined with comparativism, interest actualism gives us the view which earlier we called actualist comparativism:

> *Actualist Comparativism*: E's value for S equals the intrinsic value for S of S's life in the actual world WE, in which E occurs, minus the intrinsic value for S of S's life in the closest world, W∼E, in which E does not occur *excluding any intrinsic value S would accrue in W∼E after S ceases to be responsive in WE.*

To see that this view is as plausible as McMahan's, consider his main complaints against comparativism: it implies that a fetus's death is worse than a child's, it overestimates the harmfulness of what is done to animals with low degrees of psychological unity, and it implies that refusing the Cure is irrational.

According to actualist comparativism, dying is typically worse for a child than for a fetus. In assessing the values of their deaths, we ignore the interests which the child and the fetus would have had if they had not died. We consider only the interests each actually had, which are their *antemortem* interests: interests they had before they died. Given preferentialism, those interests are determined by their antemortem desires, or some idealization of these. Assuming that dying is against the pre-death interests of children and adults but not of fetuses, or that dying more seriously impairs the pre-death interests of children and adults than it does the pre-death interests of fetuses, then dying is worse for children than for fetuses.

The animal McMahan describes in the following passage also has little stake in remaining alive:

> *Isolated Animal*: "Imagine a sentient creature whose mental life consists of a stream of consciousness without any psychological connections. It lives entirely in the ... 'specious present' ... It is not self-conscious and has no conception of the future. Not only does it have no memory or foresight, it also has no psychological architecture to carry forward: no structure of beliefs, desires, attitudes, dispositions, or traits of character. All it has, we may suppose, are experiences. But most of these experiences are extremely pleasant." (2002, 75)

According to McMahan, "our intuitive sense is that the reason to care for its sake is absolutely minimal" (2002, 76). If this means that killing Isolated Animals does not substantially harm them, then interest actualists will concur: we cannot impair the post-death interests of Isolated Animals, since they have none, which means that the only complaint against killing them is that it would impair their pre-death interests, which are likely to be quite minimal. To be sure, not killing them benefits them. But the benefit is not great – it is not on a par with the benefit you and I enjoy from living – assuming, as interest actualists may, that wholly disconnected lives are not nearly as valuable as ones that are unified as our lives are.

As for the Cure: given actualist comparativism, you are bound to be somewhat ambivalent about such a 'treatment,' which is no objection to this view, since, I suspect, ambivalence is our intuitive response to the case. If you reject the Cure, your death within five years will impede your near-term (pre-death) interests, but at least you will have about five years to advance them. Taking the Cure will have a great impact on your near-term interests, since, immediately upon being Cured, you will be unable to advance them. Thus, considering your near-term interests only, it is better not to take the Cure. What about the interests of your future self? These are harmlessly impeded if you opt out of the Cure, since you will die before they are formed. But, once Cured, you will be greatly benefited by advancing them. Thus, from the standpoint of the interests of your future self, taking the Cure is greatly beneficial, and refusing it is harmless. If you focus on the fact that refusing the Cure is harmless to your future self and very harmful in terms of your near-term interests, you will be inclined to refuse it. If you emphasize that the Cure is greatly beneficial to you in the long run despite the fact that it seriously impedes your near-term interests, you will be inclined to take it. Now suppose that you also strongly prefer that your life be unified. Then the Cure will be correspondingly less beneficial to you; so much so, perhaps, that you *might* refuse it even if you are focusing on your long-term interests.

Present desire comparativism

David Boonin, another critic of Marquis, thinks it is wrong to deprive subjects of further life just when they *value* or *desire* that life (compare Tooley 1972 and Quinn's reservations 1984), and that his view, unlike Marquis's, supports the permissibility of abortion.

Boonin defends his analysis by noting that, although it supports abortion, it has the same implications as Marquis's in key test cases, such as infants, suicidal teenagers, temporarily comatose adults, and you and me. On Boonin's view, being deprived of a future like ours is objectionable in these test cases because the subjects involved desire to preserve their lives. Even comatose subjects desire to live, he says: their desire is *dispositional* or unconscious rather than occurrent or conscious, much like the desire you and I have while we are sleeping (2002, 64–70). Suicidal teenagers have what Boonin calls an *ideal* desire to live, which he describes as follows:

The actual content of people's desires arise under imperfect conditions, such as a lack of accurate information, and we can define their ideal desires as their actual desires idealized, where this involves 'correcting' the actual content of their actual desires to account for the various distorting effects that such imperfect conditions may have caused. (2002, 71)

What of infants? Perhaps, as Michael Tooley (1983) argued, they cannot actually desire to live because they lack the requisite conceptual apparatus, but they do have an ideal desire to live:

The newborn infant does not yet possess the concept of himself as a continuing subject of experience, and it is true that he does not understand that death involves the annihilation of such a subject ... But if he did understand these things, he would surely desire that his future personal life be preserved since he would understand that this is necessary in order for him to enjoy the experiences that he does already consciously desire to enjoy. (2002, 84)

By contrast, an early fetus lacks any actual desires, whether occurrent or dispositional. It therefore has no desires concerning its future, "whose content may have been distorted by various sorts of imperfect conditions." Hence "there is no other such desire that it would now have instead under more ideal circumstances" (2002, 83).

How plausible is Boonin's contention that abortion is permissible even though it deprives fetuses of futures like ours? He says that the wrongness of killing subjects depends on whether they "desire" or "value" their lives, but this may or may not mean that their lives are valuable *for* them. Hence it is not clear whether Boonin thinks that fetuses are harmed as badly as we are when killed. If they are, it would be odd to deny that abortion is objectionable, at least without further explanation. However, I suspect that Boonin thinks that the futures of subjects are valuable *for* them only if they *value* them, or would ideally desire them. (Others have defended views much like this; e.g., Cigman [1981] and Harris [1984].) On this interpretation, he wants to modify comparativism in something like the following way:

Present Desire Comparativism: An event or state of affairs E occurring at time T harms a subject S if and only if, at T, S ideally desires the life S would have if E did not hold and ideally prefers it to the life S would have if E held. E benefits S if and only if S ideally desires the life S would have if E held and ideally prefers it to the life S would have if E did not hold. How much E harms or benefits S depends on the strengths of S's idealized desire and preferences.

Boonin pairs this analysis with the Harm Account of killing, and concludes that the wrongness of killing a subject S at a time T turns on whether S (ideally) desires the life S would have if not killed, and prefers this to the life S would have if killed. Thus interpreted, Boonin's view still faces two serious difficulties.

The first concerns the combination of the Harm Account with present desire comparativism. My lack of even an ideal desire to live on does not show that killing me is unobjectionable. Surely, as the Consent Account suggests, it is impermissible to kill competent beings when they withhold consent. Those who lack the desire to live might still withhold consent.

Second, Boonin has not made it clear that infants have an ideal desire for further life. He attributes this desire to them on the grounds that living on would help them to satisfy some of their desires. But cats, too, have various desires that would be served by further life, yet Boonin would not say they (ideally) desire to live. Some of their desires would be better served if they were able to drive cars, too (it would be a handy way to escape the neighborhood dog), but surely it does not follow that they have an ideal desire to drive. Presumably, we think cats lack the desire to live because they are not capable of forming any preference as to whether or not to live. But that is true of infants as well. (Do we ideally desire to live at T just in case not dying at T benefits us? In that case it is hard to see why present desire comparativism is preferable to ordinary comparativism, and Boonin's case for abortion collapses since fetuses *will* benefit from further life.)

SUMMARY

The comparable lives argument makes the strongest case against the permissibility of abortion. Pairing comparativism with the Harm Account of killing, it says that abortion seriously harms fetuses by depriving them of lives like ours, and killing is directly wrong when it is seriously harmful. This claim needs revision, since the Harm Account is overly simple, but the revision does not undermine the argument. Given the Combined Account which was defended in chapter 7, the comparable lives argument can say that aborting a fetus seriously harms it by depriving it of a life like ours and that killing an individual is a serious direct wrong when it seriously harms him unless it is with his competent, informed consent, which, of course, a fetus cannot provide. But *are* fetuses deprived of lives like ours when killed? Person and mind essentialists do not think so; for them, you and I are one sort of being with one sort of life, while fetuses are another, with a different sort of life. However, mindists and personists cannot easily explain what early fetuses are, and what happens to them when they acquire minds. Animal essentialism can be deployed against abortion, since it says that you and I once were fetuses. Nevertheless, animalists do not have to reject abortion. They can accept metaphysical gradualism, which says that fetuses are human-beings-in-progress; on this view fetuses are not yet individuals whose existence can be ended, and so they cannot yet be harmed by being deprived of their lives.

There are other ways to resist the comparable lives argument. We can attack comparativism.

One way is to deploy interest actualism against it, a strategy that was criticized in chapter 5. According to actualism, what advances desires we would have developed if not killed has no bearing on our welfare. Hence abortion is not very harmful: the desires the fetus would have developed will go unfulfilled, but this is not against its interests.

Another way is to deploy interest relativism against comparativism. The relativist assesses the harmfulness of killing fetuses and infants from their standpoint at the time we act to kill them, and discounts harm done to the fetus later in life, as the former is disconnected psychologically from the latter. This is McMahan's approach. Interest relativism has implausible consequences, discussed in chapter 5. McMahan's preferred analysis of the wrongness of killing fetuses is counterintuitive as well. Worse: to respond to worries such as Prenatal Injury, he retreats to interest actualism. Yet his approach is no better than the pairing of actualism with comparativism.

Finally, we can modify comparativism drawing on the claim that depriving subjects of life is directly wrong just when they value or desire that life, or rather just when they have an ideal desire to live. Since fetuses lack this kind of desire, and infants, depressed teenagers, and you and I do not, we can conclude that killing fetuses is all right. However, this argument has flaws, one of which is that it is hard to see why infants should be attributed an ideal desire for further life. While it is true that living on would satisfy some of their actual desires, the same seems true of cats.

References

Ad Hoc Committee of the Harvard Medical School to Examine the Definition of Brain Death, 1968, "A Definition of Irreversible Coma – Report of the Ad Hoc Committee of the Harvard Medical School to Examine the Definition of Brain Death," *Journal of the American Medical Association* 205: 337–340.

Adams, Robert, 1999, *Finite and Infinite Goods: A Framework for Ethics*, Oxford: Oxford University Press.

Agich, George, and Jones, Royce, 1986, "Personal Identity and Brain Death," *Philosophy and Public Affairs* 15: 267–274.

Allsopp, Richard, Vaziri, Homayoun, Patterson, Christopher, et al., 1992, "Telomere Length Predicts Replicative Capacity of Human Fibroblasts," *Proceedings of the National Academy of Sciences USA* 89: 10114–10118.

Alvarez, A. Alfred, 1971, *The Savage God: A Study of Suicide*, London: Weidenfeld & Nicholson.

Andersson, Malte, 1984, "The Evolution of Eusociality," *Annual Review of Ecology and Systematics* 15: 165–189.

Arras, John, 1998, "Physician-Assisted Suicide: A Tragic View," in Battin, M. Pabst, Rhodes, Rosamond, and Silvers, Anita, eds., *Physician Assisted Suicide: Expanding the Debate*, New York and London: Routledge, 279–300.

Baker, Lynne, 2000, *Persons and Bodies: A Constitution View*, Cambridge: Cambridge University Press.

Barry, Robert, 1992, "The Paradoxes of 'Rational' Death," *Society* 25–28.

Bates, David, 2001, "The Prognosis of Medical Coma," *Journal of Neurology and Neurosurgical Psychiatry* 71 (suppl. I): 120–123.

Battin, M. Pabst, 1982, *Ethical Issues in Suicide*, Englewood Cliffs: Prentice-Hall.

Battin, M. Pabst, and Mayo, D.J., eds., 1980, *Suicide: The Philosophical Issues*, London: Peter Owen.

Beck, Aaron, Kovacs, Maria, and Weissman, Arlene, 1996, "Hopelessness and Suicidal Behavior: An Overview," in Maltsberger and Goldblatt 1996, 331–341. First published in *Journal of the American Medical Association* 234 (1975): 1146–1149.

Belshaw, Christopher, 2000, "Death, Pain, and Time," *Philosophical Studies* 97: 317–341.

forthcoming, *Annihilation: The Sense and Significance of Death*, Acumen Press.

Benatar, David, ed., 2004, *Life, Death, and Meaning*, Lanham: Rowman & Littlefield Publishers, Inc.

Bernard, Claude, 1878–9, *Lessons on the Phenomena of Life Common to Animals and Vegetables*, 2 vols., Paris: Librairie J. B. Bailliere et Fil.

Bernat, James, 2006, "The Whole-Brain Concept of Death Remains Optimum Public Policy," *Journal of Law, Medicine and Ethics* 34.1: 35–43.

Bernat, James, Culver, C.M., and Gert, B., 1981, "On the Definition and Criterion of Death," *Annals of Internal Medicine* 94: 389–394.

Bishop, John, 1989, *Natural Agency*, Cambridge: Cambridge University Press.

Black, Henry, 1968, *Black's Law Dictionary* (4th edn.), St. Paul, MN: West Publishing Co.

Boden, Margaret, ed., 1996, *The Philosophy of Artificial Life*, Oxford: Oxford University Press.

Bodnar, Andrea, Ouellelte, Michel, Frolkis, Maria, et al., 1998, "Extension of Life-span by Introduction of Telomerase into Normal Human Cells," *Science* 279: 349–352.

Boonin, David, 1997, "A Defense of 'A Defense of Abortion': On the Responsibility Objection to Thomson's Argument," *Ethics* 107.2: 286–313.

2002, *A Defense of Abortion*, Cambridge: Cambridge University Press.

Bostrom, Nick, 2005, "A History of Transhumanist Thought," *Journal of Evolution and Technology* 14.1: 1–25.

Bradley, B., 2004, "When Is Death Bad for the One Who Dies?," *Noûs* 38: 1–28.

Brandt, Richard, 1975, "The Morality and Rationality of Suicide," in Battin and Mayo 1980, 117–132.

Brazier, M., 1987, *Medicine, Patients and the Law*, Harmondsworth: Penguin.

Bremer, Frederic, 1929, "Cerveau 'Isole' et Physiologie du Sommeil," *Comptes Rendus des Séances de la Societé de Biologie et de ses Filiales*: 102: 1235–1241.

Brock, Dan, 1992, "Voluntary Active Euthanasia," *Hastings Center Report* 22.2: 10–22.

Brock, Dan, and Buchanan, Allen, 1989, *Deciding for Others: The Ethics of Surrogate Decision Making*, Cambridge and New York: Cambridge University Press.

Brueckner, Anthony, and Fischer, John, 1986, "Why Is Death Bad?," *Philosophical Studies* 50: 213–227.

1998, "Being Born Earlier," *Australasian Journal of Philosophy* 76.1: 110–114.

Buchanan, Allen, 1988, "Advance Directives and the Personal Identity Problem," *Philosophy and Public Affairs* 17.4: 277–302.

Butterworth, George, 1992, "Origins of Self-Perception in Infancy," *Psychological Inquiry* 3.2: 103–111.

Cairns-Smith, Graham, 1982, *Genetic Takeover and the Mineral Origins of Life*, Cambridge: Cambridge University Press.

Callahan, Joan C., 1987, "On Harming the Dead," *Ethics* 97.2: 341–352.

Carson, Thomas, 2000, *Value and the Good Life*, Notre Dame: University of Notre Dame Press.

Carter, W.R., 1982, "Do Zygotes Become People?," *Mind* 91: 77–95.

Chen, Jun, and Goligorski, Michael, 2006, "Premature Senescence of Endothelial Cells: Methuselah's Dilemma," *American Journal of Physiology, Heart and Circulatory Physiology* 290: 1729–1739.

Cholbi, Michael, 2000, "Kant and the Irrationality of Suicide," *History of Philosophy Quarterly* 17.2: 159–176.

Christman, John, ed., 1989, *The Inner Citadel: Essays on Individual Autonomy*, Oxford: Oxford University Press.

Cigman, Ruth, 1981, "Death, Misfortune, and Species Inequality," *Philosophy and Public Affairs* 10: 47–64.

Clare, Anthony, 1975, *Psychiatry in Dissent*, London: Tavistock.

Darwin, Charles, 1859, *On the Origin of Species by Means of Natural Selection*, London: John Murray.

Davidson, Donald, 1987, "Knowing One's Own Mind," in *Proceedings and Addresses of the American Philosophical Association* 61: 441–458, reprinted in Davidson, Donald, *Subjective, Intersubjective, Objective*, Oxford: Clarendon Press, 2001.

Davis, John, 2007, "Precedent Autonomy, Advance Directives, and End-of-Life Care," in *Steinbock 2007*, 349–374.

Dawkins, Richard, 1976, *The Selfish Gene*, Oxford: Oxford University Press.

1987, *The Blind Watchmaker*, New York: W.W. Norton & Company.

DeGrazia, David, 2003, "Identity, Killing and the Boundaries of Our Existence," *Philosophy and Public Affairs* 31.4: 413–442.

2005, *Human Identity and Bioethics*, Cambridge: Cambridge University Press.

Doepke, Frederick, 1996, *The Kinds of Things*, Chicago: Open Court.

Donnelly, John, ed., 1990, *Suicide: Right Or Wrong?*, Buffalo: Prometheus Books.

Draper, Kai, 1999, "Disappointment, Sadness, and Death," *Philosophical Review* 108.3: 387–414.

Dresser, R.S., 1986, "Life, Death, and Incompetent Patients: Conceptual Infirmities and Hidden Values in the Law," *Arizona Law Review* 28: 373–405.

Dresser, R.S., and Astrow, A.B., 1998, "An Alert and Incompetent Self: The Irrelevance of Advance Directives," *Hastings Center Report* 28.1: 28–30.

Drexler, Eric, 1986, *Engines of Creation: The Coming Era of Nanotechnology*, New York: Anchor Books.

Durkheim, Emile, 1952, *Suicide: A Study in Sociology*, London: Routledge & Kegan Paul.

Dworkin, G., 1981, "The Concept of Autonomy," in Haller, R., ed., *Science and Ethics*, Amsterdam and Atlanta: Rodopi Press. Reprinted in Christman 1989, 54–62.

1988, *The Theory and Practice of Autonomy*, New York: Cambridge University Press.

Dworkin, Ronald, 1993, *Life's Dominion*, New York: Alfred A. Knopf.

Epicurus, 1966a. *Principal Doctrines*, in Saunders, J., ed., *Greek and Roman Philosophy after Aristotle*, New York: Free Press.

Epicurus, 1966b, *Letter to Menoeceus*, in Saunders, J., ed., *Greek and Roman Philosophy after Aristotle*, New York: Free Press.

Ereshefsky, Mark, 2001, *The Poverty of the Linnaean Hierarchy: A Philosophical Study of Biological Taxonomy*, Cambridge: Cambridge University Press.

Eyre, J.A., Miller, S., Clowry, G.J., Conway, E.A., Watts, C., 2000, "Functional Corticospinal Projections are Established Prenatally in the Human Foetus Permitting Involvement in the Development of Spinal Motor Centres," *Brain* 123: 51–64.

Faden, R., and Childress, T., 1986, *A History and Theory of Informed Consent*, New York: Oxford University Press.

Fairbairn, Gavin, 1995, *Contemplating Suicide: The Language and Ethics of Self Harm*, London: Routledge.

Farberow, Norman, and Schneidman, Edwin, 1957, "The Logic of Suicide," in Farberow, Norman, Schneidman, Edwin, and Menninger, Karl, eds., *Clues to Suicide*, New York: McGraw-Hill.

Feezell, Randolph, 1987, "Potentiality, Death, and Abortion," *Southern Journal of Philosophy* 25.1: 39–48.

Feinberg, Joel, ed., 1973, *The Problem of Abortion*, California: Wadsworth Publishing Company.

    1984, "Harm to Others," in Feinberg, Joel, *Harm to Others*, Oxford: Oxford University Press, 79–95. Reprinted in Fischer 1993, 171–190.

    1986, *Harm to Self*, Oxford: Oxford University Press.

Feit, Neil, 2002, "The Time of Death's Misfortune," *Noûs* 36: 359–383.

Feldman, Fred, 1991, "Some Puzzles About the Evil of Death," *Philosophical Review* 100.2: 205–227. Reprinted in Fischer 1993, 307–326.

    1992, *Confrontations with the Reaper*, New York: Oxford University Press.

    2000, "The Termination Thesis," *Midwest Studies in Philosophy* 24: 98–115.

    2004, *Pleasure and the Good Life: Concerning the Nature, Varieties, and Plausibility of Hedonism*, New York: Oxford University Press.

Fine, Robert, 2005, "From Quinlan to Schiavo: Medical, Ethical, and Legal Issues in Severe Brain Injury," *Proceedings (Baylor University Medical Centre)* 18.4: 303–310.

Finnis, John, 1995, "A Philosophical Case Against Euthanasia," in Keown, J., ed., *Euthanasia Examined: Ethical, Clinical, and Legal Perspectives*, Cambridge: Cambridge University Press, 23–35.

Fischer, John, ed., 1993, *The Metaphysics of Death*, Stanford: Stanford University Press.

    1997, "Death, Badness, and the Impossibility of Experience," *Journal of Ethics* 1: 341–353.

Frankfurt, Harry, 1971, "Freedom of the Will and the Concept of a Person," *Journal of Philosophy* 68.1: 5–20. Reprinted in Christman 1989, 63–76.

Frey, R.G., 1978, "Did Socrates Commit Suicide?," *Philosophy* 53. Reprinted in Battin and Mayo 1980, 35–39.

    1981, "Suicide and Self-Inflicted Death," *Philosophy* 56: 193–202.

Furley, D., 1986, "Nothing to Us?," in Schofield, M., and Striker, G., eds., *The Norms of Nature*, Cambridge: Cambridge University Press, 75–91.

Gallup, Gordon, Jr., 1970, "Chimpanzees: Self-recognition," *Science* 167: 86–87.

Gazini, Linda, Dobscha, Steven, Heintz, Ronald, and Press, Nancy, 2003, "Oregon Physicians' Perceptions of Patients Who Request Assisted Suicide and Their Families," *Journal of Palliative Medicine* 6: 381–390.

Gilbert, Walter, 1986, "The RNA World," *Nature* 319: 618.

Glannon, Walter, 1994, "Temporal Asymmetry, Life, and Death," *American Philosophical Quarterly* 31: 235–244.

Glover, Jonathan, 1984, *What Sort of People Should There Be?*, Harmondsworth: Pelican Books.

1990, *Causing Death and Saving Lives*, Harmondsworth: Penguin Books.

Goldman, Alvin, 1970, *A Theory of Human Action*, Englewood Cliffs, NJ: Prentice-Hall.

Gorsuch, Neil, 2006, *The Future of Assisted Suicide and Euthanasia*, Princeton: Princeton University Press.

Gosling, J.C.B., 1969, *Pleasure and Desire: The Case for Hedonism Reviewed*, Oxford: Oxford University Press.

Green, Michael, and Wikler, Daniel, 1980, "Brain Death and Personal Identity," *Philosophy and Public Affairs* 9: 105–133.

Grey, W., 1999, "Epicurus and the Harm of Death," *Australasian Journal of Philosophy* 77: 358–364.

Griffin, James, 1986, *Well-Being*, Oxford: Clarendon Press.

Grisez, Germain, and Boyle, Joseph, Jr., 1979, *Life and Death with Liberty and Justice: A Contribution to the Euthanasia Debate*, Notre Dame: University of Notre Dame Press.

Gunderson, Martin, 2004, "A Kantian View of Suicide and End-of-Life Treatment," *Journal of Social Philosophy* 35.2: 277–287.

Haji, Ishtiyaque, 1991, "Pre-Vital and Post-Vital Times," *Pacific Philosophical Quarterly* 72: 171–180.

Haldane, J.B.S., 1954, "The Origin of Life" (1929) in *New Biology* 16.12: 12–27.

Halevy, Amir, and Brody, Baruch, 1993, "Brain Death: Reconciling Definitions, Criteria, and Tests," *Annals of Internal Medicine* 119.6, 519–525.

Harley, Calvin B., 2001, "Telomerase and Cell Immortality: Applications in Research and Medicine," *Scientific World Journal* 1.1 (1 Supplement 3): 115.

Harley, Calvin B., Vaziri, Homayoun, Counter, Christopher M., and Allsopp, Richard C., 1992, "The Telomere Hypothesis of Cellular Aging," *Experimental Gerontology* 27: 375–382.

Harris, John, 1984, *The Value of Life*, London: Routledge & Kegan Paul.

Hasker, W., 1999, *The Emergent Self*, Ithaca, NY: Cornell University Press.

Hayflick, Leonard, 1965, "The Limited *In Vitro* Lifetime of Human Diploid Cell Strains," *Experimental Cell Research* 37: 614–636.

Hendin, Herbert, 1991, "Psychodynamics of Suicide, with Particular Reference to the Young," in Maltsberger and Goldblatt 1996, 612–632.

Hetherington, Stephen, 2001, "Deathly Harm," *American Philosophical Quarterly* 38: 349–362.

Hill, Thomas, 1980, "Humanity as an End in Itself," *Ethics* 91: 84–99.

1991, *Autonomy and Self-Respect*, Cambridge: Cambridge University Press.

Holland, R.F., 1971, "Suicide," (1969), reprinted in Rachels, James, ed., *Moral Problems*, New York: Harper & Row.

Hölldobler, Bert, and Wilson, E.O., 1990, *The Ants*, Cambridge, MA: Harvard University Press.

Hume, David, 1826, "On Suicide," *The Philosophical Works of David Hume*, London: Adam & Charles Black.

Inwald, David, Jacobovits, Immanuel, Petros, Andy, Fisher, Malcolm, and Raper, Raymond F., 2000, "Brain Stem Death," *BMJ* 320: 1266–1267.

Jones, B.E., 1998, "The Neural Basis of Consciousness Across the Sleep-waking Cycle," in Jasper, H., Descarries, L., Castelucci, V.F., Rossignol, S., eds., *Consciousness: At the Frontiers of Neureoscience*, Advances in Neurology 77, Philadelphia: Lippincott-Raven, 75–94.

Kagan, Shelly, 1999, *The Limits of Morality*, New York: Oxford University Press.

Kamm, Frances, 1988, "Why Is Death Bad and Worse than Pre-Natal Non-Existence?," *Pacific Philosophical Quarterly* 69: 161–164.

1998, *Morality Mortality*, vol. 1, Oxford: Oxford University Press.

Kant, Immanuel, 1963, *Lectures in Ethics*, trans. Louis Infield, New York: Harper & Row, 147–157.

Katz, Leonard, 2006, "Pleasure," *The Stanford Encyclopedia of Philosophy*, ed. Zalta, Edward N., http://plato.stanford.edu/entries/pleasure.

Kaufman, Frederik, 1996, "Death and Deprivation; or Why Lucretius' Symmetry Argument Fails," *Australasian Journal of Philosophy* 74.2: 305–312.

1999, "Pre-vital and Post-mortem Non-existence," *American Philosophical Quarterly* 36: 1–19.

Keller, Simon, 2004, "Welfare and the Achievement of Goals," *Philosophical Studies* 121.1: 27–41.

Keown, John, 2002, *Euthanasia, Ethics and Public Policy: An Argument Against Legalisation*, Cambridge: Cambridge University Press.

Kierkegaard, Søren, 1843, *Either/Or*, ed. Hong, Howard, and Hong, Edna, Princeton: Princeton University Press.

Kluge, Eike-Henner, 1975, *The Practice of Death*, New Haven: Yale University Press.

Kobayashi, K., Hua, L.-L., Gehrke, C.W., Gerhardt, K.O., and Ponnamperuma, C., 1986, "Abiotic Synthesis of Nucleic Acid Bases by Electric Discharge in a Simulated Primitive Atmosphere," *Origins of Life and Evolution of Biospheres* 16.3–4: 299–300.

Kraut, Richard, 1994, "Desire and the Human Good," *Proceedings and Addresses of the American Philosophical Association* 68.2: 39–54.

Kripke, Saul, 1980, *Naming and Necessity*, Cambridge, MA: Harvard University Press.

Kuhse, Helga, 1987, *The Sanctity-of-Life Doctrine in Medicine: A Critique*, Oxford: Clarendon Press.

Kurzweil, Ray, 2005, *The Singularity Is Near: When Humans Transcend Biology*, New York: Viking Press.

Lamb, David, 1983, *Review of Medicine and Moral Philosophy*, *Journal of Medical Ethics* 9: 175.

Lamont, Julian, 1998, "A Solution to the Puzzle of When Death Harms its Victims," *Australasian Journal of Philosophy* 76: 198–212.

Lander, E.S., Linton, L.M., Birren, B., et al., 2001, "Initial Sequencing and Analysis of the Human Genome," *Nature* 409: 860–921.

Lange, Marc, 1996, "Life, 'Artificial Life,' and Scientific Explanation," *Philosophy of Science* 63: 225–244.

Langton, Christopher, 1992, "Artificial Life," in Nadel, L., and Stein, D., eds., *1991 Lectures in Complex Systems*, Santa Fe Institute Studies in the Sciences of Complexity, Lectures, 4; Reading, MA: Addison Wesley, 189 241. Reprinted in Boden 1996, 39–94.

Lee, Patrick, 1996, *Abortion and Unborn Human Life*, Washington, DC: Catholic University of America Press.

Levenbook, B, 1984, "Harming Someone After His Death," *Ethics* 94: 407–419.

Levy, D.E., Bates, D., Caronna, J.J., et al., 1981, "Prognosis in Non-Traumatic Coma," *Annals of Internal Medicine* 94: 293–301.

Lewis, D., 1973, *Counterfactuals*, Cambridge, MA: Harvard University Press.
   1976, "Survival and Identity," in Rorty, Amelie, ed., *The Identities of Persons*, Berkeley: University of California Press, 17–40. Reprinted in Lewis, D., *Philosophical Papers*, vol. 1, Oxford University Press, 1983, 55–77.
   1983, "Extrinsic Properties," *Philosophical Studies* 44, 197–200.

Lippert-Rasmussen, Kasper, 2007, "Why Killing Some People Is More Seriously Wrong than Killing Others," *Ethics* 117: 716–738.

Locke, John, 1975, *Essay Concerning Human Understanding* (1690), ed. P. Nidditch, Oxford: Clarendon Press. Reprinted in Perry 1975, 33–52.

Lucretius, 1951, *On the Nature of the Universe*, trans. Latham, R., Harmondsworth: Penguin.

Luper(-Foy), Steven, 1987, "Annihilation," *Philosophical Quarterly* 37.148: 233–252. Reprinted in Fischer 1993: 269–290.

Luper, Steven, 2002, "Death," *The Stanford Encyclopedia of Philosophy (Winter 2002 Edition)*, ed. Zalta, Edward N., http://plato.stanford.edu/archives/win2002/entries/death.
   2004, "Posthumous Harm," *American Philosophical Quarterly* 41: 63–72.
   2005, "Past Desires and the Dead," *Philosophical Studies* 126.3: 331–345.
   2007, "Mortal Harm," *Philosophical Quarterly* 57: 239–251.

McCarley, R.W., 1999, "Sleep Neurophysiology: Basic Mechanisms Underlying Control of Wakefulness and Sleep," in Chokroverty, S., ed., *Sleep Disorders Medicine*, Boston: Butterworth Heinemann, 21–50.

McInerney, P., 1990, "Does a Fetus Already Have a Future Like Ours?," *Journal of Philosophy* 87: 264–268.

MacIntyre, Alasdair, 1981, *After Virtue*, Notre Dame: University of Notre Dame Press.

Mackie, David, 1999, "Personal Identity and Dead People," *Philosophical Studies* 95: 219–242.

McMahan, Jeff, 1988, "Death and the Value of Life," *Ethics* 99.1: 32–61. Reprinted in Fischer 1993, 231–267.

1995, "Killing and Equality," *Utilitas* 7: 1–29.

2002, *The Ethics of Killing*, Oxford: Oxford University Press.

Maltsberger, John, and Goldblatt, Mark, eds., 1996, *Essential Papers on Suicide*, New York: New York University Press.

Margolis, Joseph, 1978, "Suicide," in Beauchamp, T.L., and Perlin, S., eds., *Ethical Issues in Death and Dying*, Englewood Cliffs, NJ: Prentice-Hall, 92–97.

Margulis (a.k.a. Sagan), Lynn, 1967, "On the Origin of Mitosing Cells," *Journal of Theoretical Biology* 14.3, 255–274.

1991, *Symbiosis as a Source of Evolutionary Innovation: Speciation and Morphogenesis*, Cambridge, MA: MIT Press.

Marquis, Don, 1989, "Why Abortion is Immoral," *Journal of Philosophy* 86: 183–203.

1994, "A Future Like Ours and the Concept of Person: A Reply to McInerney and Paske," in Pojman, L., and Beckwith, F., eds., *The Abortion Controversy*, Boston: Jones and Bartlett Publishers, 354–369.

1995, "Fetuses, Futures, and Values: A Reply to Shirley," *Southwest Philosophy Review* 6.2: 263–265.

Marten, Ken, and Psarakos, Suchi, 1994, "Evidence of Self-awareness in the Bottlenose Dolphin (*Tursiops truncatus*)," in Parker, S., Boccia, M., and Mitchell, R., eds., *Self-Awareness in Animals and Humans: Developmental Perspectives*, New York: Cambridge University Press, 361–379.

Mayo, David, 1980, "Irrational Suicide," in Battin and Mayo 1980, 133–143.

Mele, Alfred, ed., 1997, *The Philosophy of Action*, Oxford: Oxford University Press.

Meltzoff, A.N., and Moore, M.K., 1983, "New Born Infants Imitate Adult Facial Gestures," *Child Development* 54: 702–709.

Mill, J.S., 1863, *Utilitarianism*, London: Parker, Son, & Bourn.

Miller, Stanley, 1953, "A Production of Amino Acids under Possible Primitive Earth Conditions," *Science*, n.s. 117.3046, 528–529.

Mitsis, Phillip, 1988, "Epicurus on Death and the Duration of Life," *Proceedings of the Boston Area Colloquium in Ancient Philosophy* 4: 303–322.

Mollaret, P., and Goulon, M., 1959, "Le coma dépassé," *Revue Neurologique* 101: 5–15.

Moruzzi, G., and Magoun, H.W., 1949, "Brain Stem Reticular Formation and the Activation of the EEG," *Electroencephalography and Clinical Neurophysiology* 1: 455–473.

Nagel, Thomas, 1993, "Death," in Fischer 1993, 61–69. First published in *Noûs* 4.1 (1970): 73–80. Also reprinted in Nagel, Thomas, *Mortal Questions*, Cambridge: Cambridge University Press, 1979.

Nakamura, Ken-Ichi, Izumiyama-Shimomura, Naotaka, Sawabe, Motoji, et al., 2002, "Comparative Analysis of Telomere Lengths and Erosion with Age in

Human Epidermis and Lingual Epithelium," *Journal of Investigative Dermatology* 119: 1014–1019.

Nimchinsky, E.A., Sabatini, B.L., and Svoboda, K., 2002, "Structure and Function of Dendritic Spines," *Annual Review Physics* 64: 313–353.

Nozick, Robert, 1971, "On the Randian Argument," *The Personalist* 52: 282–304. Reprinted in Paul, J., ed., *Reading Nozick: Essays on Anarchy, State, and Utopia*, Totowa, NJ: Rowman & Littlefield, 206–232.

  1974, *Anarchy, State, and Utopia*, New York: Basic Books.

Nussbaum, Martha, 1996, *The Therapy of Desire*, Princeton: Princeton University Press.

Okamoto, Noriko, and Inouye, Isao, 2005, "A Secondary Symbiosis in Progress?," *Science* 14.310: 287.

O'Keeffe, Terence, 1984, "Suicide and Self Starvation," *Philosophy* 59.229: 349–363.

Olson, Eric, 1997, *The Human Animal*, Oxford: Oxford University Press.

  2007, *What Are We? A Study in Personal Ontology*, Oxford: Oxford University Press.

Oparin, Alexander, 1952, *The Origin of Life*, New York: Dover, 1952. First published in Russian, 1924.

Overvold, Mark, 1980, "Self-Interest and the Concept of Self-Sacrifice," *Canadian Journal of Philosophy* 10: 105–118.

  1982, "Self-Interest and Getting What You Want," in Miller, H., and Williams, W., eds., *The Limits of Utilitarianism*, Minneapolis: University of Minnesota Press, 185–194.

Pahel, Kenneth, 1987, "Michael Tooley on Abortion and Potentiality," *Southern Journal of Philosophy* 25.1: 95–96.

Pallis, Christopher, 1982, "ABC of Brain Stem Death," *British Medical Journal* 285: 1487–1490.

  1994, "Brain (Stem) Death," in Walton, John, et al., *The Oxford Medical Companion*, Oxford: Oxford University Press, 95–97.

Parfit, Derek, 1984, *Reasons and Persons*, Oxford: Clarendon Press. Reprinted with note, 1985.

Perry, John, ed., 1975, *Personal Identity*, Berkeley: University of California Press.

Pirie, N.W., 1938, "The Meaninglessness of the Terms Life and Living," in Needham, J., and Green, E.E., eds., *Perspectives in Biochemistry*, Cambridge: Cambridge University Press, 11–22.

Pitcher, G., 1984, "The Misfortunes of the Dead," *American Philosophical Quarterly* 21.2: 217–225. Reprinted in Fischer 1993, 119–134.

Plum, Fred, 1991, "Coma and Related Global Disturbances of the Human Conscious State," in Peters, A., and Jones, E.G., eds., *Cerebral Cortex*, New York: Plenum Press, 359–425.

Portmore, Douglas, 2007, "Desire Fulfillment and Posthumous Harm," *American Philosophical Quarterly* 44: 27–38.

Potten, Christopher, and Wilson, James, 2004, *Apoptosis: The Life and Death of Cells*, Cambridge: Cambridge University Press.

Prado, C.G., 2008, *Choosing to Die*, Cambridge: Cambridge University Press.

President's Commission for the Study of Ethical Problems in Medicine and Biomedical and Behavioral Research, 1981, *Report*.

Quinn, Warren, 1984, "Abortion: Identity and Loss," *Philosophy and Public Affairs* 13.1: 24–54.

Rachels, James, 1975, "Active and Passive Euthanasia," *New England Journal of Medicine* 292: 78–80.

   1983, "The Sanctity of Life," in Humber, J.M., ed., *Biomedical Ethics Reviews*, Clifton, NJ: Humana Press, 29–42.

   1986, *The End of Life*, Oxford: Oxford University Press.

Rakic, P., 2002, "Pre- and Post-developmental Neurogenesis in Primates," *Clinical Neuroscience Research* 2: 29–39.

Rawls, John, 1971, *A Theory of Justice*, Cambridge, MA: Harvard University Press.

Rea, M., 2005, "Four Dimensionalism," *The Oxford Handbook of Metaphysics*, Oxford: Oxford University Press, 246–281.

Rhoden, Nancy, 1990, "The Limits of Legal Objectivity," *North Carolina Law Review* 68: 845–865.

Robins, Eli, Murphy, George E., Wilkinson, Robert H., Gassner, Seymour, and Kayes, Jack, 1959, "Some Clinical Considerations in the Prevention of Suicide Based on a Study of One Hundred and Thirty-Four Successful Suicides," *American Journal of Public Health* 49: 888–899. Reprinted in Maltsberger and Goldblatt 1996, 142–160.

Rosenbaum, Stephen, 1986, "How to be Dead and not Care: A Defense of Epicurus," *American Philosophical Quarterly* 23: 217–225.

   1989a, "The Symmetry Argument: Lucretius Against the Fear of Death," *Philosophy and Phenomenological Research* 50.2: 353–373.

   1989b, "Epicurus and Annihilation," *Philosophical Quarterly* 39.154: 81–90. Reprinted in Fischer 1993, 293–304.

Rosenberg, Jay, 1983, *Thinking Clearly About Death*, New Jersey: Prentice-Hall.

Roy, Alec, 1982, "Suicide in Chronic Schizophrenia," *British Journal of Psychiatry* 141: 171–177. Reprinted in Maltsberger and Goldblatt 1996, 442–456.

Royce, Josiah, 1908, *The Philosophy of Loyalty*, New York: Macmillan.

Ruben, D.-H., 1988, "A Puzzle about Posthumous Predication," *Philosophical Review* 97.2: 211–236.

Scanlon, Thomas, 1998, *What We Owe to Each Other*, Cambridge, MA: Harvard University Press.

Scarre, Geoffrey, 2007, *Death*, Stocksfield: Acumen Press.

Schopenhauer, Arthur, 1851, "On Suicide," *Parerga und Paralipomena*, Berlin: A.W. Hayn.

Schroedinger, Erwin, 1944, *What is Life? The Physical Aspect of the Living Cell*, Cambridge: Cambridge University Press.

Schwarz, Stephen, 1990, *The Moral Question of Abortion*, Chicago: Loyola University Press.

Scott, D., 2000, "Aristotle on Posthumous Fortune," *Oxford Studies in Ancient Philosophy* 18: 211–229.

Sedley, D., 1998, *Lucretius and the Transformation of Greek Wisdom*, Cambridge: Cambridge University Press.

Segal, C., 1990, *Lucretius on Death and Anxiety*, Princeton: Princeton University Press.

Shewmon, Alan, 1997, "Recovery From 'Brain Death': A Neurologist's Apologia," *Linacre Quarterly* 64: 30–96.

1998, "Chronic Brain Death: Meta-analysis and Conceptual Consequences," *Neurology* 51: 1538–1545.

2001, "The Brain and Somatic Integration: Insights into the Standard Biological Rationale for Equating 'Brain Death' with Death," *Journal of Medicine and Philosophy* 26: 457–478.

Shneidman, Edwin, 1965, "Preventing Suicide," *American Journal of Nursing* 65: 111–116. Reprinted in Donnelly 1990.

Silverstein, H., 1980, "The Evil of Death," *Journal of Philosophy* 77.7: 401–424. Reprinted in Fischer 1993, 95–116.

2000, "The Evil of Death Revisited," *Midwest Studies in Philosophy* 24: 116–135.

Singer, Peter, 1980, "Animals and the Value of Life," in Regan, Tom, ed., *Matters of Life and Death*, 2nd edn., New York: Random House, 338–380.

1994, *Rethinking Life and Death: The Collapse of Our Traditional Ethics*, New York: St. Martin's Griffin.

Snowdon, Paul, 1990, "Persons, Animals, and Ourselves," in Gill, C., ed., *The Person and the Human Mind: Issues in Ancient and Modern Philosophy*, Oxford: Oxford University Press.

Sober, Elliott, 1992, "Learning From Functionalism – Prospects for Strong Artificial Life," in Langton, C.G., et al., eds., *Artificial Life II*, Santa Fe Institute Studies in the Sciences of Complexity, Proceedings, 10; Redwood City, CA: Addison-Wesley, 749–66.

Stalnaker, Robert, 1968, "A Theory of Counditionals," in Rescher, N., ed., *Studies in Logical Theory*, Oxford: Basil Blackwell, 1968.

Steinbock, Bonnie, 1992, *Life Before Birth: The Moral and Legal Status of Embryos and Fetuses*, New York: Oxford University Press.

2007, *The Oxford Handbook of Bioethics*, Oxford: Oxford University Press.

Stone, Jim, 1987, "Why Potentiality Matters," *Canadian Journal of Philosophy* 17.4: 815–830.

1994, "Why Potentiality Still Matters," *Canadian Journal of Philosophy* 24.2, 281–294.

Stretton, Dean, 2004, "The Deprivation Argument Against Abortion," *Bioethics* 18.2: 144–180.

Suits, David, 2001, "Why Death Is Not Bad for the One Who Died," *American Philosophical Quarterly* 38.1: 69–84. Reprinted in Benatar 2004, 265–284.

Super, H., Soriano, E., and Uylings, H.B., 1998, "The Functions of the Preplate in Development and Evolution of the Neocortex and Hippocampus," *Brain Research Reviews* 27: 40–64.

Szasz, Thomas, 1999, *Fatal Freedom: The Ethics and Politics of Suicide*, Syracuse: Syracuse University Press.

Taylor, James, 2008, "Harming the Dead," *Journal of Philosophical Research* 33: 185–202.

Thomas Aquinas, 1925, "Whether It is Lawful to Kill Oneself?," *Summa Theologica*, New York: Benziger Brothers, Inc.; London: Burns & Oaks, Ltd., Part 2, Question 64, A5.

Thomas, Lewis, 1974, *The Lives of a Cell: Notes of a Biology Watcher*, New York: Viking Press.

Thomson, Judith, 1971, "A Defense of Abortion," *Philosophy and Public Affairs* 1.1: 47–66.

Tolhurst, William E., 1983, "Suicide, Self-Sacrifice, and Coercion," *Southern Journal of Philosophy* 21: 109–121. Reprinted in Donnelly, John, ed., *Suicide: Right or Wrong*, Buffalo: Prometheus Books, 77–92.

Tooley, Michael, 1972, "Abortion and Infanticide," *Philosophy and Public Affairs* 2.1: 37–65.

  1983, *Abortion and Infanticide*, Oxford: Clarendon Press.

Truog, R.D., and Facler, J.C., 1992, "Rethinking Brain Death," *Critical Care Medicine* 20: 1705–1713.

Tye, Michael, 2003, *Consciousness and Persons: Unity and Identity*, Cambridge, MA: MIT Press.

Unamuno, Miguel, 1954, *The Tragic Sense of Life*, New York: Dover.

US Department of Health and Human Services, 2007, www.cdc.gov/nchs/datawh/statab/unpubd/mortabs/lcwk9_10.htm.

Van Inwagen, Peter, 1990, *Material Beings*, Ithaca: Cornell University Press.

Veatch, Robert M., 1975, "The Whole-Brain-Oriented Concept of Death: An Outmoded Philosophical Formulation," *Journal of Thanatology* 3: 13–30.

  ed., 1979, *Life Span: Values and Life-extending Technologies*, San Francisco: Harper & Row.

Velleman, David, 1991, "Well-Being and Time," *Pacific Philosophical Quarterly* 72: 48–77. Reprinted in Fischer 1993, 329–357.

  1993, *Morality and Action*, New York: Cambridge University Press.

  1999, "A Right of Self-termination?," *Ethics* 109: 606–628.

Von Economo, Constantin, 1931, *Encephalitis Lethargica: Its Sequelae and Treatment*, London: Oxford University Press.

Vorobej, M., 1998, "Past Desires," *Philosophical Studies* 90: 305–318.

Wade, Nicholas, 2007, "Scientists Transplant Genome of Bacteria," *New York Times*, June 29.

Waluchow, W.J., 1986, "Feinberg's Theory of 'Preposthumous' Harm," *Dialogue* 25: 727–734.

Warren, James, 2001, "Lucretius, Symmetry Arguments, and Fearing Death," *Phronesis* 46: 466–491.

  2004, *Facing Death: Epicurus and His Critics*, Oxford: Oxford University Press.

Warren, Mary Ann, 1973, "On the Moral and Legal Status of Abortion," *Monist* 57.1: 43–61.

Warwick, Kevin, 2002, *I, Cyborg*, London: Century.

Wiggins, David, 1967, *Identity and Spatio-Temporal Continuity*, Oxford: Basil Blackwell.

1980, *Sameness and Substance*, Oxford: Basil Blackwell.

Williams, Bernard, 1970, "The Self and the Future," *Philosophical Review* 79.2: 161–180. Reprinted in Williams, Bernard, *Problems of the Self*, Cambridge: Cambridge University Press, and in Perry, John, ed., *Personal Identity*, Berkeley, CA: University of California Press, 1975, 179–198.

1973, "The Makropulos Case: Reflections on the Tedium of Immortality," in Williams, Bernard, *Problems of the Self*, Cambridge: Cambridge University Press.

Williams, Christopher, 2007, "Death and Deprivation," *Pacific Philosophical Quarterly* 88.2: 265–283.

Wilson, Edward, and Hölldobler, Bert, 2005, "Eusociality: Origin and Consequences," *Proceedings of the National Academy of Sciences, USA*: 102: 13367–13371.

Windt, Peter, 1980, "The Concept of Suicide," in Battin and Mayo 1980, 39–48.

Young, Robert, 2007, *Medically Assisted Death*, Cambridge: Cambridge University Press.

Index

232